If Olaya Street Could Talk

Saudi Arabia:
The Heartland of Oil and Islam

John Paul Jones

The Taza Press
Albuquerque, New Mexico, USA

The Taza Press
Albuquerque, New Mexico, USA

(www.tazapress.com)

Library of Congress Control Number: 2006909033

Includes bibliographical references, glossary of Arabic
terms, and index.

ISBN-13: 978-0-9790436-0-4
ISBN-10: 0-9790436-0-3

Cover Design: A Joint Production

Printed in the United States of America

First Edition

Table of Contents

Lyrics of Beale Street Blues

I've seen the lights of gay Broadway,
Old Market Street down by the Frisco Bay,
I've strolled the Prado, I've gambled on the Bourse;
The seven wonders of the world I've seen,
And many are the places I have been,
Take my advice, folks, and see Beale Street first!

You'll see pretty browns in beautiful gowns,
You'll see tailor-mades and hand-me-downs,
You'll meet honest men, and pick-pockets skilled,
You'll find that business never ceases 'til somebody gets
killed!

If Beale Street could talk, if Beale Street could talk,
Married men would have to take their beds and walk,
Except one or two who never drink booze,
And the blind man on the corner singing "Beale Street
Blues!"

I'd rather be there than any place I know,
I'd rather be there than any place I know,
It's gonna take a sergeant for to make me go!

I'm goin' to the river, maybe by and by,
Yes, I'm goin' to the river, maybe by and by,
Because the river's wet, and Beale Street's done gone dry!

Introduction

If Olaya Street Could Talk

Saudi Arabia – The Heartland of Oil and Islam

Oil and Islam. There may be more important issues that will ultimately affect the well-being of the world's citizens, but these issues dominate today's headlines as well as the political imperatives of many countries' leadership. One prevalent school of thought now projects that these will be foremost considerations for the next two or three generations.

These considerations certainly did not motivate my travel to Saudi Arabia in 1978. There was an element of, "let's-just-see-what-happens-whimsy-if-we-do-something-different," in that decision. When I ventured to the Kingdom, there was the very real possibility that the visit might last only three months. Yet it lasted almost a quarter of a century, with a four year "sabbatical" in the middle. The first ten year period was from December, 1978 to March, 1989. The second ten year period was from May, 1993 to June, 2003. During this period I married; both of my children would be born in the Kingdom and grow up there until their college years. We made a number of solid, long-term friends. The Kingdom became home, and its rhythms became our own. We had to make modest adjustments in our western "lifestyles," yet the amount of vacation, the healthcare, the schooling, and a country where you could run "free and clear" more than compensated for those adjustments.

During this period Saudi Arabia experienced a remarkable economic and social transformation. Upon my arrival in the Kingdom, goats grazed along Olaya Street, a road which soon became Riyadh's principal commercial thoroughfare. Every facet of Saudi society experienced dynamic change, perhaps at ten times the rate of change in the Western world. Various Saudis would become my friends, and a few, my adversaries. It was often an exciting, dynamic place to live.

Thomas Friedman, the New York Times columnist, once told me that I had lived in Saudi Arabia "way too long," as though I had somehow become a lesser person for doing so. The possibility that it might have been a broadening educational and developmental experience did not seem to have occurred to him. His comment was a far more telling reflection on his own mindset than my own. No, overall it was a very positive experience, and it was only during the last year when the regrets and the sadness would occur, as my family, my western friends, and the Saudis themselves were overwhelmed by forces that seemed beyond the power of any of us to control, as the contagion of violence spread into the Kingdom.

In my youth I had been a soldier—not by choice—and at that time this contagion was overwhelming Vietnam, a country that is now at peace. Mankind's understanding of the epidemiology of physical diseases is so much greater than its understanding of the rise and fall of tribal conflicts and violence. Some speak of ideologies, the abstract word for ideas, and there is no question that herein rests the source of the problem, but we are far from explaining how the problem can remain dormant for long periods and then suddenly erupt. I am bewildered as to how it all happened. In times of scarcity, one might understand how tribes would fight over good land and food. But now, what is the underlining imperative for conflict? Can it be a deep psychological need, exacerbated by the pursuit of financial advantage?

France is another country that I have learned to appreciate. With a few exceptions, the books and articles that I've read on France reflect my own experiences in the country. But with Saudi Arabia, it is only the exceptional book or article that reflects my experience. The others seem a crude caricature, like wartime propaganda, and much of this was even before 9/11. Americans have also used coarse caricature to portray their own citizens, blacks and Indians for example. Over time, for various reasons, those caricatures have largely disappeared, and an entirely different portrayal is the norm. I hope that my book is a step in changing American perceptions of Saudi Arabia in particular, and the Arabs in general, and further an examination of how and why those shifts in "tribal thinking" occur.

Part of that examination involves reviewing past tribal conflicts that are now resolved. At one time it appeared that there would be eternal conflict between the "children of Charlemagne," France and Germany. There were three bitter wars in a seventy year period. Now a war between these two countries is a virtual impossibility. Perhaps the most famous book about the second of those three conflicts, World War I, is Erich Maria Remarque's *All Quiet on the Western Front.* In one memorable scene, the German infantrymen are discussing the origins of the war, and if the Kaiser had said "No," might there not have been a war? The consensus was that the "No" of one man would not have been enough, but if twenty or thirty people—yes, those with the power—had said "No," the war would have been avoided. A prime factor in examining tribal conflict is the concentration of power in the hands of a few in the decision-making process.

I have never been in, nor reported to, the CIA, as various Saudis suspected. ("Why else would he travel so much in our country when we take all our vacations abroad"?) I certainly never intended to write a book on the experience. Yet it eventually became an imperative. To contribute to ending the ideology of war without end should be a sufficient reason.

Note: In most cases the names of individuals in the book have been changed.

If Olaya Street Could Talk

Saudi Arabia:

The Heartland of Oil and Islam

How We Got Back There

I hear that you are building your little house deep in the desert
You're living for nothing at all now
I hope you are keeping some kind of record.

—Leonard Cohen
Famous Blue Raincoat

In April 1993 I found myself on Beale Street, in Memphis, courtesy of King Faisal Specialist Hospital. Beale Street had become a tourist destination, and like so many others, it contained only hints of the cultural and social forces that it represented. Sure, you could pay the cover charge, ease past the bouncer, and listen to the Blues. But could you really understand the lyrics if you had not also lived the anguish?

Earlier in the week, on my drive from Atlanta to Memphis, I had stopped at Rowan Oaks, William Faulkner's historical home in Oxford. The home was closed for renovation. It was early on a spring Sunday, the mist was lifting, and I wandered the grounds, blessedly alone, and contemplated how this one man had captured the anguish—the lives of dirt poor blacks and whites who had lived in the Mississippi hill country—and committed it all, not to music, but to words and paper, much to the regret of his fellow citizens, who thought that he had told far too much about them.

Northern Mississippi, with its unofficial capital in Memphis, contained the forces behind America's greatest cultural divide, the one between the immigrants whose ancestors had come to America voluntarily and those who had not. And it was here where the conflict over that divide had been the most profound, the most raw.

All Americans have lived with that divide. When I lived as a child in a lily-white suburb of Pittsburgh in the 50's, my only window to the other side of that divide, darkly if you will, was the *Amos and Andy Show*. In the 60's I attended university in Atlanta, witnessing the heady days of desegregation, the caving in of the old order and the formation of the new. A time when the rules governing race relations would be dramatically re-ordered, and the seeming tranquility of the Eisenhower 50's ended. I made occasional forays across that divide and was once told, along with several other whites, by Martin Luther King Sr. in his Ebenezer Baptist Church, that we were welcome in his church, but we should yield our seats to his regular black parishioners. We obliged, savoring the delicious irony of such a "Rosa Parks" moment.

It never was separate but equal. And the word "divide" carries a bit too much of that connotation. James Baldwin famously captured so much of the anguish of that division's underside, including what Beale Street represented—an initial place of refuge for the Blacks fleeing the rural areas and the harsh life of a sharecropper without rights. But Baldwin had two strikes against him, he was Black; he was homosexual. One day he decided he could no longer wait for America's society to ever so slowly rectify the many injustices that he had experienced and like Richard Wright before him, sought solace in France. Baldwin's final resting place is high in the hills overlooking the Mediterranean, in St. Paul de Vence. What would he think of America today, its erratic, good-spirited or half-hearted—depending on your perspective—efforts at trying to resolve America's Dilemma?

My companion on Beale Street was an Arab, one who had hired me to return to the Kingdom of Saudi Arabia, one who would be my boss for ten days until yet another organizational upheaval at King Faisal Specialist Hospital whisked him away. Abdul Karim's life began as an Iraqi, a nation formed as a result of guilt in the British Foreign Office at the end of the First World War, guilt over the fate of King Hussein of the Hejaz who had been their ally and who had lost in the political struggles of *Al Jazeera* ("The Peninsula" in

Arabic). The British cobbled together two countries just to the north of the peninsula as kingdoms for King Hussein's sons, Faisal and Abdullah. These "countries" were formed from disparate parts of the now dissolved Ottoman Empire, often referred to as the "Sick Man of Europe." Abdullah received Jordan; Faisal was awarded Iraq. Abdul Karim now had a new nationality, he was a Saudi, but not a "real" Saudi, as was whispered against him, for like Baldwin, he had two strikes against him. He could not trace his family's roots deep into the tribes of Al Jazeera, and he was a Shia. Such distinctions I was barely beginning to comprehend, and today much of America is learning of these divisions.

So Abdul Karim and I sat together, listening to the Blues, and I thought how little of the historical and cultural background he must understand of this musical expression and of our location. This reflected my own ignorance of the cultural and historical forces in his background. But underlying the divisions in Abdul Karim's background is an inequality as deep as the black/white divide in America. How profoundly had Abdul Karim's life been affected by ill-informed decisions taken, presumptively on his behalf, in far-off London or Washington?

An illness had brought us together in this Blues club, an illness that neither of us had had the misfortune to experience—leukemia. Of the afflictions that strike humans, leukemia is one of the more cruel when it attacks a child. At one time, the disease was universally fatal. Now it is only fatal sometimes, and those who labor in the field of treating leukemia have one of the more meaningful careers, interweaving intense sadness with professional triumphs. Survival rates continue to improve. A number of years prior, leukemia had struck a small Saudi child, the son of Dr. Al-Rashid. Dr. Al-Rashid sought help for his son at St. Jude's Hospital in Memphis, where the leukemia was treated and was brought into remission.

Dr. Al-Rashid was a wealthy man and an embodiment of the reconciliation that had occurred in *Al Jazeera* after Abdul-Aziz ibn Saud conquered and, through means of the sword and marriage, unified the country. The first step in Abdul-Aziz's efforts to create what would become the Kingdom of Saudi Arabia was the famous 1902 battle for Musmak Fort in Riyadh, when at the age of 21 he returned from exile in Kuwait and traveled via Yabrin to defeat Dr. Al-Rashid's ancestors.

Eight decades later Dr. Al-Rashid thanked Allah for his son's cure by building a hospital on the outskirts of Riyadh, modeled on St. Jude's. Municipal utilities were nonexistent in that area, so he built a power plant and drilled a well over a mile deep, drawing water that was so hot it had to be placed in cooling ponds before it could be treated and used at the hospital. A loose advisory relationship existed among members of St. Jude's staff, the King Faisal Specialist Hospital and Dr. Al-Rashid. Abdul Karim and I were in Memphis for a week to gain additional insights into St. Jude's operation. We were scheduled to return to Riyadh to open and operate the new hospital, which had already been delayed by the First Iraq War. Much later the hospital actually opened and treated patients, but this would be accomplished by others.

***

I returned to Riyadh in May 1993, after an absence of four years and two months. I had missed the First Iraq War's direct impact on the Kingdom, not by design but by accident. My wife, Mary, and I were exceedingly fortunate in leaving as we did; eventually fulfilling a dream few people with children are able to experience—a two-and-a-half-year trip around Europe and the Middle East, tiptoeing through the narrowest of biological windows. Our children, Paris and John, were born less than a year apart on the Gregorian calendar—in fact they were born on the same Hijerian day, the sixth of Ramadan, 1405 and 1406, respectively. And by having "Ramadan babies," we were doubly blessed, as the Arabs say. We had arrived at the window in our kids' lives when diapers were no longer necessary but before first grade was a must. We were traveling north into Europe, expanding normal springtime by a month or so. But I will only mention the first ten days of that trip, carefully selected for the phase of the moon, the ten days we spent camping in the deserts of Saudi Arabia prior to our departure.

We left Riyadh not in the most normal direction for traveling to Europe. We headed southwest, toward what the Romans called "Arabia Felix," the Yemen. Our first objective was Aflaj and Lake Layla. We had heard rumors that this wonderful lake, where Mary and I had water-skied years before, now had a fence and holiday chalets, and that the water level was dropping precipitously. It was true; the water level had dropped 20 meters. The drive in the direction of Abha was now all asphalt, unlike a trip I had taken ten years previously—a 500-kilometer struggle through open desert. The town of Taithlith, for which I had previously searched in order to find petrol, was now marked by a sign of interstate highway proportions and was just one more exit off the highway. There was a new "shortcut" between Taithlith and Bisha, a 90-kilometer trek through the desert, which would have saved us several hundred kilometers of driving over terrain that we had previously seen. Normally I would never have contemplated such a trip because the golden rule of desert treks is to always travel with at least one other vehicle. A good Saudi friend cut through the rumors about the actual status of the road and gave me the definitive condition. The road was not paved, but it was a well-graded dirt track with signposts every kilometer, and in the event of automotive problems it was heavily traveled. The weather was cool, there was no way we could get lost; we made the decision to go for it.

About eight kilometers up the track, a sandstorm, the likes of which we had never experienced in ten years, slammed into us. Visibility was no further than the hood of our 4-wheel drive vehicle. We strained to detect signposts, knowing if we missed one, we could be in deep trouble. We tried not to let our small children feel the fear we felt or sense the danger we were in; we struggled back, and finally, the asphalt was under our tires. We gladly drove on through the storm to Abha on the main highway.

Our hotel reservations were in the "igloo hotel," chalets designed like igloos and scattered on the hillside near Al-Baha, considerably to the north. I was simply too tired to drive through the mountains and in those more gentle days in the Kingdom, Mary drove the roads for a couple of hours. This area of Saudi Arabia is still considered "Yemen's lost provinces," by the more nationalistic, Manifest

Destiny–minded Yemenis. Years later it birthed numerous recruits for Al-Qaeda, including a number of the Saudis who steered the planes into the World Trade Center. At the time though, as it is now, it was simply one of the loveliest parts of the Kingdom—dramatic mountains and valleys, cool climate, and massive cumulus clouds, where snow is possible, even in the Saudi summer.

After a bit of R & R in Al-Baha, we ambled down the escarpment to Jeddah, to re-provision and let our little boy play in the Red Sea as we had done with our daughter two years previously. We drove around Madinah, and on to Madain Salah to visit the Nabatean tombs. These tombs were the most famous archaeological site in the Kingdom, yet were a shadow of the more famous Nabatean ruins at Jordan's Petra. Before reaching Madain Salah, however, we followed our standard practice for this lone car trip and camped behind hills, but no more than one kilometer from the asphalt in case of vehicle problems. We found a nice spot on the backside of some sand dunes, a full moon was rising and an intense sunset was fading. Our two domed tents were set up and the kids were playing in the sand. An old Datsun pickup truck came bouncing through the dunes, a Bedouin using the fading light to get home. Those two tents signaled that we were from Mars or beyond, something completely alien to his world. But we were in "his territory," and he stopped. *As salaam Alaykoum*'s were exchanged, as is the customary greeting, and he inquired if we were okay. When I indicated that we were, he simply waved and drove on, respecting our privacy.

The next day we finally saw, explored, and picnicked among the tombs of a civilization of which nothing is recorded. Our drive north above Tabuk and toward Wadi Zaytah revealed another area of stunning beauty, massive sandstone outcrops arranged with an appealing visual gradient and made famous by Wadi Rum, an area immediately adjacent and just over the border in Jordan where *Lawrence of Arabia* was filmed. This was our last night in what so many expats (expatriates) called the Magic Kingdom. If you are lucky enough to grow up in one place, in peace and tranquility, the topography and landscape becomes your inertial reference frame, the "real world." All other landscapes become exotic. My inertial reference frame is the lush green wooded rolling hills of western

Pennsylvania. My family and I had our final campfire that night, burning the wood we had hauled on the roof rack. In a ritualistic fashion I poured the dregs of the last beer that I had made from malt, freely sold in the Kingdom nine years previously, but now illegal, over the embers of that last campfire. One of my standard quips was that when the malt ran out, I was leaving the Kingdom. Then I sat down with my kids who were kicking the soccer ball around in the desert and told them that today we would be departing the Kingdom for good, crossing into another country. Life would be different there, and I told them to watch for the differences; that is what makes life interesting. Eventually we would travel far enough that we would be in a country where the trees were so thick one might not be able to see the sun, like where I grew up, a place we reached 25 days later, on an infrequently traveled road along the pine-covered Syrian coast, north of Al-Ladhiqiyah.

At age three, my daughter, sensing that her own inertial reference frame might be slipping away, could only plaintively ask the question that many other expats had asked upon leaving: "Yes, but how are we going to get back here?"

Where The Story All Began

There is a leafless tree in Asia
Under the stars there is a homeless man
There is a forest fire in the valley
Where the story all began

—The Moody Blues
You and Me

It was March 1969, and I was seven months into my government-sponsored, all-expenses-paid tour of Southeast Asia, with a particular focus on the more rural areas. We had three meals a day, of sorts. The government wanted us to be self-reliant, so much of our accommodation we constructed ourselves. Free transportation was always provided, though. As a beneficiary of the government's largesse, however, there were certain corresponding obligations. One in particular that I recall was that I was supposed to be "winning the hearts and minds" of the native population. Things were not going very well in that regard.

For those who have participated, war has often been described as long periods of boredom punctuated by moments of sheer terror. Adrenaline would have to handle the terror, but I had a plan for the boredom. The United States Army is forever hyping its "educational opportunities," and I must give them credit, though perhaps not in the way they want. My 21 months in the Army was one of the most intensely educational periods of my life. Certainly it provided deep insights into power relations, a doctorate's worth, but it was also a wonderful opportunity to read whatever I wanted. I read almost 100 books in that year I was in Vietnam. My reading list was suitably eclectic, and the books arrived from a variety of sources, including the US Army itself.

Americans generally use the lighter, airier term "draftee," but I always preferred the more guttural European designation "conscript," which seems to carry the darker connotations associated with the only alternative to retain one's citizenship—five years in prison. It was as a conscript that I received Advanced Individual Training at Fort Sam Houston, Texas, and *theoretically* became a Medical Corpsman. Part of that training involved one of the longest days of my life, the eight-hour block of instruction on bed making: four hours on the making of the occupied bed, four hours on the making of the unoccupied bed. The beds were tightly made, the quarters would dutifully bounce as required, and that particular skill set would certainly grow rusty in 'Nam. Much of the rest of the training was similarly irrelevant.

When I arrived in Vietnam, September 1968, I was quickly assigned to the 1/69th Armor, a tank unit with the 4th Infantry Division, in the Central Highlands. As part of the orientation to the Division, I was to learn that the Highlands were strategic and if they were "lost," all of South Vietnam would fall. It was one of the shibboleths of the war that would actually come true seven and a half years later. But the "communists" never quite reached the suburbs of Sydney, as the more aggressive advocates of the domino theory postulated.

With our impeccable bed-making skills, was it any wonder that new arrivals were designated as "FNGs," which Ollie North in his book, *One More Mission*, claimed (I would assume with a straight face), meant "funny new guy." Another effort to rewrite history, or at least make it palatable to his conservative base. This particular FNG was most fortunate in obtaining a desperately needed mentor, Keith, the company's senior medic, an east Tennessee farm boy.

"Forget all that other stuff, this is what is really going on here, this is what you need to know to do your job and to stay alive," Keith would tell me. And, "You city boys could not possibly understand what it is like to be attached to the land, and how these peasants must resent our destruction of it."

The battalion doctor at the time, also an FNG, was appalled at our lack of basic medical education and gave the four new arrivals an intensive three-day course, ever so wisely selecting what we needed to know to become the "Doc," including much of what he had recently learned himself and which was certainly not taught in his medical school.

Keith also explained the book arrangement. The Army actually sent the company 200-300 books every couple of weeks. "Almost all of it is trash—Westerns, war and pulp sex novels, mysteries, but each box contains a few decent books."

"How do we have first crack at the box?" I asked. Yet another FNG comment.

"That's the last thing you want to do. Look around you—we're surrounded by DATs (dumb ass tankers). Let them sort out the trash, and the real books will be the only ones left."

Sure enough, we would rummage through the box after the others and down at the bottom would lay, for example, Ellison's *Invisible Man*, or Gibbon's *The History of the Decline and Fall of the Roman Empire*. Time proved that Keith overstated the case a bit, a couple of the DATs were anything but, and we honorably shared the decent books and always had more than we could read.

Aside from his medic role, Keith was also an Operational Assessment Specialist, at least an informal one. In October 1968 Charlie Company was committed to a Search and Destroy Operation on the Bong Son plain. We rode along in the medic's APC (armored personnel carrier). It was a use of tanks never envisioned on the battlefields of Western Europe. The tanks plowed right through flooded rice fields. In order to minimize their chances of bogging down in the mud, the tanks had to fan out to avoid running in each other's tracks. The inadvertent consequence was to cause maximum damage to the rice fields. The peasants stood by with an implacable expression of resignation. Allegedly we were surrounding villages and searching for suspicious individuals and activity. If suspects were there, they were long gone, amply warned by the noise of the tanks. After two weeks, and many destroyed fields and hedgerows,

Keith laconically observed, "If these people weren't VC before we arrived, they sure are now."

It would be a most useful metric for any military action, but the simple question is never on any of those after-action report forms: "Have we created more enemies than we neutralized?"

The Army War College in Carlisle, Pennsylvania has faculty members who can easily explain how an impossibly remote jungle valley (when it was a jungle and not upgraded to a rain forest), precisely 12 time zones away, in the tri-border area where Vietnam, Laos, and Cambodia meet, was once vital to the security of the United States and is now no longer vital. The faculty could also explain how we took advantage of other cultural divisions, specifically those between the ethnic Vietnamese and the more indigenous people, (the people who "ate the forest," a reference to their slash-and-burn agricultural techniques) whom the French simply called the Montagnards. Or explain how it made sense for a few very well-trained soldiers who wore green berets to lead two or three companies of Montangards (paid by the United States) to kill their historic adversary, the Vietnamese. Most of America has long forgotten, but the debacle continues to be very much a part of the institutional memory at the AWC—MacArthur's ill-advised, nay, unbelievably arrogant, push to the Yalu far too late in the fall of 1950, and the correspondingly disastrous retreat of American forces, some across the frozen Changjin Reservoir, others through the aptly named "Gauntlet." The image was indelibly etched: "our boys" being overrun by "Asian hordes." Lyndon Baines Johnson had his fears too, and he specifically told Gen. Westmoreland, "Just make damn sure there are no goddamn Dien Bien Phus."

Antecedents enough, I suppose, for my arrival, along with a company of tanks, at the Special Forces Camp at Polei Klang in March 1969. We represented firepower. The majority of the shells in the tanks were canister, containing "fleshettes"—ten to some unbelievably high power of tiny metal arrows, designed specifically as an antipersonnel weapon with those "Asian hordes" in mind, which would hopefully deter some North Vietnamese Army (NVA) commander from committing troops to overrun one of our remote firebases. Though it may have been required reading for the faculty in Carlisle, I was probably the only one at Polei Klang who had previously read Bernard Fall's classic account of the siege of Dien Bien Phu, entitled, *Hell in a Very Small Place*. Maybe I was jumping to conclusions, and I'm sure the colonel in the TOC (tactical operations center) would have considered me unqualified to kibitz over his shoulder, but I didn't like what I saw. Rockets had completely destroyed the perforated steel plate runway, making re-supply by fixed-wing aircraft impossible. Helicopters continued to re-supply us, but we needed a tremendous amount more than the proverbial ball of rice and bandolier of ammo on which our worthy adversaries seemed to get by. Agent Orange had created so many "leafless trees in Asia," and in particular, pushed back the vegetation from such roads as Highway 19, making ambushes much more difficult. But vegetation hugged the narrow, rugged dirt track into Polei Klang, creating a continuous border of ambush sites. Finally, we were squarely in the middle of the valley, and the NVA held all the surrounding hills and rained 122-millimeter rockets on us almost daily. Everything considered it all had a very familiar ring, and I suspect Bernard Fall, who had died two years previously by stepping on a land mine along the "Street Without Joy," would have been concerned.

During my year in Vietnam the battalion had five real doctors. The five reflected the wide spectrum of medical types, with different hopes, aspirations, and outlooks on this war. The one that I just missed had placed the "McCarthy for President" bumper sticker on the medic's jeep. One of the gentlest was Hispanic, lacking a single fiber of the military mind. During one of the rocket attacks, he retreated into a corner, pulling some sandbags over himself. He left on a medical evacuation helicopter, a "Dust Off," pumped full of Thorazine, never to return. A Sp6 medic, Gary Miller, was told he was in charge.

My orders were to dig deep, very deep, though nothing would stop a direct hit from a 122. Task accomplished, it was back to the waiting, the boredom, and the books. Ironically, I was beginning Thomas Merton's *Seven Storey Mountain*. I had been compelled to read it for school when I was fifteen. I knew that I understood very little of the book, but I remained intrigued by the blurb on the back, about a young man who had led a full and worldly life and at the age of 26 had decided to chuck it all and enter a Trappist monastery to contemplate in silence God's existence. I was probably more interested in the full and worldly life part, but I still remember his observation that perhaps the only reason that God did not destroy the entire world, due to the overwhelming evil in it, was the existence of a few monks who contemplated His existence full time. Immersed in the book, Gary interrupted me with a, "You know he died last year, in Bangkok. He was electrocuted; a fan fell in his tub when he was taking a bath."

A near hit from a 122 could not have stunned me more! How could this man even know who Merton was, not to mention the circumstances of his death? Gary was an "old man" for this war, like Merton when he entered the monastery, 26 or so himself, and his story came out: He had also been a Trappist monk at Gethsemani, in Kentucky, decided the contemplative life was not for him, and soon thereafter entered another sort of brotherhood, the Army. He had already reached the same conclusion about his latest brotherhood and told me that if we ever got out of here, he was going deep into the desert to build a bunker and live the rest of his life.

To me the idea was incomprehensible. One did not go live in a desert if you grew up surrounded by green hills; deserts were hot, full of dangers, many poisonous. If absolutely necessary, one might struggle through them to find a Promised Land on the far side. But one did not actually *live* in them.

Meanwhile, way out in the middle of the Pacific Ocean, other men lived on a tropical island, far from their homes in the continental United States. All their creature comforts were met, but there was still the boredom. They had a couple of beers the night before, watched a free movie, and turned in early. The next morning they showered, shaved, applied deodorant, and were in the fully loaded B-52s as they lumbered down a very long runway, eventually obtaining lift-off speed, and pulling up from Guam. These men were going to the war also.

John Foster Dulles had offered French Foreign Minister George Bidault two atomic bombs to solve the French problems at Dien Bien Phu. Bidault declined and, among the other reasons, decided that these bombs might also eliminate the French as well as the Viet Minh. A final solution, of sorts. These B-52s carried no atomic bombs, only high explosives, and some five hours later, the hills around Polei Klang erupted in explosions. The mission went under the rubric Operation Arc Light, and those on the ground could barely make out the silver glints so high in the sky. The 122s stopped. A *deus ex machina*, though not exactly what the ancient Greek playwrights had in mind. One more successful application of American air power. Or maybe the NVA had just been playing with us, had pulled out a couple of days earlier, and only so many "daisies" had been cut that day. Those "Asian hordes" were held at bay, we were pulled out, and Gary was closer to building that bunker, one of his own choosing and design, deep in the desert.

Slouching Towards Olaya Street

> Had we returned home in 1916, out of the suffering and the strength of our experience we might have unleashed a storm. Now if we go back we will be weary, broken, burnt out, rootless and without hope. We will not be able to find our way any more.
>
> —Erich Maria Remarque
> *All Quiet on the Western Front*

To my way of thinking, I had returned home in the fall of 1915. The war might have been forever for the Vietnamese, but for me it had lasted one year, and only the memories would be carried forever. The ex-soldier's storm was meant to transform American society, rectifying its inequities, as well as ensuring that it understood the enormous, serious mistake this foreign adventure had been. Of course it didn't work out that way. Inertia and the countervailing forces were stronger, and troubled-Vietnam-War-veteran became one word. Although well-adjusted-Vietnam-War-veteran never gained quite the same traction, it was a worthwhile goal for me. I finished college in one field and stumbled thereafter into what the rest of society would call a respectable job in health-care administration. The work in this "real world" was meaningful, even exhilarating at times. So many of my fellow twenty-somethings weren't as lucky.

There were the many comforts of the Atlanta social scene. I even made a stab at settling down, bought a tumbledown house in

Atlanta's first suburb, Inman Park, and attempted very half-heartedly to restore it to its previous Victorian grandeur. Guess it was mainly the trees and that fantasy of a simpler time at the turn of the century that gave me comfort. And with the neighbors I had, any identifiable eccentricity of my own did not make me stick out so far that I had to be hammered down. An entire decade had almost slipped away since Gary had his dreams of a bunker of his own design, in arid surroundings.

Oscar Wilde once famously observed that work was made for those who couldn't figure out anything else to do with their lives. I had once found some work exhilarating, but still there were all those other things life should be about, and you can hardly achieve self-actualization as a wage slave to the corporate master. In my gadfly moments I'd throw out quips like, "If Americans are masters of efficiency, why is it that everyone is working all the time?" The resonance to this observation was never really strong—too many were racing, racing, and consuming, consuming.

Serendipity, as in most people's careers, made the next delivery. A friend suggested that I might be interested in a job in Saudi Arabia. There was no long deliberation. The answer was NO. Like most of my fellow Americans, I had a negative impression of the place. At the time I never really questioned why, having had no personal experience there, knowing no one who had ever been there, never having met anyone from there, and not even having read a single book on the country. The answer was simply NO. And I had a more solid basis for saying no than most, for at least I had been through Turkey, Iran, Afghanistan, and Pakistan. Turkey and Iran I gave a mixed rating, Afghanistan I was positively excited about, but it was Pakistan, and in particular the treatment of the women, most specifically the one I was with, that gave me a more solid basis for my refusal.

There is certainly something to be said for persistence, and thank goodness the former head of the Georgia Tech placement center—when it was still in the building that had once been Lester Maddox's old restaurant—pressed the issue, with a, "It could not possibly harm you to interview with this guy, he has actually lived there."

I must have passed the interview, but more importantly, so did the interviewer. The enormous carrot was dangled in front of me—two months off a year! A career objective, so easily obtained. Realistically, I would never achieve this in the United States, with a corporate culture that assumed disloyalty if you took two weeks' vacation in a row. Now just how bad could the other ten months be? He wanted me to sign a two-year contract—I said NO. "Look, I'll give it a try for a year." He said that was impossible; there were no one-year contracts. But he assured me that if things got too bad, just wait until after payday, apply for a visa to Bahrain, and I could then easily cut out, losing very little.

So, like many governments from time immemorial, I decided to take my mind off my "domestic problems" and sought a foreign adventure. The carrot was the pull: I no longer had to struggle to reorganize America's work-obsessed priorities. I could just grab my two months a year vacation by moving to a different country. And there was the push also, that indigestible lump somewhere in my soul, that our country had committed an unrepentant sin in that narrow, sinuous country on the other side of the world. Our reasons were quite different, but James Baldwin, I understand you.

Breaking on Through to the Other Side

You know the day destroys the night
Night divides the day
Tried to run
Tried to hide
Break on through to the other side
Break on through to the other side
Break on through to the other side, yeah

—The Doors
Break On Through (To the Other Side)

In the late 70's Hospital Corporation of America, or more precisely HCI, its international subsidiary, held the management contract for King Faisal Specialist Hospital. We were told at the time that this contract alone contributed something like 12 percent of the total revenues for HCA. A significant contribution to the bottom line and no doubt, in closely guarded ways, an important contributing factor to making Senator Bill Frist a Senate Majority Leader. Before embarking for Riyadh, an orientation was conducted in Nashville, some of which was executed with admirable skill, like when we were told that alcohol was strictly illegal in the Kingdom, yet assured that it seemed to be freely available at parties.

Other parts of the orientation were wildly inadequate. An "authentic Arab" had been hired to give us a talk about the culture, and inter alia, he assured us that the Kingdom had just reconstructed the entire Hejaz Railway, which connected Istanbul to Medina, as seen in the movie *Lawrence of Arabia*. It proved to be a fantasy worthy of the Iraqi Information Minister Mohammed Saeed Al-Sahaf during the Second Iraq War!

The long-range 747 was not operational, so the flight to Riyadh was via Chicago, New York, London, Rome, and Athens. Recruiters had told us that accommodation for single men might, for a time, be in the considerably less than upscale Batha Hotel. Fortunately, that "intermediate stop" was not necessary. I moved directly into the recently completed Sahara Towers on Olaya Street. In a few short years' time, the desert along this road exchanged hands at two to three times the price of land on Fifth Avenue in New York City. Today Olaya Street is one of the prime commercial arteries of the city. But in the late 70's, goats grazed on the opposite side of this two-lane dusty street and Bedouin were encamped a few hundred meters away on a hill. HCI had already cautioned us about taking photographs, and among other concerns, it was thought that the Saudis would believe the photographs would be used to ridicule them—no doubt because many people did exactly that.

So I had FNG status again. In my mental baggage, I was carrying many more misconceptions than the allegedly reconstructed Hejaz Railway. I didn't find the wise mentor this time who could give me the inside scoop. Thus, discarding the old mindset would take some time. Time I had plenty of, along with a view from my fourth-floor apartment of brown desolation and the grazing goats on the other side of Olaya Street.

Many Western expatriates quickly purchased a vehicle, quite often a four-wheel drive. I was to be no exception. But the hospital also provided regular bus transportation for its employees. Sahara Towers was located about five kilometers away, and I rode the shuttle for the first month or so, until I decided it was safe enough to stay longer, and I could afford an investment in personal transportation.

It was a relaxed time, and looking back it is difficult to believe that men and women freely cohabitated in this housing unit and many others. One of the American construction companies sent a bus through the hospital's female housing compound each morning to pick up its employees for work. A young Saudi physician and his Canadian girlfriend rode on the hospital bus from Sahara Towers to the hospital each morning. In the next six months he would depart for what seemed like an impossibly long seven-year training program in Canada. He eventually returned, rising to a senior administrative post within the hospital and acquiring the mantle of respectability and authority that such a post carried.

Not long before I left on my final "exit-only" visa, in early 2003, I was in his office and decided to allude to those times in Sahara Towers a quarter century before. Would he want to reminisce about those freer, perhaps better times, or would he prefer to ignore them, thinking his current position could not admit to such a cavalier youth and, furthermore, embarrassed that a foreigner had raised the subject? He was polite but evasive, and I quickly sensed he did not "want to go there." Like Faulkner, I knew too much about them, and reminisces would be too embarrassing.

I arrived in December 1978, during the gloriously cool Riyadh winter. Some days I would walk across the open desert to the hospital. I had been warned that packs of wild dogs roamed the intervening area, so I always picked up a suitably sized stone to hurl at them if they attacked. Fortunately my ammunition was never required. Today, in the Riyadh of five million people, that entire intervening area is solidly covered with housing, commercial establishments, and a national expressway. Like many others at the time, I purchased an old canvas-covered Daihatsu jeep, a vehicle as useful in the city, with its roads always under construction, as it was in the desert.

My first desert adventure, an overnight camping trip, was a ten-kilometer or so run down Olaya Street, with the asphalt and any remaining buildings fading out in five kilometers, after which I took a dirt track and aimed for a small hill that some expats, for unexplained reasons, had dubbed "Bunny Hill." We would roll out a thick blanket from the jeep to sleep on, something that the expats, again for unexplained reasons, called a "Yemen blanket." No tent was required, after all you were in the desert, and it never rained, or so I thought. Today, the location of "Bunny Hill" is just inside the north perimeter expressway; the hill was half demolished when I left in 2003, and it is safe to assume that the location of "Bunny Hill" is now covered by villas.

Riyadh was a frontier town, along many different dimensions. The "national bird" was the construction crane. The entire city sported just a couple of traffic lights. With the constant road construction, if one took a six-week leave, one literally had to relearn the detours from point A to point B. Fresh meat consisted of lamb or goat. There was no fresh milk. Electrical power failures were not uncommon. The tap water was not considered potable. I experienced the exhilarating freedom of having neither a residential phone nor television for three years. A few of the familiar props of late 20th Century Western existence were removed, and we rediscovered what people did before such distractions. To the expats who have returned to their home country, there is universal agreement that they will never achieve the intensity of the social interactions and the camaraderie which evolved during that time.

There were the dinner parties—the ritual of breaking bread with one's fellow men and women. I acquired a reputation for making sweet and sour pork, doubly delicious in a land that proscribes the eating of the meat of the pig. We played volleyball, softball, tennis, and we also swam and scuba dived. Some remained inside their safe cocoon, and others decided to explore their surroundings.

Though it was never my intention to leave this cocoon when I initially signed on, the wonder of the Arabian Peninsula filled me with awe. And move over Atlanta, for there was the Riyadh social scene in the fading days of my youth. "Take me on a trip upon your magic swirling ship. . . to dance beneath the diamond sky, with one hand waving free . . . " Did Bob Dylan pay us a visit and I missed it on one of my leaves? His allusions captured the essence of this scene. We might have been turning into rustic bumpkins who would later be out of place in our respective countries, but we had the music, much of it of our own creation. Some of the music was the creation of others, and in these innocent days, there would be professional chamber music concerts at the Intercontinental Hotel, with performers flown in from Europe. The concerts were open to the public where men and women, Saudi and non-Saudi, would sit together and enjoy.

***

King Faisal was a man of the desert, pious and ascetic. He had a few quirky beliefs, but from the historical record, and his actions, one senses that he had his heart in the right place. He understood the value of a life unburdened by the goods deemed necessary in modern life. Yet he realized that his Kingdom must come to terms with the modern world. Among his other actions, he wrestled with the Islamic prohibition against reproducing images of living forms and came down on the side of introducing television into the Kingdom, which would greatly aid in the education of his people. Not everyone in King Faisal's family shared his view, including his nephew, Khalid bin Musaid. King Faisal also firmly believed that everyone in his country was entitled to sophisticated, quality medical care based on the most elementary of criteria—they needed it. It is a belief that has still not gained acceptance in the ruling classes of the United States.

Many people lose their life to television so to speak, as that life is slowly drained away in mindless addiction. King Faisal lost his life to television in much more dramatic fashion. Khalid bin Musaid had been killed in an attack, led by him, trying to destroy the recently operational TV transmitter. Khalid's younger brother, also named Faisal, had his own run at that often sought "full and worldly life," and among other escapades, was convicted of conspiring to sell the drug LSD when he was a student at the University of Colorado in 1970. However, his youthful indiscretions would not be redeemed by the contemplative life in a Trappist monastery but by a golden sword on "chop-chop" square. In the time-honored traditions of the Peninsula, if not elsewhere, the young Faisal set out to avenge his brother's death. As a prince he had "access," and with a .38 caliber pistol, he put three bullets in the King, killing him almost instantly.

Royal succession quickly passed to Faisal's brother, Khalid. Among other actions, in order to commemorate his predecessor, Khalid named the new hospital, in its final stages of construction, after the late King Faisal. A grimmer monument was also left across the street from the hospital: the half-finished palace under construction by Musaid's family was left standing, in the exact state of completion it was in when King Faisal was assassinated by his nephew. As the years passed, the unfinished palace was repeatedly vandalized and covered in graffiti. Occupying very expensive real estate on one of the busiest corners in the city, it was finally torn down in 2003. It is reminiscent of how the Japanese left one building, dubbed the "A-Bomb Dome," standing in Hiroshima as an historical memorial to that catastrophic event in 1945 while they completely rebuilt the rest of the city.

Many of these facts were poorly understood, or unknown, to the expats who poured into the Kingdom to work at the new King Faisal Specialist Hospital, though as part of the three-day orientation program, all were dutifully shown the late King's somewhat idealized portrait crafted in lapis lazuli which was displayed in the hospital's lobby. The hospital was a mini-city, and like the US Army before, assumed the function of caring for many of the social needs of its employees and their families. It also provided to its Western employees fully furnished and equipped housing, including everything from trash baskets to table linens. In addition to its own power plant and water treatment plant, the hospital had a significant security department and even its own fire trucks. It provided subsidized meals in the cafeteria and recreation facilities. It functioned as a post office and telephone exchange, had its own laundry, transportation and travel departments, and obtained the visas necessary for travel. For numerous Western expats, the many buffers the Hospital provided made it possible to ignore the larger, developing society in Riyadh, which included avoiding the need to learn Arabic.

But someone was "invisible" in this earlier picture, in the Ralph Ellison sense—the Saudis. Here we were, in the very heart of their country, one of the more socially conservative countries on earth, and they were at the very periphery of our existence. The very poor Saudis drove the hospital buses and the local taxis. More affluent Saudis were shopkeepers, particularly in the gold *souks*. A small group of Saudis worked at the hospital in administrative posts but were kept at the extreme edges of power. They were like so much cardamom sprinkled in the coffee, an exotic presence sufficient to suggest that one was not actually in a hospital in Peoria. The hospital was run by Americans, plain and simple, to the consternation of the many other nationalities employed by the hospital. Saudi students studied at night, sitting along the wall of what we called "Gerrin Village," named after the original builder of the townhouses, which housed many of the single women and married couples who worked at the hospital. It was a couple of years before I discovered why—the student's own homes lacked electricity, thus light and air conditioning, so what better place to study on a summer evening than outside, in the cool air, reading by the lights on top of the wall?

There were occasional chance encounters with Saudis. One day we were playing softball in a rocky vacant lot, and a Saudi was sitting, watching us. He came up to me, quietly observing in well-spoken English, and obviously making reference to the game's long periods of boredom vis-à-vis soccer, "I think you must have a lot of patience to play this game."

5

Searching for Taithlith

The congestion of Yemen, therefore, becoming extreme, found its only relief in the east, by forcing the weaker aggregations of its border down and down the slopes of the hills along the Widian, the half-waste district of the great water-bearing valleys of Bisha, Dawasir, Ranya and Taraba, which ran out towards the deserts of Nedj. These weaker clans had continually to exchange good springs and fertile palms for poorer springs and scantier palms, till at last they reached an area where a proper agricultural life became impossible. They then began to eke out their precarious husbandry by breeding sheep and camels, and in time came to depend more and more on these herds for their living. . . . There were few, if indeed there was a single northern Semite, whose ancestors had not at some dark age passed through the desert. The mark of nomadism, that most deep and biting social discipline, was on each of them in his degree.

—T. E. Lawrence,
Seven Pillars of Wisdom

Was Lawrence just making this stuff up? Overpopulation in the Yemen settled the entire Arabian peninsula, and beyond? Furthermore, in reading other portions of his book, the modern reader should experience a profound unease arising from his casual assessment of the racial characteristics of another people. He speaks of Semites, and it is clear that he is speaking of both Arabs and Jews: "Semites had no half-tones in their register of vision."... "They were a limited, narrow-minded people, whose inert intellect lay fallow in incurious resignation." ..."The common base of all the Semitic creeds, winners or losers, was in the ever present idea of world-worthlessness." ..."The Semite hovered between lust and self-denial." One might ask of the latter statement: Yeah? More so or less so than the English? David Fromkin, in his classic study of the making of the modern Middle East entitled *A Peace to End All Peace*, said that "Lawrence possessed many virtues but honesty was not among them; he passed off fantasies as the truth. A few months before, he had sent a letter to General Clayton that contained an almost certainly fictitious account of an expedition he claimed to have undertaken as his own."

All these observers, with their impressions of Arabia, sliced and diced. Lawrence, and Wilfred Thesiger after him, were profoundly flawed individuals. In the latter's case, it was often rumored, his "character flaws" would have resulted in lengthy prison sentences and universal revulsion in most Western countries. The issue of the motive and perspective of the observer, and his "reference frame," which is far from inertial, was one of Edward Said's central concerns in his seminal work *Orientalism*, the preeminent scholarly work on the manner in which the West's ideas of the Muslim world are created and transmitted.

For me, many of these considerations would only evolve years into the future. I had my own priorities and places I had to visit, or revisit, during that 60 days a year of vacation. And so within the first year and a half I had visited Paris for two weeks, Bali for two, South Africa for three, and New Zealand for ten days. That was before a ten-day visit to the States. But of all the trips, it was the "accidental" one that I remember with the most intensity. Certainly it was not on my list of destinations when I departed from Nashville. The Ministry of Information was giving away coffee-table picture books of the Kingdom, which included pictures of the houses in the Asir—tall towers with crenellations and horizontal slates placed in the walls every two feet or so to retard the erosion of the mud walls during the rainy season. I had the opportunity to travel in the reverse direction of all this supposed population flow that Lawrence described, back up from the desert to the very gates of the Yemen, indeed, into those famous "lost provinces" of the Yemen—the Asir. The trip was not originally my idea—one of the hospital administrators wanted to take this trip before he departed the country, in his own tattered Daihatsu jeep, and he was taking his wife and two small children. Well, if he could do it, I could come along for the ride also, driving my own Daihatsu. Plus, the first week in November is the perfect camping time, finally cool enough in the lower regions around Riyadh, but not yet too cold in the mountains of the Asir.

The trip was charted in the shape of one big triangle, Riyadh to Abha, Abha up the recently completed mountain road to Taif, and then back to Riyadh, approximately 3,000 kilometers. The first night's campsite had already been selected: Lake Layla. In the very early months of my FNG status, when the "old timers" talked of water-skiing at Layla, I thought it had to be one of those folklore myths, like the alligators in the sewers of New York City. The next morning I would be taking a bath in that myth, the last one for another eight days—the lake certainly did exist. We knew that the asphalt evaporated at Wadi Dewasir, and we would be faced with the daunting task of trying to negotiate a further 500 kilometers of open desert (long before the days of a GPS), with only the sun and a simple compass as our guides, before we would become acquainted with the asphalt again outside Khamis Mushayt, near Abha. We stopped at the police station at Wadi Dewasir and asked the police chief about the best way across this expanse. He strongly advised us not to try it. "There are many paths in the desert, and unless you know which one to take, you'll get hopelessly lost, and might even die." He was wise; he had done his duty as he was gaining an understanding of these foreigners who had so recently started invading his country. He even probably suspected what we actually did—pretend to go back toward Riyadh, swing around the town, and continue heading southwest into the open desert.

It was to be my introduction to campsites selected for their aesthetics. Did they have the right feel—partially secluded, usually with a view including the desert landscape gradient, near hills fading into distant mountains, the essence of why the desert appears so immense? It was also an introduction to the wonderful concept of "running free and clear." Like the dream expressed in so many automobile ads, driving anywhere, the absence of fences that proclaimed this is mine, keep out—is perhaps the one aspect that I miss the most. Saudi Arabia is one of the very few places on earth where you can really run free and clear—paradoxically in a country that one does not immediately associate with the word *freedom*. And many years before I became aware of the existence of the Dark Earth Society, the organization dedicated to reducing light pollution, there was the desert sky and the complete lack of light pollution.

We were carrying extra petrol, but not enough to make it all the way to Abha. We *had* to obtain more petrol in the desert town of Taithlith. The compass, and our standard rule that when the path forked, to ignore Robert Frost and take the road more heavily traveled, got us there. The buildings were beginning to change; they had more color, even bright colors, and thus a resemblance to Mexico. With the essential petrol cans full, and with ice and good food in our coolers, we were content. That night, though, our dreams were interrupted by the grinding of the gears of a Mercedes-Benz truck, loaded with goods. Traveling at night, most likely since that was the way things were done in the desert, the truck continually became stuck in the sand, and the driver had to dig his way out. He might have driven only ten kilometers the entire night. In contrast, our light Daihatsus skimmed across the desert's surface.

The next day we stopped at a Bedouin tent, carefully observing the desert protocol for such a meeting, which is none other than one would use in meeting the local SWAT team in the United States—no sudden moves. We parked our vehicles about 25 meters away and one person walked up to the tent, empty-handed. Once it was ascertained that no harm was meant, the coffee flowed. Thesiger should have been with us. The man had a classic hawklike nose and that etched, hard-lined profile of a man of the desert. On this cool November day his surroundings were appealing, with judiciously spaced, low rock outcrops, both yielding a sense of privacy but also providing dramatic vistas, depending on the direction one faced. The bedu told us that his life was *mush quais* (not good). The freedom from authority, the vistas, and the stars were overwhelmed by the heat of summer and the evasive, blowing sand that entered everything. His dream was to obtain one of those cinder block homes the government was building, AC in the summer, and windows that, more or less, prevented the sand's invasion. Like almost all of the Bedouin population in the Kingdom, over the course of the next 20 years they would abandon millennium-old ways and embrace the sedentary lifestyle, creating problems of its own, such as an epidemic of diabetes.

The mountains rose in the west. We were fortunate to meet another expat worker, a non-Westerner, who also said that there were too many desert paths and volunteered to lead us for 50 kilometers or so, guiding us to the right passage that would take us to Abha.

We were late. It had taken us two and half days to travel the 500 kilometers. We had agreed to meet a couple who had flown from Riyadh to Abha. They intended to go scuba diving, of sorts, in a place where it had never been done before. They had been at the airport about five hours when we finally arrived, and we squeezed them into the back of the jeeps with their gear, specifically, a hookah apparatus that could be floated, and via its engine, supply air down a tube to someone underwater.

At 10,000 feet, Abha is removed from the water by 90 horizontal kilometers. But it was being connected by a dramatic road that dropped off the high escarpment to the Red Sea. To expedite the building process, the entire road was closed until 5:00 p.m. every day, and then something akin to the Oklahoma land rush occurred. Precisely at the designated time, the road opened, a perilous plunge to the sea down a dirt track began. One was quickly enveloped in dust as vehicles raced to pass each other. About two-thirds of the way, an additional complication developed when the downward propelled vehicles met the vehicles struggling up the escarpment. Finally, all was compounded by the deepening dusk and switchback after switchback, we drove downhill for one and a half hours, arriving on the coastal plain as night rapidly approached.

This coastal plain is called the Tihama and is strikingly similar to Africa, with its conical huts made of straw and the coal-black people.

Like Africa, diseases such as malaria and what would later be discovered in the '90's, Rift Valley fever, unknown in the rest of the Kingdom, are found here. We strove to find the beach, and our idealized campsite, but couldn't find the path in the darkness. Finally, utterly exhausted and mindful of his two little kids, my partner in this adventure said he could go no farther, and we threw down our blankets, sleep overtaking us immediately.

The next morning we awoke to see a farmer quietly watching us. We were asleep in his field, and he had indeed been invaded by Martians. I looked down at my dirty blue jeans, covered in flies, the most lethargic flies in the world, and if so inclined, one could eliminate 50 in a slow swat.

We spied an extinct volcano balanced on the edge of the sea, 15 kilometers or so to the north. It seemed a likely spot for our hookah diving, which quickly ended in failure when a wave flipped the inner tube carrying the engine, drowning it. The engine wouldn't start again. But the warm salt water felt good after the cold of the mountains, and an assessment of our freshwater supplies allowed for a quick rinse-off. The next day we snaked our way up the dirt road back into the mountains. We drove on an asphalt road all the way back to Riyadh, first traveling north along the mountain road through Al-Baha to Taif. We moved into the anticlimactic part of the trip, for although the vistas along this road, built in the very early days of the oil boom to bind these provinces with the north, are as dramatic as any along California's coastal highway, they could not compare with the earlier unknown of 500 kilometers of open desert. We arrived in Riyadh in mid-November, 1979. We felt a real sense of achievement and satisfaction. It was a fitting way to end the 1300s, since we were in the closing days of 1399 on the Hijerian calendar. However, in a few days, at the beginning of 1400, things would not go as well for the House of Saud. In fact, all hell was going to break loose.

* * *

Our paths may have in fact crossed on those mountain roads. He and his followers didn't like our presence in the Kingdom, being infidels and all as we were, but we were too small to attract his attention. His target was much larger and may have been the King himself, who might quite possibly be in Mecca (or, as officially decreed in the Kingdom, Makkah) for prayers on the first day of 1400. His name was Juhaiman bin Mohammed Al Ataybi. And he was from the heartland, Qassim.

The House of Saud had formed a loose alliance with the religious movement, whose incarnation in the 1800s (mid-1200s on a Hijerian basis) was led by a charismatic preacher named Abdul Wahab, who advocated a return to the simpler forms of "true Islam." In the 1900s, Abdul Aziz made use of the Wahabites in their latest form—the Ikhwan, the Brotherhood, whose fearless warriors were unbeatable in battle—to unify much of the Arabian Peninsula for the first time in history and create the Kingdom of Saudi Arabia. But it was always an uneasy alliance; religious fundamentalists have that tendency for extending their messianic vision too far for the practicalities of temporal rulers, even for Abdul Aziz, who had to borrow a few machine guns from the British and return to Qassim in the late 1920's and mow the Ikhwan down.

Juhaiman was born in 1940, growing up in the spirit of martyrdom that permeated the air of these defeated Ikhwan settlements. He co-opted messianic religious themes from Christianity and Judaism, as well as the Shia branch of Islam. He had proclaimed one from his band of followers as the expected Mahdi, a concept that had appeared on most Westerners' consciousness only once before. In this prior incarnation another "Mahdi" had defeated General Gordon at Khartoum in 1881. That event corresponded with the year 1300 on the Hijerian calendar, which reflected the centenary component of the Mahdi legend.

In a very well-provisioned and carefully executed plan, Juhaiman and several hundred of his followers seized the Grand Mosque in Makkah—and dug in to stay. It took the better part of two weeks, and the rumored use of French mercenaries quickly converted to Islam, to defeat this latest coming of the Mahdi. The use of weapons at the Grand Mosque is forbidden, and so the official Saudi media stuck with the line that Saudi forces had used no gunfire to remove the "deviants." The wounded piling up in the hospitals of Riyadh belied this contention. But there was a palatable sense of relief in the cafeteria at the hospital that the Saudi authorities saw no "foreign hand" in this event.

As with so many other events in life, timing is crucial. We had just returned to the relative safety of our hospital-provided refuge. An American department head was commencing his trip, also in an old Daihatsu jeep, as we ended ours. His trip was at least as ambitious. Jeff intended to cross the mountains north of Medina and arrive at the Red Sea somewhere around Wedj, where Lawrence had landed in 1916 to commence his march north, the initiation of the "Arab revolt." Our colleague didn't make it, and although he carried extra wheels, he was defeated by tires shredded by the sharp rocks while traveling in the *wadis* (dry water courses, similar to arroyos in the western United States). When Jeff returned to the main asphalt road, he was quickly apprehended by Bedouin irregulars who had recently been activated with orders to arrest suspected "terrorists" who were creating the havoc in Makkah and possibly other places as well. An old Bedouin pointed a flintlock rifle at Jeff and indicated he was getting in the jeep; Jeff was under arrest, and the destination was north, the town of Tabuk.

Fortuitously, in heading north Jeff and his uninvited companion met a convoy, including the governor of Tabuk, heading south. The prince already had information about the true nature of the taking of the Grand Mosque; Americans weren't behind this one, so he wrote a safe conduct pass for Jeff and his party to return to Riyadh. It was most useful since the Saudis had placed roadblocks every 100 kilometers along the Jeddah–Riyadh road.

Executions in the Kingdom are normally carried out on the Islamic holy day, Friday. To forestall any reaction from the perpetrator's supporters, a Tuesday in early January was selected, and 63 heads of the followers of Juhaiman rolled into the dirt, justice dispensed in eight different towns. It seemed that peace had returned to the Kingdom.

***

Many dimensions separate the Café Flore in Paris (a city that also has a historical reputation for rolling a few heads) from those dusty towns scattered across *Al Jazeera*. It was half a year after the events surrounding the taking of the Grand Mosque, and the long twilight of a late Parisian spring was fading in the west. My objective was probably no more than the tourists on Beale Street. I was chasing a few ghosts myself, trying to savor the atmosphere, now long since changed, where Sartre and de Beauvoir had established themselves as writers. While nursing a beer I thought back over the past eighteen months. All my original travel objectives in going to the Kingdom had been met. I still intended to return to Atlanta in six months. Life in the Kingdom was not so bad, and I hadn't once planned to flee to Bahrain. Complications were setting in though, among them the fact that I now had double the travel destinations than when I set out on this adventure. A number of them were inside the Kingdom itself. So, I made a decision, like many others had. The decision would be the subject of wry smiles from the desk staff at the hotel in Paris that I visited annually. It would even be made into a T-shirt sold at the expat bazaars in Riyadh—an old man sitting in his wheelchair and underneath the slogan: "Just one more year."

And that was how, almost exactly a year after the original trip, on a crisp November day, I again set off for Wadi Dewasir and that 500-kilometer stretch of open desert to Abha. The faces of my traveling companions had changed. There were two other vehicles, a married couple in one, and two men, one with the two children in the other. Jeanette, a Canadian nurse, was traveling with me. Before we reached Wadi Dewasir we drove through the town of Sulaiyil. Wilfred Thesiger had been detained and arrested in this town during his historic '47 crossing of the *Rub al-Khali* (Empty Quarter). Remnants of the Ikhwan lived here, and the hostility was especially palatable due to the fact that Thesiger was Christian. King Abdul-Aziz himself granted permission to release Thesiger and allowed him to continue on to Abu Dhabi. Knowing that technically, under the laws of the Kingdom, I should not be traveling with a single woman, I adopted moderately cautious tactics—like ensuring that the real married couple was first in line at any checkpoint. I knew that I should be particularly cautious around the town of Sulaiyil, keeping Thesiger's arrest in mind. In the middle of the town, at a stoplight, a rather hostile looking policeman approached me first, in the second vehicle, asking for our *iqamas* (residency papers). In these early days the iqamas were not clear as to marital status, and it was possible for a married couple, each working, to have individual iqamas, with no dependents shown. He asked if Jeanette was my wife—I indicted yes. He wanted her iqama, and I gave it to him. He again asked if she was my wife. Yes, I said, knowing that nothing in the iqama system contradicted this. Then he pointed at me first and said "American," and at her and said "Canadian." My response was one that Americans use which endears them to Canadians: "Canada—America, same-same." He knew I was lying about the marital status, but was unsure of the procedures for dealing with the matter, and so waved us on with a snarl. The open desert was looking better.

When we reached Wadi Dewasir, we didn't even stop at the police station before plunging into the desert. I had long since lost my FNG status. I would be the pathfinder, my sense of dead reckoning well tested. Taithlith was again the mandatory destination for petrol. Dead reckoning and Robert Frost failed me this time, though. I must have missed it by a good 30 kilometers. We stopped a Bedouin, a very well-armed one with his AK-47, and I asked him how much farther to Taithlith. Another smile as he pointed 90 degrees away from the direction I was pointing. We might have been Martians, but he knew his obligations to lost desert travelers. He motioned for us to follow him, and we bounced along at high speed for 20 kilometers or so. At the top of a hill he pointed ahead, "Taithlith," and so it was, our promised petrol land. He vanished with our thanks.

My dead reckoning actually proved much better getting us up the right passageway through the mountains toward Abha. So much better, in fact, that the Saudi authorities knew the path also and had placed a police checkpoint on this narrow dirt track through the hills. Our papers were in order, so there was no problem in that regard, and we were unlikely suspects to storm the mosque in Makkah. But there was that look of incomprehension on the policeman's face: What could possibly be our motives for coming to such a desolate location? We airily replied *"ijhaza"* (vacation). We bridged that vast cultural gulf with a man who was unlikely to ever sit in the Café Flore. A companion quickly added *"mafi mouk"* (no brains). And you just knew that was exactly what he had been thinking because he immediately became embarrassed, thrust his best manners forward, and insisted that we join him and his buddies in the tent for tea. They went out of their way to assure us that it was the most natural thing in the world, coming here on vacation, not realizing, and certainly not believing, if told, that Lawrence had once postulated that the surplus of Yemen's population had once poured down this dirt track into the open desert, toward those poor wells and palm trees.

6

Abdul Aziz ibn Saud Lived and Slept Here: Yabrin

> To return to the Empty Quarter would be to answer a challenge, and to remain there for long would be to test myself to the limit. Much of it was unexplored. It was one of the very few places left where I could satisfy an urge to go where others had not been. The circumstances of my life had so trained me that I was qualified to travel there. The Empty Quarter offered me the chance to win distinction as a traveler; but I believed that it could give me more than this, that in those empty wastes I could find the peace that comes with solitude, and, among the Bedu, comradeship in a hostile world.
>
> —Wilfred Thesiger,
> *Arabian Sands*

Obtaining information on the Kingdom and its developments was a very happenstance affair. Little was written about the country in English, and even less was actually available within the Kingdom. There was the small bookstore at the Intercontinental Hotel, and part of its meager fare was the Bartholomew map of the Kingdom and Thesiger's classic account of how he conned the Middle East Anti-Locust Unit into funding his personal obsession, a crossing of the *Rub Al-Khali* (the Empty Quarter) just after the Second World War, under the pretext of looking for the breeding grounds of the locust that occasionally overwhelmed India. The book, *Arabian Sands*, was obligatory reading for anyone in Saudi Arabia with the least interest in the world beyond the gates of the hospital.

After reading *Arabian Sands,* at least a weekend brush with the vastness and emptiness of the *Rub Al-Khali* seemed obligatory. But we were not masochist enough for the whole pain, life and death thrills that Thesiger undertook with his beloved "faithful companions." We wanted more of a small tasting in the winter, via jeep, and with a cooler full of ice in the back. The Bartholomew map indicated a small village named Al-Ubalayla and a dotted trail going 500 kilometers south, southeast of the village of Harrad. Now a veteran of two 500-kilometer cross-desert trips, it was worth at least an attempt, though even at the outset we suspected the trip would be daunting, with the need for petrol paramount.

We traveled three hours to Harrad by car, along a two-lane asphalt road, which included the forty minutes required to grind out of the increasing traffic of the Riyadh of old. We started out on Wednesday evening, after work, at the beginning of our weekend. We set up camp in the dark, near Harrad, ready for the push south on Thursday morning.

It was a bit more of a push than we bargained for. There was a series of low, wide, sand-filled *wadis* that had to be crossed with just the right touch—fast enough to get through them without flipping the jeep, but not slow enough to get stuck. We did a lot of digging and pushing. Over five hours later, the beginning of the afternoon, we had struggled almost 90 kilometers, and the petrol was almost half consumed. Then it appeared, just beyond the twin buttes: The village of Yabrin. Two white minarets rose visible against the dusty green background of palm trees.

The founder of modern Saudi Arabia, Abdul Aziz ibn Saud, had grown up here as a boy after his father grew tired of living in exile in Kuwait. It was also here that he stayed prior to his attack on Riyadh in 1902. Much later, thanks to that Anti-Locust Board, Thesiger had reached this oasis 32 years prior to our arrival. Due to the drought, Thesiger and his three traveling companions could find no one else. After eight days on the trail from Layla there were only the wells, still full of the much-needed water. Thesiger knew that he was in the heartland of the Murrah tribe, the famed desert trackers of Arabia. Saudi governors employed one or two of the Murrah tribe on their staff for the sole purpose of desert tracking, because the trackers had the ability to judge the speed and length of time since camels had passed through, based on their footprints and the freshness of their dung. Thesiger described the Murrah as one of the great tribes of the Nedj, the central region of Saudi Arabia and estimated their number at 5,000-10,000, and reported that they lived in an area the size of France.

The "real estate developers" had been active in the intervening 32 years, and a fair settlement of mud and cinder block homes had been built. Unlike Thesiger, our needs were not water, of which we always carried a more than adequate supply, but petrol. We saw the back of a tanker truck perched on a small hill and the hose that would gravity-feed the petrol into our jeeps, operated by a Yemeni and sold at prices not much higher than in Riyadh.

With full tanks and sighting the Saudi flag fluttering from a nearby building, we decided to "pay our respects" to the local governmental official. He introduced himself as Emir Hamad, a young, thin man in his late twenties who had acquired his position upon the death of his father a couple of years earlier. Emir Hamad was polite, invited us in, offered us tea, but quickly cut to the purpose of our visit. We did our *ijhaza* (vacation) routine. He had heard this before, as we learned many years later, from travelers who worked at Aramco. "Always avoid Yabrin," these travelers said, because the Emir takes a hard line on such casual wanderings." And he did so with us. He told us we were in a border region (we would have agreed if we assumed the border was 500 kilometers thick) and that we required special government permission to be in the area.

Actually, in some ways the border was 500 kilometers thick! It wasn't so many years previous that territorial claims concerning the Buramyi oasis with Oman and the United Arab Emirates had been settled. There remained continued disputes over who controlled this vast region, with limited permanent human settlement and immense oil reserves.

By instinct, and quite possibly acting under orders, we received a very firmly implied, "White boy, I don't want the sun to set on you in

Yabrin tonight." And there was an implicit "no further south" in his tone. We quickly agreed that we were really bound for the village of Khunn toward the northeast. That was just fine with Emir Hamad, as long as we were out of his area of responsibility. To aid us in reaching our destination, Hamad summoned his "first lieutenant," pointedly armed, and told him to follow us. He followed us for around ten kilometers or so and finally turned around with the setting sun, heading back to Yabrin. We set up camp, figuring we had had our taste of the Empty Quarter, and it was more sour than sweet. We thought it would be our last visit, but it turned out to be the first of many.

7

The Wilder Shores of Love

"…and the old castle thousands of years old yes and those handsome Moors all in white and turbans like kings asking you to sit down in their little shop and…the night we missed the boat at Algeciras the watchman going about serene with his lamp and O that awful deep down torrent O and the sea the sea crimson sometimes like fire and the glorious sunsets and the fig trees in the Alameda gardens yes and all the queer little streets and pink and blue and yellow houses and the rose gardens and the Jessamine and geraniums and cactuses and Gibraltar as a girl where I was a Flower of the mountain yes when I put the rose in my hair like the Andalusian girls used or shall I wear a red yes and how he kissed me under the Moorish wall and I thought well as well him as another and then I asked him with my eyes to ask again yes and then he asked me would I yes to say yes my mountain flower and first I put my arms around him yes and drew him down to me so he could feel my breasts all perfume yes and his heart was going like mad and yes I said yes I will Yes."

—James Joyce,
Ulysses

There were those who did catch the boat in Algeciras and made it all the way to Tangiers, leaving behind the fig trees there, or the magnolia trees in Marseilles, or the olive trees in Salonika landing on the south shore of the Mediterranean. Leslie Blanch, in her book *The Wilder Shores of Love,* chronicles the lives of four Western European women who crossed to the southern and eastern shores of the Mediterranean and immersed themselves in another culture, with variable results in their love lives.

Ms. Blanch addressed the most common intercultural relationship: northern European women with Arab men. But there were those small countercurrents too, all the more interesting due to their uniqueness. The official policy in Saudi Arabia was to strongly discourage Western women from developing relationships with Saudi men within the country. Those who were too open in ignoring these warnings could suddenly be deported. Some stayed under the radar, but this rarely led to long-term relationships. And there were those who were simply manifesting their entrepreneurial skills, as it were.

The relationships that seemed to be the most enduring developed when the Saudi men were attending university in a Western country. In general, the men faced the disapproval of their families, but some persevered and married, bringing their new wives to a very different environment. In the early 80's a Saudi colleague approached me at work one day. He told me that he had just gotten married, that his new 19-year-old American wife would be coming to the Kingdom, and that she had previously never been out of Wisconsin. Hum! Like Dorothy in the Wizard of Oz, she would be a bit dazed when assessing her new landscape and realizing that "she was no longer in Sheboygan." "Could my wife and I help with the transition?" he asked.

And that was how it came to be that we were the only "non-mixed" couple at a Thanksgiving dinner held in their apartment with ten other couples, all of whom were Saudi men with Western wives. Some of the women had embraced Islam, others had remained Christian. There were a few fruits of the marriages there too, none of the kids much older than three. Of necessity this group had to band together, more so than other trans-cultural marriages, due to the generally observed prohibition against the mixing of the sexes within the Saudi culture.

The party was alcohol-free, but the general festive atmosphere and the turkey and dressing led me to let my cultural-sensitivity guard down too much. One of the Saudis was from Buraydah, which is by far the most conservative large town in the Kingdom. By comparison, Riyadh would be as culturally liberal as San Francisco. I joked that I had had a wonderful time in the discos of Buraydah. He looked a bit puzzled, and so I dug myself in deeper. "Well, of course the discos are underground, even some of the residents of Buraydah don't know of their existence." To which I received only a scowl. At *saleh* (prayer time), he was the only Saudi who prayed. His was one of the marriages that did not last.

Years in the future, I sat with some of those mixed couples whose marriages were intact as I watched my son play baseball at the beautiful ball field at the Arizona compound. Their sons were straddling one of the sharpest cultural divides in the world today, between the Western and Islamic cultures. The kids probably didn't think of themselves in that way as they picked up ground balls at shortstop. The Saudi dads quietly sat in the stands and watched their kids play a game so alien to their own youth—whose subtle rules they still did not understand. Their wives had successfully made the transition to Riyadh, some as flourishing businesswomen.

The countercurrents were much more unusual and certainly the more interesting for it. Truly the eyes have it, heart-stopping kohl-outlined eyes, the only part of the body visible, peering from behind the veil and looking right through you. The ultimate definition of exotic. As Joyce said: " . . . and then I asked him with my eyes to ask again . . . " Something to tease, maybe even torment the back of your brain. Dale Walker wrote a whimsical tale of the expat experience in Saudi Arabia entitled *Fool's Paradise*. Instead of the more common books on the Saudis, the sour, "let's look down our noses at these backward people" books, his book concentrates on the foibles of the expats themselves, in the Magic Kingdom. In one vignette, almost certainly apocryphal, he tells the tale of a particularly macho Western male who liked to notch his bedpost, one for each different nationality. The finals of the World Cup of such a sport would be a Saudi woman, universally "seeded" in the top place. In the city of Taif, this macho male's friend "fixed" the match for him by arranging an Egyptian prostitute to assume the Saudi nationality.

Such whimsy aside, real Saudi women meeting and even marrying Western men occurred also. I knew of perhaps two and a half cases. One was a very attractive Saudi woman, a Shia, who dressed as fashionably as any other Western woman—not as a Western woman in Saudi Arabia, with their loose-fitting clothes, but as a Western woman living in the West. She taught Arabic at the hospital for a period of time and had married a famous German movie actor. The other was the daughter of a very prominent business family, a woman of inherited wealth who directed major companies in the Kingdom but took the time to quietly contribute to the operation of the American School in Riyadh, which her children attended. In both cases, for the marriage to be legal in Saudi Arabia the men had to embrace Islam, which they must have done with varying degrees of sincerity.

As to the half case, like so many of those stories that fell under the rubric of expat folklore, you could never be absolutely certain that the story was true—even if you heard it from the originator's mouth, as I did. The guy was wild and crazy and he may have actually done it—dated a Saudi woman in Riyadh. How they actually got together was never fully explained, but when you are dealing with a force akin to gravity, well, water somehow figures out how to run downhill. Her brothers had picked him up one day, drove him to the desert, and made it very clear, in no uncertain terms, that if he ever saw their sister again, the next trip to the desert would be a one-way trip for him. Even "wild and crazy" as he was, the message was clear, and he opted to leave the country shortly thereafter.

***

When I left Nashville, on an adventure that might have lasted only a month or so before I fled to Bahrain, I knew I was going to a Kingdom, but I had no idea that I would be meeting the Queen. No, not the Queen of Saudi Arabia, the "Queen" of a country and western music band, the lead female singer. "Coat of Many Colors," "Stand by Your Man," "Queen of the Silver Dollar," and "Long, Black Veil," were part of the standard maudlin fare, some of the many songs that make C&W what it is. Fifteen years before she literally took the boat from Algeciras, she caught the figurative one and arrived in Riyadh in 1975 by plane. The courtship in Riyadh lasted almost two years, and she finally said "and yes I said yes I will Yes," "....as well him as another." So it was Bahrain that we fled to in early 1982, to be married by the Reverend Scutter, minister of one of the churches on the island. It was all part of the Saudi labor law: three days' vacation on the occasion of one's marriage. Those three days coupled with a weekend would have meant five days on the island, perhaps too long, perhaps too conventional.

After the simple ceremony, we flew back to Riyadh and drove across the country to Al-Hasi inlet, 48 kilometers south of Umm Lajj, where we honeymooned in a tent, almost certainly the first couple to ever honeymoon there. It is a lovely inlet on the Red Sea, and perhaps in 20 years or so, if the Minister of Tourism is successful, an appropriate five-star hotel will be built there for other couples' honeymoons. But it could never be the same as when we "ran free and clear," just as the Kingdom was beginning to assume all the accoutrements that we today believe are essential to enter the modern world.

8

Saudiazation—A Trial Run

Old bureaucrat, my comrade, it is not you who are to blame. No one ever helped you to escape. You, like a termite, built your peace by blocking up with cement every chink and cranny through which the light might pierce. You rolled yourself up into a ball in your genteel security, in routine, in the stifling conventions of provincial life, raising a modest rampart against the winds and the tides and the stars. You have chosen not to be perturbed by great problems, having trouble enough to forget your own fate as man. You are not the dweller upon an errant planet and do not ask yourself questions to which there are no answers. You are a petty bourgeois of Toulouse. Nobody grasped you by the shoulder while there was still time. Now the clay of which you were shaped has dried and hardened, and naught in you will ever awaken the sleeping musician, the poet, the astronomer that possibly inhabited you in the beginning.

—Antoine de Saint-Exupéry,
Wind, Sand and Stars

Health-care administration can actually be thrilling and give one a profound sense of satisfaction. More often than not, a human being enters the facility and emerges better than when he or she entered; sometimes radical, life-changing improvements are made, frequently it is the gift of life itself that is preserved. Of course there are also the failures and the incompetence. And it always struck me that advances in the information technology field has covered car maintenance, both in Saudi Arabia as well as in the United States, so much better than "human maintenance." King Faisal Specialist Hospital seemed more special than a corresponding facility in the United States, certainly due to its uniqueness, as well as to the abiding faith that the citizens of the country, particularly those from the rural areas, would be treated appropriately and well. The Arabic word *takassusi*, meaning "specialist," carries almost a magical quality throughout the country. One of the principal roads in Riyadh was so named, and when camping in the remote areas, the word meant you were all right. When requesting the requisite permission from the Coast Guard in order to dive, it was always granted once you said that magical word, *takassusi*.

Administrative policy and procedures, APPs, were the downside of such work. It is true of most bureaucratic institutions, and it was certainly true of KFSH—the endless arguments trying to determine the meaning of *'is'* and much more. Even if you perfected the document, you knew that many employees were going to do their own thing anyhow. Saint-Exupery knew the mindset so well. The clay that had dried and hardened, every opening that might let in the light blocked up with cement. Those endless, tedious committee meetings—others working in bureaucratic institutions have certainly shared this fate. But we experienced far worse than tedium and boredom after the final days of the American administration.

There was a coup of sorts in 1981 within the administration at KFSH. The American executive director took leave back to the United States, and a young Saudi physician he had befriended saw his chance and grabbed for the brass ring. As one Saudi said to me many years later, we had such a small core of educated, talented people back then; so many things were possible for the young and ambitious. You didn't have to be there in the antechamber of one of Riyadh's palaces to understand what happened. You could almost hear the affirmations of "you'll have our full support," and although both sides in the dialogue were fluent in Arabic, that phrase was mistranslated as, "you'll have carte blanche." The American administrator was never permitted to return.

The new administration, in reality one person, started out like so many, saying all the right things, which included dutifully "changing the wallpaper in the lobby," as the management books sardonically advocate. Some of that wallpaper involved "Muslim issues," and how conditions at this American implant in the heartland of Arabia might be ameliorated.

On one issue, the rank and file Muslims took direct political action in a country that strongly forbids demonstrations. Religion was their vehicle. Around 50 Muslim men occupied the pool area at the Amenities Center and used it for their prayer area. Would anyone, particularly the Western-led security force, attempt to remove them? Not even they were that stupid. The takeover was really about being granted access to this Amenities Center—incredibly the center was only for non-Muslims. Naturally the swimming pool was the thorniest issue—how do you reconcile swimming in a mixed-sex environment with Islamic precepts? The administration worked out a modus vivendi whereby two days a week the pool was reserved for females only, two days were reserved for males only, and the other three days were for "families," the code word for men and women together, though not necessarily married. This arrangement lasted through my departure in 2003.

Perhaps even more incredibly, the hospital did not have its own mosque. There were two mosques in Yabrin in the *Rub Al-Khali*, but the most prestigious hospital in the country didn't have ONE. The administration quickly made efforts to remedy this oversight and proudly displayed the plans for the new mosque at the entrance to the hospital. In the meantime, temporary prayer areas throughout the hospital proliferated. Which raised yet another political question—bluntly—did women have souls?

The vast majority of Muslims working at this modern hospital were on the affirmative side of this question. This same bias applied to the writers in the *Arab News*, "the leading English language newspaper in the Kingdom," whose cover page was green and thus was universally referred to as the Green Truth in the expat community. But these folks were arguing with someone, and despite all those Koranic verses about women's status and rights, there was that short *thobe*, anti-radio, anti-TV, flat-earth believing, and no doubt anti-Darwin group on the other side of those arguments. Men and women could not pray together, that was forbidden, and therefore the women soon obtained the first of numerous separate female prayer areas.

The director consolidated power rapidly, no alliances had to be made, particularly as he played to his political base. Although he was already in charge of everything, he REALLY wanted to be in charge of everything. He collected titles with the avidity of an 11-year-old collecting baseball cards. He wrote memos to himself, from one position to another, asking for approval on various matters. Much to the consternation of those termites in Personnel, he kicked a small chink in one of their mud walls. He examined job descriptions for positions such as messenger, and changed the qualifications of previous work experience from two years to three after the high school degree, and carefully initialed the change. The more perceptive doctors on the medical staff diagnosed an early form of a disease that can spread so rapidly: megalomania.

Of course, there were the normal problems too. One never asked why such and such was being built when the answer was always, "If you were getting ten percent off the top, you'd see a lot of reasons." The services of various relatives became indispensable to the smooth functioning of the hospital. Even the director's salacious inclinations would be forgiven by the country's Saudi leadership, given the normally assumed discretion.

But the megalomania was metastasizing. Discretion only gets in the way, if not being an absolute sign of weakness. Throughout human history progress had been made in the treatment of varying diseases, but the prognosis of this one remains predictable: this disease remains terminal, at least in terms of one's career. The particulars of megalomania as it spreads are the variables. In this case, the director made a seemingly odd alliance with foreigners. These foreigners all worked in the Security Department, half of them British (often via Rhodesia, when it was Rhodesia) and the other half American (usually via Vietnam). He in turn gave them carte blanche. They, too, tasted unbridled power, and savored it as they had never been able to do before.

What would seem an odd alliance has occurred many times: the reliance on foreigners to do one's bidding. It is the reason that the Mamelukes ruled Egypt for over three centuries. It was why the British hired the Gurkhas. And it is why the American workforce is now dependent on 11-20 million illegal foreigners. If you have no real rights in a country, it is hard to complain. But with the boys in Security, one did not sense that they were working under duress. Their inner instinct had been unleashed, like cops gone bad. And in a country particularly concerned about security, loyalty, and sovereignty, the director issued a specific directive that Saudi nationals could *not* be hired in the Security Department.

The director's disease destroyed even the fig leaf of discretion. His Western mistresses, with the emphasis on the plural, openly proclaimed their new status. The *ragum wahead* (number one) mistress had her own townhouse when the norm at the time was for single women to live three to a townhouse. The Grounds Maintenance Department provided her with a lovely garden. Security personnel drove her to horseback riding lessons. She strutted down the main corridor in the hospital and stated: "I can have anyone fired at this hospital that I want." And there were others like her. Meanwhile, so as to indicate the special perks of his position, the essence of any exclusive club, the director unleashed his Security boys on single Western men and women engaged in courtship rituals ordained since time immemorial. Security personnel hid in bushes and stood on rooftops, binoculars in hand, spying on single men and women meeting, allegedly to uphold Islamic morality. They thrived on it. All hospital employees, in the lingo of the Security boys, had become, if not actual, then at least potential "perps" (perpetrators, as in, of a crime).

Their power grew, as the director felt threatened by other individuals, Saudis and non-Saudis, who were speaking out against his reign. Only his closest Security personnel could be trusted, and he put them in charge of various hospital departments, such as Food Service, in which they had absolutely no background. Freud would have had a great time analyzing the base reasons, but the director also greatly feared that his mistresses might be "cheating on him."

So, in a very fateful move, he decided to have the suspects' phones tapped.

The Security force didn't have the intellectual candlepower to tap phones, so a special position was created and a suitably skilled technician was hired. He was so different from the other Security personnel, competent and mild-mannered; he could have been your next-door neighbor. But he had a job to do: verifying if certain Western women were receiving "unauthorized" phone calls from men. He was universally called Dick the Wiretapper.

The megalomania continued to spread, and its handmaiden, paranoia, grew. For the "King" of the hospital, any disagreement with him became a lèse-majesté. A distinguished British physician who had apparently stuck his tongue out at these goings-on was arrested by the hospital Security forces, turned over to the Saudi police, and placed in a jail with numerous street criminals for three days. Another person who had proclaimed that the emperor had no clothes was the British Chairman of Medicine. The head of Security went to his house one night and demanded that the chairman accompany him. The Chairman of Medicine knew the rules in the Kingdom—Security personnel could not enter a person's private home except in very specified circumstances, even stricter than having a search warrant in the United States. The Head of Security violated this rule, crossed the threshold, and took the chairman into custody. He, too, was turned over to the Saudi police, who placed him under interrogation. Later, upon release, retaining his sense of humor, he said that he resisted their various interrogation techniques, including the constant bright light, but when they turned on the Arabic music he claimed that he "broke," and was willing to tell all. Of course, there was nothing to tell. It was a grim, even scary time. My wife and I knew we didn't rank in the top five in terms of lèse-majesté, but we had given the boys in Security, not to mention the director, our own "Bronx cheer" from time to time and therefore probably were in the top ten. Thoughts again turned to Bahrain.

Meanwhile, one didn't have to be in that palace antechamber to sense what was going on from the Saudi perspective. No doubt the first reports of the director's excesses were dismissed as so many sour grapes by those loyal to the previous American administrator.

Eventually, though, the picture became clear and irrefutable. One of the government's first major efforts at the famed Saudiazation of the workforce was grievously flawed. Aside from the very public show of indiscretion and flaunting of the norms of Saudi society, particularly worrisome was the wiretapping. If the director could wiretap his Western mistresses, what would prevent him from wiretapping various royals when they were patients in the hospital and blackmailing them later?

Dr. Ghazi Al Ghosabi, the Minster of Health, was viewed as the prime mover in establishing a Royal Commission to formally investigate the hospital, which itself was viewed as a contest of wills between the director and Ghosabi. Many foreigners, through choice or by default, took sides in this conflict, unaware of the complexities involved. Having lived through the excesses of the new director's regime, and having personally felt the jackboot of the Security Department stepping on our hands, if not our backs, our side was pre-selected. We viewed Ghosabi as riding a white horse.

Mary and I left on a 45-day vacation, hoping all would be resolved by our return. While sitting on the front porch of the house of some good friends in Inman Park in Atlanta, an ex-KFSHer brought over the news clipping. Ghosabi had been summarily fired. So it was true, what the director had boasted: "he had the King in his back pocket." It turned out that Ghosabi was guilty of his own lèse-majesté, having published a pastiche of an Arab folk story concerning the fox who advises the lion who the real enemies in the jungle are. Reliable sources said that the poem was aimed at the advisors to the King, but the advisors convinced the King that it was aimed at his own personage. Our time in the Kingdom was now over, and there was only one question remaining—could we safely return to the Kingdom and retrieve our personal possessions, and sell the car, or was it best to abandon everything? I picked up the phone and called our good American physician friend, whom I knew to be in the top five on the hit list. Yes, he said, he had been fired within hours of the Ghosabi termination. He was in his apartment packing his belongings when the doorbell rang. A Saudi gentleman introduced himself as a member of the Royal Commission. He politely asked why the doctor was not at work. After the explanation, the Saudi politely asked the doctor to return to work—saying that no one could be terminated without the approval of the Royal Commission, and "we continue to value your services." Though Ghosabi was a prime force behind the appointment of the Royal Commission, it had other supporters who understood the seriousness of the hospital's problems.

I called again from Paris before boarding the Saudia plane to Riyadh. My physician friend laughed at my caution and assured me that things were safe and fine. The Royal Commission was now in charge. In reality, the power struggle continued for another year, but they held the upper hand since no one, absolutely no one, could leave the hospital's service without first seeing one of the commission's representatives, stating that they were leaving of their own free will. Security's reign of fear ended. Although the propaganda wars between the factions continued on a daily basis, the director was obviously damaged merchandise. The hospital floundered for a year, just marking time, much as the United States did during the Watergate period.

Just when it seemed the investigation had become a permanent state of affairs and that the Saudis would never make up their minds, the decision came down suddenly, with the finality of a terrible swift sword. I received an agitated phone call from the Western "press secretary," or propagandist, for the director. We had grown estranged of late, having been on opposite sides in this power struggle. But in the old days when I first arrived we had played poker every Saturday night. So he was playing on that when he called, saying that he knew I had grown up in Pittsburgh and did I know the name of the hospital there.

"Well, there are many hospitals there."

"Well, which one would the Queen be in?"

"Now how should I know?" It seems that the director had been sent with the Queen to attend to her medical needs while she was receiving treatment in Pittsburgh. It was a one-way ticket more or less, as it would be a number of years until he was allowed to return to the Kingdom. Over the same weekend six Western members of the Security Department received a Royal Order granting 72 hours to pack their bags before they would be formally deported from the country. One of the six was Bernie Kerik, whom President George

W. Bush would nominate to be the Director of Homeland Security over 20 years later. Purportedly Kerik withdrew his name due to problems with the taxes relating to an illegal nanny.

The "press secretary" eventually located the director by calling enough hospitals but was told by the director that there was nothing he could do for them. Forty-eight hours later a green and white KFSH coaster bus drove the six deportees to the airport. I took a picture of them leaving, much to the consternation of the wife of the former head of Security. Several years later, I was told that the Ministry of the Interior had a picture of me taking that picture. Apparently they had not disapproved of my actions, or I, too, could have been deported. Bernie Kerik, in his book *Lost Son*, claims that he was picked up in a black van, "the kind of vehicle they use to carry people to their beheadings." Perhaps the most charitable explanation for mistaking this routine hospital bus for a black van headed for a beheading was his postpartum blues, being now separated from the megalomaniac whom he had so faithfully served.

"*Après moi, le déluge*," is the battle cry of every strong man on the way out, who never thinks he is to blame for anything. Of course it never works out that way. The world goes on, and in this case, it went on *particularly* well. It would be almost 20 years until I would again look to Bahrain, or neighboring countries, as a place of possible refuge.

The new administration assumed control after the weekend. They, too, said all the right things, "changed the wallpaper in the lobby," and set out to make more substantive changes. And they made some changes that reflected their natural style. They also tried to hide their belief that they were entering Sodom and Gomorrah, with everyone associated with the hospital's ancien régime so tainted.

Three principal themes became readily apparent, reflecting the palace decisions:

1. The Security Department could no longer act without restraint in a manner that disregarded all authority and all laws of the Kingdom. Furthermore, it would be transformed from a department that excluded all Saudis to one that would be exclusively Saudi.

2. As much as possible, all Westerners with line authority would be replaced. Those with needed expertise could be retained, but in general they would not be giving the orders.

3. One Saudi was placed in charge of the hospital, but two others held appointments within the hospital, independent of him. And the Security Department was an entity totally separate, reporting to the Ministry of the Interior with its own man in charge. In short, the classic checks and balances of the division of power were adapted.

The remnants of the former director's regime tried to instill the fear that all of the change was for the worse. Just imagine, the "dreaded" Ministry of the Interior in charge of security—house-to-house searches for booze, Bibles, and uncensored *Time* magazines would surely follow. None of that came to pass. In fact what was to occur was the development of a Security force that should be a model for any other, particularly in a trans-cultural setting.

One need not have bugged the conversation that occurred in the bubble-shaped protrusion, situated at the top of the very distinctive inverted pyramid of a building that was the headquarters of the Ministry of the Interior. The content of the conversation became quite clear in the actions of the "new and improved" Security Department, "We have invited these Westerners, almost all of whom are non-Muslims, to this country to help us care medically for our citizens until the time that we have trained a sufficient number of our own citizens to render this care. It is not our job to impose our lifestyle on them. If they can be discreet, are reasonably respectful of us, and help us care for our people, then by all means they should have their booze, their so-called uncensored magazines, and they can conduct their religious services, and have their holidays. On the other hand they should not try to change our lifestyle, culture, manner of doing things . . . "

A most reasonable modus vivendi was established, which endured for almost two decades.

In those gentler days of the mid-80's the hospital director wished his non-Muslim staff "Merry Christmas," and he even sent out

Christmas cards one year. To make potential physician hires more comfortable with the thought of adapting to the "rigors" of living in Riyadh, he told them that he had more winemakers working on his staff than there were in the entire Napa Valley. Though the overall quality of the wine was certainly deficient, it was a very true statement. In later years the Saudi in charge of the Guard Force delivered the orientation to newly arriving female nurses in such a manner: "Ladies, we have a curfew at the hospital—it's 1:00 a.m. We don't think it looks good if you are coming back to hospital accommodation at 3:00 and 4:00 a.m. So, if it is a new date, sometime reasonably early in the evening you must decide how much you really like this guy—be back before one, or come back in the daylight." . . . " No hiding in the bushes for this chief of the guard! The latter vignette was told to me by a newly hired Saudi, with a beard, with more than a little distaste, even disgust, at this open tolerance of "sin." The ominous implications of the new hire's reaction didn't register on me at the time—I thought this live-and-let-live attitude would be eternal.

And there is was. It was the Saudis who were respectful of one's private dwelling, treated the hospital employees with a fundamental respect, and made allowances for one's lifestyle if one exhibited discretion in public and reciprocated the respect—in other words, what one thought were quintessential American values. And it was the British and the Americans who were the thugs and goons, devoid of that internal gyroscope that said, "this is right, and this is wrong." Sure, their defense, as Kerik explained in his book, was that they were just acting under orders, the classic defense of the enablers of a corrupt regime. But for those of us who were there, we know that they gleefully followed, and enhanced those orders.

Yet another "American dilemma" would be posed, one that would intensify 20 years in the future: How does one deal with one's fellow Americans, who have no real belief in the freedoms outlined in the Constitution, and have no fundamental respect for an individual's privacy, and yet invariably are the first to wrap themselves in the flag?

Although I had been on the winning side in this power struggle, I still felt that my days in the Kingdom were coming to a close, since I was one of those Westerners who had "line authority." A sea container was sailing to the States, and although it was six months prior to the end of my contract, friends asked if Mary and I would be interested in sharing the container with them. A freight forwarder came to the apartment and hauled the boxes past the office of the newly appointed Head of Housing. He also had the "I've just arrived in Sodom and Gomorrah" syndrome. A quick confirmation proved that I was not on the list of current terminations, and the most likely explanation was that I was stealing hospital property from my housing unit. He quickly sent two of his minions to investigate.

"Yes, those are my boxes," I replied. "Don't I have the right to send my personal possessions back to the States at my own expense? Please, come in, and do an inventory of all hospital-owned items." They backed off their implicit accusations. My seemingly aberrant behavior quickly came to the attention of the hospital director, who in turn sent one of his minions to see me.

"Wasn't I happy working at the hospital?"

"Didn't I think the new administration was an improvement over the old?"

I gave solid affirmative replies to both questions.

"Then why leave?"

"Well, it seems like you're terminating every other Westerner with line authority."

"Er, ah . . . well, we're just cleaning up a little of the dead wood, but we'd like you to stay—you did support the Royal Commission, and we appreciate that."

And, "Er, ah, of course you can't still have line authority, but we'd like for you to work in an advisory role, and we'd be happy to pay you the same amount of money, and the hassles would be less."

So, as with many "career moves," serendipity was a major factor, and we signed on for "just one more year," which we knew at the time would be about three, until the next-born was diaper-free.

We had survived the "interesting times" of the Chinese proverb and fully concurred that it was best to live in boring times—and that would be the major downside of the next few years—those hideously boring committee meetings that Saint-Exupery understood so well—

but I would still be allowed to nurture my "wind, sand and stars" on the weekends and vacations.

9

The Return to Yabrin

On the eighth morning we climbed a final ridge. I had calculated that if we were ever to see Yabrin we should see it now; and there it lay straight in front of us, the splashes of the palm-groves dark on the khaki-plain.

—Wilfred Thesiger,
Arabian Sands

Wind, sand, and stars would be exemplified by Yabrin. There were only barren rocky plains and high sand dunes for the 1,000 kilometers south to the Indian Ocean. Of course, there was this "little problem" that the Emir had run us out of his town on our last visit and told us never to come back. Well, as they say in management circles, this wasn't a problem, this was a challenge. The solution came from a most unlikely source. Some Saudi bureaucrat, trying to fill in all the chinks in his little world in the quest for greater order and control, had helped convince the powers that be that you just couldn't have all these foreigners running around the country footloose and fancy-free. No, they should have a permission letter from their sponsor (read: their employer) if they wanted to travel within the country beyond an unspecified radius from the place of their employment.

We must travel back in time from 1984 when the new administration assumed control at KFSH. The year was 1981 when the permission letter business started. There were those dark mutterings in the expat community about the "fascist state we're living in," but not requiring too much reflection, I realized that these "lemon" permission letters might just be made into lemonade. I inquired in our Personnel Department, which was delegated this responsibility along with the official new forms.

"Is there any place in the Kingdom that I am not permitted to go?"

"Well, of course, being a non-Muslim, you can't go to Makkah or Madinah, but anywhere else is fine, provided you have a valid leave, or it is the weekend."

"Anywhere?"

"Yes."

"Well, how about Yabrin?"

"I don't know where that is, but if you'll spell it for me, I'll be happy to type it in the form, both in English and Arabic."

"And would you mind adding Al-Khunn?"

And so the Emir discovered he wasn't dealing with just any old expat. He was dealing with one who had *wasta* ("connections" or "influence"). My *wasta* was the Sudanese clerk working in Personnel who cheerfully typed in anything I wanted, but the key element was the King Faisal Specialist Hospital letterhead. Emir Hamad was standing outside his house when the jeeps arrived. I saw the scowl on his face and could seemingly read his mind—he was dealing with the dumbest expat ever and sterner measures would be required this time to discourage our return. We hadn't even exchanged greetings when I thrust the permission letter into his hands—his face connoted equal measures of amazement and repugnance. I worked hard on suppressing the "Gotcha!" on my face. The letter said "Yabrin," and the dates were equally correct, in the Hijerian calendar, today and tomorrow. He choked out an *"Ahlan wa Sahlan"* (You are most welcome.).

We were soon sitting on cushions in his unassuming majlis room with another cushion placed under my elbow, in the place of honor. The Emir offered us coffee, tea, and some sand-encrusted dates. And so commenced our annual wintertime pilgrimage to Yabrin, and as a consequence, we witnessed the dramatic transformation of one village as the entire country was swept along on its remarkable path to modernization.

In the very early days of these pilgrimages, my wife, or wife-to-be, depending on the date, was "just one of the boys," and, along with the other women in the party, sat in the *majlis* room (a room used to entertain guests) with us. It took the Emir a couple of years to decide that although foreign, these were really women and should be hustled off to the women's quarters to interact with his own wife and discuss domestic matters.

In the back of his mind, and in the minds of so many other Saudis, there was always the *why*?

Why would we travel in the desert? Why on earth would we find flat, dusty, Allah-forsaken Yabrin a place of interest? Even if I could have expressed "wind, sand, and stars" perfectly in Arabic, it just wouldn't translate properly to those who lived in this very harsh environment. And it should be remembered that although we journeyed to Yabrin numerous times, perhaps 15 in all, we never visited in the summer, which we considered a six-month period. In the Emir's mind, the only possible explanation was that it was an official government assignment and that I must work for the CIA. It was an accusation, implicit and explicit, that I faced on numerous occasions.

We dealt with the delicate issue of where we would spend the night, since his role as host required offering accommodations, and there was that palatable sense of relief when we indicated that we wanted to sleep on top of the butte, about five kilometers to the northwest of his village, a formula that would serve us well through our final trip there in the winter of 2002–3.

With my limited Arabic and my unwillingness to venture onto topics the Emir might consider sensitive (which I thought of in quite broad terms), we quickly reached a conversational impasse. He broke it by showing me his short-wave radio. He listened to the BBC, Arabic station, every evening. He introduced the game of trying to name a country and then see if the other party could name the leader. It was a game I felt at least qualified to play, since at the time I probably knew fifty leaders and their countries. Emir Hamad easily beat me in a virtuoso command of the current political state of the world. And with that game developed in me a profound appreciation for one of the cultural differences between numerous Saudis and

Americans. On the surface, it appeared that he was quite insular and closed-minded. Paradoxically, though, he represented the many Saudis who assumed there was something useful to learn from another country, another people, and were more fully informed of world developments than the average American. Yes, even in Yabrin, which took four to five hours to cover 90 kilometers of sandy tracks down from Harrad, there was a man cognizant of events in the Central African Republic. On the other side of this cultural divide, there was the vast majority of Americans who measured a foreign country's progress by how closely it resembled the United States.

Meanwhile, in the "women's quarters," Mary and the other women who accompanied us were treated much more warmly than the cordial, if frosty around the edges, relationship I and the other men enjoyed with the Emir. The quarters of the Emir's wife were dark and cramped, but she appeared to enjoy entertaining the foreign women, offering tea, dates and Arabic coffee. The women showed her pictures of their children, and on one trip, she rummaged around in an old trunk, unearthing a Polaroid picture Mary had given her a few years previously, and proudly showed it to her guests. In the very early days of our marriage, on the most fundamental topic, my wife was thought to be *kharbaan* (broken, nonfunctioning) since we had no children. On more than one occasion, the Arab women expressed concern and sympathy for Mary's plight. *"Inta kabeera!"* You are old, why don't you have babies? *Kabeera* can mean big (which she wasn't) or old, and in the sense that Mary was north of 19, well, she was guilty. It was just one of those matter-of-fact observations about the most essential aspect of the Saudi woman's existence. But we were working at the most prestigious hospital in the Kingdom; surely this could be "fixed." It finally was, though there was nothing the matter medically, and in quick succession two Ramadan babies were born. Finally, finally, these Westerners seemed to have gotten the hang of it. The Emir's wife celebrated the ending of the *kharbaan* status, and on one of our visits we even brought the living proof, much to her delight. Still, it wasn't a recovery from *kharbaan* to full functionality. And it wasn't just my wife who seemed to have this "problem." In fact, virtually all Western women had it. It was a syndrome best summed up in the expression: "Well, you know

Westerners, it is *itnaan*, and *kalaas*," (two, and we're finished). Yes, a cultural difference.

Many years later, one of the numerous *Abu Sabbah*s (father of seven) that I knew, a cheerful Sudanese man who worked at the hospital, pushed me on this cultural difference. "Why, why is it that you Westerners only have two?" I pointed at my elbows, swinging them around a bit. The concept that the world was too crowded did not translate well, despite the fact that we were speaking the same language. Once again I would hear "*Allah Karim*," (Allah is generous.) "He provides you with these many children, each one to love, the central aspect of life, and He will provide for them." Faith.

***

The top of the butte outside Yabrin provided a wonderful view of the stars, and one year we observed Halley's Comet in the heavens. But it also dished up ample portions of Saint-Exupery's wind and sand. In fact, a few times I fantasized that if I actually worked for the CIA, I would return to Riyadh, slam my fist down on my taskmaster's desk, and demand double the pay before I would return to Yabrin, such were the hardships endured there. But when it was a weekend lark, and we were just having fun, we rolled with the meteorological punches. On one trip, dinner on top of the butte was cut short by a gathering sandstorm. We slept intermittently inside sleeping bags, covered by the thick Yemen blankets, as the wind howled around us. In the morning all was calm, but we were covered by at least an inch of sand. On another trip, one of the few on which my wife did not accompany me, a traveling companion, a 6'4" man weighing around 250 pounds, and I were asleep in the tent. Suddenly our legs were almost vertical as another sandstorm slammed into us with winds so strong that we felt we might start rolling in the desert like so much tumbleweed—a tent with 450 pounds of ballast. On yet another trip we were soaked, even inside the tents, by torrential rains.

Perhaps the strangest meteorological event occurred one other cold night just north of Yabrin. We awoke, unzipped the tent door, and were absolutely dumbfounded to find ourselves enveloped in thick fog, like on a Scottish moor. Astonishment aside, we knew we had serious problems. We had always found Yabrin, in those pre-GPS days, by dead reckoning, desert tracks, and our sole compass. But the visibility was 20 meters at best. Slowly, very slowly, with that simple compass, we picked a point 20 meters ahead and moved forward, eventually reaching Harrad as the fog was lifting. Years later I was to read that under certain unusual meteorological conditions, fog could roll in from the Arabian Gulf, penetrating up to 200 kilometers and bringing with it much needed moisture to the desert plants. Coastal fog, the result of cool coastal currents, waters the desert regions of Chile, Baja, and Namibia. The Arabian Gulf is not cool, so the conditions that bring the fog inland are more unusual.

***

The names Al-Khunn and Mutlaq designated the straggle of cinder block homes between 15-30 kilometers from Yabrin. The former was the town we drove toward after our first Yabrin visit, the "get out of town" trip. The latter was across a vast salt flat, passable on a single track, and impassable when it rained. Mutlaq was built against a wall of impenetrable sand dunes, and therefore, was the last Saudi settlement in this eastern direction—the next habitation would be in the United Arab Emirates. Agriculture was being attempted in this region, with the help of deeper, permanent wells.

I was intrigued to listen to the story of a Mutlaq resident. He had obviously visited Manhattan—this wasn't something he had seen in the movies. For example, he knew the prices of many things there. His experiences rang too true of being the ultimate country bumpkin. Like so many NYC cabdrivers, this man traveled the island with little to no English. He further explained that his trip was totally paid for by the government—it was the government's incentive to encourage people to live in the Empty Quarter, thereby reinforcing the Saudi's claim to the area. The crops so laboriously grown were irrelevant; it was the government's assertion of its rights to the gas and oil that lay under these sands that was of true interest. And it was also the government's answer to the eternal question: How do you keep them down on the farm once they've seen Riyadh?

It was in Al-Khunn though, where we ran into those proverbial wilder shores of love. After visiting Mutlaq, it was easiest to go to Al-Khunn to quench our most common and strongest thirst—petrol. There we met Rashid, sporting a long snow white beard. In an area where men carried the mien of seriousness, if not sternness, he was positively amiable and jovial. He invited us in to his plywood shack. The floor was sand, and a small open fire blazed in the middle. He and his wife's few possessions were neatly placed within this domain. Was this by preference, indifference to his surroundings, or had he, or one of his relatives, committed a grievous crime? If it was the latter, given his nature, I could only imagine the one of lèse-majesté, and thus he would have been a soul mate. The shack was small, so there was not the normal division separating the women's side. His wife was simply in the background, preparing tea, and speaking with the women in our party. Like many in the area, Rashid was proud of his camels and was happy to be photographed with them. We carried our standard Polaroid and gave people their pictures as we retained others with our SLR cameras. Rashid's countenance was special though, and I made a point of having a few 8 × 10 glossies printed for our next visit.

The following winter we returned to the village with the pictures. My political and cultural antenna was still in its developmental stage, and I didn't immediately pick up on and register the shorter *thobe*, more straggly beard, and sterner mien of Rashid's companion. But when I said *soura* (picture), the reaction was swift as the admonishments about *souras* being *haram* (forbidden) flew in Rashid's direction. Rashid made a valiant, if implausible, effort at covering things up. He explained that any *souras* that were available had been fed to the camels. If the imam of the mosque under construction in the background actually believed Rashid, we'll never know. Rashid invited us in for tea, something the imam could not expressly forbid, so he grumped off, probably urging Rashid to give an extra washing to the glasses when the infidels were finished.

On this visit that we were introduced to Rashid's daughter, who, it was explained, was the second wife of some "city slicker" up in Hofuf, a fair-sized town about 200 kilometers to the north. The daughter also had those haunting kohl-outlined eyes, visible behind the veil. There were a number of women around, and my wife persuaded them to have their pictures taken. This was no problem, and although they wore their veils, the more colorful dresses of the Bedu women showed. Later, when I was developing the pictures, I noticed that one of the women was giving the camera an obscene gesture. Not the standard Western one, but a most distinctive gesture nonetheless. Was this gesture aimed at us? It seemed unlikely, as they almost avidly sought to have their pictures taken. Or was it done to hint at a more libertine lifestyle that could be found along the frontier? Was it any wonder that one of the sterner imams had been sent to get these people back on the true path?

The following year we again returned to see Rashid. The mosque was now complete, as were a few more cinder block houses, but the plywood shack remained on the southern edge of the village. We noticed the lack of camels in the nearby pen as we, my wife and I and another American couple, approached the shack. Rashid's wife came out to greet us, insisting that we come in for coffee. My political and cultural antennae had developed a bit more over the past year, but it did not require much astuteness to realize that all this was not quite normal. In fact, being alone with her in the dwelling made us down right nervous. We quickly inquired about Rashid's health. Well, it wasn't, because Rashid was *maut* (dead). We wanted to leave then, but she insisted that we stay, the coffee was almost ready and natural politeness prevailed. Still, it was just she, her daughter and her daughter's daughter. No men present. With our limited Arabic, and no doubt perceiving our nervousness, she realized nuance and protracted negotiations would not work, so she "popped the question," and asked if either I or my friend would marry her daughter. The city slicker up in Hofuf had divorced her. Mama knew what a tough sell she had on her hands, since our own wives were present, but she quickly put her hand on each of their arms and assured them that they would be *ragam wahead*. Each would still be the number one wife, so they should not feel threatened. As is well known in the Kingdom, this argument doesn't go very far with Saudi women either. The four of us exchanged stunned looks and unanimously agreed there was only one course of action that was appropriate—damn the coffee, damn the politeness, and with visions of the imam descending on us, along with a bunch of males in this village, we left, and in the rearview mirror, cast our final looks at yet another "wilder shore of love." We would never return to Al-Khunn; Emir Hamad's frostiness was preferable to the desperation of these women and the misfortunes life had thrown their way. As both Barbara Ehrenreich and Susan Faludi have so well documented, each in their own way, a thirty-five-year-old single mother, with two kids, working at Wal-Mart, would have understood them well.

Though Emir Hamad may have been concerned about why we were *really* coming to his domain, numerous members of the Al-Murrah tribe did not seem to have the same reservations and opened their hearts and lives to these somewhat eccentric foreigners, in our "colorful native costumes." In our own way, we had entertainment value.

The Saudis knew the expats had a particular fascination for their "work horse," the camel, as it was already losing its status as a work horse. My wife and I enjoyed riding their camels, and the obligatory pictures were taken, with "one hand waving free." Ali Salem was particularly helpful with Mary, the two of them riding together much to the amusement of the group that quickly collected to watch the spectacle. Many years later during our final year in the Kingdom, a picture was taken of me with one hand waving free, for a TV show produced by other Saudis who understood that this was one of the "rites of passage" for expats living in the Kingdom.

One weekend we were the sole expat witnesses to a magnificent camel race with substantial prize money, sponsored by one of the princes who lived in Riyadh. It was a 15-kilometer race in the open desert. The rules were rather loose, and if your camel was lagging, it seemed perfectly acceptable to drive your pickup truck right behind in order to encourage it to quicken the pace. On the domestic front, all of us were able to witness some of the women of the Murrah tribe as they wove cloth for their tents from goat hair, as had been done even in the *jahaliya* (the "time of darkness," before the Prophet Mohammed, PBUH).

In order to arrive at the camel race on time, the Saudis decided to drive the vehicles. There was always the thorny issue of alcohol. My standard rule was that I would drink with Saudis, but they had to offer it to me first. On one trip, I was riding in a red GMC truck, as another Saudi was driving my jeep with Mary as his passenger. Abdul Mutib reached in the back, pulled out a bottle of Johnny Walker, and offered it to me. I respectfully declined, claiming I didn't drink. Meanwhile, his brother, who was a police officer and driving my vehicle, asked Mary if I drank. She gave the same answer, and he was comforted, saying that was a good thing, he knew I was really a "good man." Fortunately, even though having a drink with Abdul Mutib would have fit under my self-imposed guidelines, I knew that there were simply too many other people around, some of whom would have objected to alcohol.

But our fondest memories revolve around a weekend in 1984 when we were invited to spend the night with one of the Bedu families. It was a sincere invitation and interesting enough to pry us off our normal camping spot atop the butte. No one at KFSH was motivated enough to accompany us that weekend, so it was just Mary and I. Rashid, a different Rashid, was the actual host, and given the range of the tribe, he was located substantially north of the town of Harrad, whereas Yabrin was 90 kilometers south. They agreed to meet us at the gas station in Harrad and lead us to their encampment.

At 4:00 p.m. on Thursday, our hosts met us as agreed at the gas station. Off to the north they headed with our jeep racing behind. Bedus simply don't make what we would consider to be normal allowances for driving off-road—they race along at top speed, just as though they were on asphalt, and so we struggled to keep up. Finally, in a cloud of dust, we arrived at the camp.

Our friends had set up a large white tent that would be ours for the night. It had carpets on the floor, cushions to lean on, and it was high enough for one to stand up in. They must have wondered why foreigners used those small, domed, shock-corded tents that one had to crawl into. There were the camels and the goats, of course, and we had learned the protocols of Bedouin small-talk to inquire about their numbers, the prospects for rain, and grazing. Of course, the rain was never really enough, but Allah provides. Their encampment also had a large tanker truck which provided water and a noisy generator supplied the lighting that was strung around the camp. Their babies wore Pampers. The delicacy for the dinner was goat's liver, cooked over embers buried in the sand—the goat's liver was wrapped in aluminum foil. Not much speculation would be required to ascertain Thesiger's thoughts about the corrupting influence of these modern intrusions into the traditional Bedu way of life. Thesiger said it all in his concluding remarks in *Arabian Sands*:

"I realized that the Bedu with whom I had lived and traveled were doomed. Some people maintain that they will be better off when they have exchanged the hardship and poverty of the desert for the security of a materialistic world. This I do not believe. I shall always remember how often I was humbled by those illiterate herdsmen who possessed, in so much greater measure than I, generosity and courage, endurance, patience, and lighthearted gallantry. Among no other people have I ever felt the same sense of personal inferiority."

But it would be much more than aluminum foil that would have disturbed Thesiger. One of Rashid's brothers, Saleem, was a Gulf Airlines pilot. He was still a Murrah though, proudly explaining that they might accept many things of the modern world but they were reluctant to accept newfangled inventions like borders drawn in far off London, Riyadh, Doha, and Kuwait City. Eastern Arabia was theirs and they freely roamed over these invisible lines as they wished. Saleem took great pleasure in his desert weekends.

Another of Rashid's brothers, Abdullah, was studying electrical engineering at King Saud University in Riyadh. He had driven to the camp for the weekend, his textbooks with him. I asked Abdullah how he had located the camp—it had been a couple of months since he had visited, and they had moved camp since. Basically, it all boiled down to Bedouin instincts. He knew the most likely grazing places. I flipped through his textbooks, a remarkable example of a cultural and linguistic straddle—the text was nominally written in Arabic, but every third or fourth word was in English. Words like *resistor*, *capacitor*, and all the technical terminology of the trade. It appeared the Arabs needed their own *Académie française* to invent suitable Arabic equivalents of English technological words. But language standardization was not a strong Arab attribute. The generator was eventually killed, and we enjoyed the silence and the stars. I even survived drinking a bowl of frothy, warm camel milk, which not infrequently transmits brucella, a most unpleasant bacterial disease.

The visits with the Al-Murrah tribe were not all one way, though. Sometimes they ventured into my world at the hospital, and I helped them overcome the various bureaucratic hurdles that were thrown at them. Most interesting was a visit from Emir Hamad himself. I was to learn the distinction between the "emir" appointed by the government and the "emir" who was the hereditary tribal chief. Hamad was the former, and the hereditary tribal chief was a patient, dying in the hospital's VIP unit. It was obligatory that Hamad and his entourage pay a visit, but Hamad had run headlong into another of those newfangled concepts called "visiting hours." It was after 9:00 p.m., and the hospital Security personnel would not allow him to enter. He called me for help.

After tea and coffee in our housing unit, and overcoming such faux pas that certain protocol-lacking Americans seem capable of, like not serving tea to the Emir first, I put on my suit. Okay, buddy, let me show you some *wasta* in action. Around 10:00 p.m. we went back to the VIP suites, and of course everything was okay with Security, who was only too happy to accommodate "Mr. Jones." After greeting the hereditary Emir myself, I was about to take my leave, but remembered my own obligations about the Emir's accommodations that night, although I lacked the capacity to house the entourage. It was *mafi mushkila* (no problem); they were driving back to Yabrin that night. It seemed a bit unbelievable to me, since my best time had been about seven hours—three hours on asphalt, four on the dirt track. He assured me they could make the whole trip in no more than four hours. Maybe that explained all the carnage on the road.

Our last trip to Yabrin in the 80's was undertaken with a Saudi travel companion. Khalid was a man of independent thought and significant curiosity. Instead of idly speculating exactly *why* these expats roamed in the desert, why not just tag along and find out?

After all, it really was his heritage. So, he and his kids, my wife and I, and our kids drove to Yabrin. During the eight years since my first visit, the road had slowly improved. First, sand-filled 55-gallon drums marked the way. Then a grader had defined the dirt road with a slight edge. Finally, signposts indicating the distance to Yabrin were placed every ten kilometers.

"Saudi" was then, and continues to be, a fairly loose concept. It works mainly when dealing with foreigners, but it is the tribal connections that define the main groups within the country. The Emir knew that Khalid was not an Al Murrah, and therefore he was almost as foreign as I. The Emir did remember my *wasta* from the Riyadh visit, and so I do think the dates came out of his very top drawer. It wasn't long until he was homing in on the *why* question. Khalid tried his best at the "wind, sand, and stars" concept in Arabic, but from the Emir's face, I could tell he'd be having the same thoughts if the explanation was in Chinese. I gave the Emir what I thought would be our last handshake, no doubt much to his relief, and we retreated to our butte for the night. Of the whimsical benchmarks that I used for determining when it was time to finally leave the Kingdom, one was "when they pave the road to Yabrin." It looked like I would be getting out ahead of time.

10

Papa Joe and the Animals

> Corn won't grow at all on rocky top,
> Dirt's too rocky by far.
> That's why all the folks on rocky top
> Get their corn from a jar.
>
> Rocky top, you'll always be
> Home sweet home to me.
> Good ole rocky top,
> Rocky top Tennessee, Rocky top Tennessee.
>
> —Boudleaux and Felice Bryant,
> *Rocky Top*

Without those crutches of phones, television, and various family obligations, many things are possible. One of those was the creation of a country and western band, "Papa Joe and the Animals." Papa Joe was a supervisor in the Power Plant and a man of true musical talent, making the fiddle sing, and possessing the ability to play the mandolin behind his head. Mama June, his wife, played a mighty powerful electric bass guitar. And, as already mentioned, there was the Queen herself, my wife, who could make the audience weak-kneed with her renditions of "Coat of Many Colors," as well as the plethora of other heartbreaking songs that makes C & W what it is. In the early days the band was led by a British guitar-playing, Dylan-worshipping MC, whose wit, wisdom, and enthusiasm helped pump up both the band and the audience. The band's composition included the "Red Man," an EMT (Emergency Medical Technologist), and members of the medical staff, with varying degrees of musical talent.

Care had to be taken in the band's operation. The antecedent was not good. In the mid- to late 70's there was an aptly named band called the Exit Visas. Most of their songs openly ridiculed the Saudi culture, people, and religion. Songs like Chuck Berry's "Roll Over Beethoven" were made into "Roll Over Mohammed," and the "Twelve Days of Christmas" became the "Twelve Days of Ramadan" with such lines as " . . . seven worthless princes . . . " In the West, there was an outside possibility the lyrics could all be viewed as "good satire," as long as the various taboos in the West were omitted. But in the Kingdom they represented the obtuseness of guests and the arrogant behavior of the weaker members of a dominant culture. Though the Exit Visas seemed eternal and even played at the hospital in the very early days, the Saudi authorities eventually caught up with them, issuing them namesake visas. Even people who possessed Exit Visa tapes were nervous and kept them well hidden.

So Papa Joe and company had to have a clean break with the past, and fortunately, the natural inclination of the band members was aligned with this objective. This was to be just what it seemed, a slice of the American culture, primarily directed at the expat community, but certainly everyone was welcome. The Red Man, so called due to his hair, made a point of explaining, before he sang "Long Black Veil," that it had absolutely nothing to do with where we were. A song like "Rocky Top" resonated in an audience composed of people who had to make their own alcohol. If there was to be any parody, then I would play a leading role, one of self-parody. I decided to model myself on Loretta Lynn's sleazy husband/manager as portrayed in Robert Altman's movie *Nashville*. Like the character in the movie, I'd wear a silk smoking jacket, a bow tie that hung loosely from the collar, and for the southern traditions of C & W music, I'd wear a Yankee Civil War hat.

We had the music, and it served to open some unlikely doors.

"Ladies and Gentlemen, this is our first stop on our round-the-world tour, for Papa Joe and the Animals, here in Buraydah," the MC announced. We weren't actually in downtown Buraydah, but rather 10 kilometers south. We were in a compound built for Canadians who were managing the electrification project for Qassim province, 300 kilometers north of Riyadh, a four-hour drive before the expressway was completed. Even in this conservative area of central Arabia, these foreign workers were generally highly respected, as they installed the pylons and high-tension electrical wires that would extinguish the kerosene lanterns. The limited entertainment resources in Riyadh appeared like the West End theater district of London when compared to those available in Qassim. Consequently, the band was treated like royalty.

Our Canadian hosts showed us "the sights." One of the more remarkable was the mud-walled villages, which are nostalgically remembered in various paintings and postcards. They had been abandoned a few years previously, and one could freely wander through the ruins. The inhabitants had been given "proper" cinder block homes, with wall AC units and tiled floors. No one forced the move. The villagers were happy to leave the dirt and the annual wall-reconstruction projects after the rains. Ten kilometers south of us stood the other major city in Qassim, Unayzah. A prominent Saudi in the town heard we were in the area and proudly showed off some of the old mud homes of the town's dignitaries, decorated with elaborate abstract decorations painted on the interior walls. Since our visit fell during the date harvest season, the man gave us a tour of his palm groves. It was there that I learned date protocol: always praise the quality of the dates from the inhabitant's town, and always say that they are the finest in all of Arabia.

In the early evening we stopped at a sidewalk café in Unayzah. I don't want to overstate the ambiance of the place, but we had good, simple, freshly prepared chicken and a Pepsi. Normally only men sat outside to eat, but since we were expats, and if we didn't mind "exposing" our wives, this was just fine with them. Many years later I had a Saudi boss from Unayzah who told me how they liked to consider themselves the "Parisians of Arabia." I said I know—we once ate at one of your sidewalk cafés. His expression indicated that he thought I was pulling his leg, but I made a point on my next annual leave, when he asked about my trip to the States, to say that first we were getting off in the Unayzah of France.

For those who like to paint the Saudis with a broad brush, I highly recommend a visit to the area where that Canadian compound stood, which was exactly halfway between the twin towns of Qassim province, Buraydah and Unayzah. How very different were the people in these two places. Unayzah was outgoing, friendly, and had a relaxed atmosphere. Buraydah was diametrically the opposite.

Mary and I had actually been in Buraydah previously. We stayed at the Canadian compound, but our traveling friends stayed in the fancy four-star hotel in town, which was nearly empty. We arranged for a tour of the town with the beleaguered bellboy from the Indian subcontinent who spoke excellent English. He had been harassed by the religious fanatics in the town recently—apparently his bellboy uniform jacket was too brightly colored and violated some of their precepts. Mary wore the *abaya*, the black external cloak, for the very first time on this trip. She did not have a veil. She thought she saw an old blind man with a stick coming up the street and felt sorry for him. He was hardly blind, though, and had an eye for exposed flesh, and the next thing she knew, she was being tapped on the legs with his stick. "Cover your face." The only thing she could do was to pull up the abaya, covering her head and exposing a fair amount of dress in the process. We quickly moved on and OUT of the town.

The following year Mary was the veteran, and the other women in the group looked to her for guidance. Western women did not wear an abaya at the time. It would have been frowned upon to wear one— maybe you were even making fun. Abayas were for Muslim women. Non-Muslim women were only to wear loose-fitting, non-form-revealing clothes, as was suggested in the Koran. Buraydah was the only place in the entire Kingdom where these different rules applied, and in the subsequent years they had done a marvelous job of proselytizing their views throughout the country. But no one was envisioning the future as the women prepared for the Halloween-like experience of this costume party shopping trip. None of them could quite get the hang of things, so it must have been quite a spectacle as they entered the old souk area. Some of the merchants couldn't help suppressing a smile. They, unlike the fanatics, actually wanted us there, if not us, certainly our money. One of the *souk* owners merrily helped Mary fix up her costume properly.

We were amazingly well rewarded for being willing to play such games. We were looking at a beautiful 1 × 2 meter hand-woven Bedouin carpet. We asked the price. *"Talatah mia."* Surely I had misunderstood something here. I asked again, the same reply. I knew there had to be an *alf* somewhere. Where was the "thousand"? The exasperated merchant finally pulled out 300 riyals from his wallet, or about $80, and showed the dense foreigner. I immediately paid it. Stupid me, again! I hadn't even bargained. So, the carpet salesman immediately dragged us off to his warehouse where there was a stack of carpets to the ceiling. I could have had them all at that price. We knew something was profoundly the matter with all this and declined. With a little more knowledge, I could have had one of the great bargains of all time. For these carpets were part of the "old life" in the mud homes, to be disposed of when the villagers moved into the proper cinder block homes with their brightly colored, acrylic, machine-made, wall-to-wall carpets. Alas!

The concert was well received that evening including by our Saudi friends. Of course for a band that routinely sang songs like "Pancho and Lefty," "Folsom Prison Blues," and other songs that spoke of experiences outside the straight and narrow, it was hard in the face of dire provocations not to at least throw out a raspberry or two. And few times were the provocations greater than during the reign of the first Saudi hospital director when the Western Security goons harassed regular hospital employees.

A concert was held at the hospital's Amenities Center, and we knew the Security goons would be present, ready to report any infraction, real or imagined. The challenge was irresistible—calibrate some raspberry that most of the audience would understand but which would sail over the heads of the goons. The more cynical members of the hospital staff claimed that was not much of a challenge. The Queen herself broke from her normal routine and talked about her favorite singer, proclaimed for the night to be Judy Garland, which she followed with a powerful performance of "Somewhere over the Rainbow." After the song, she said: "But we all remember Judy in her most memorable roll, that of Dorothy in the

Wizard of Oz. Here was this little girl, so far from home in a strange land, all frightened. With the help of her friends, she eventually made it to the Emerald City. She went to see the big and powerful wizard, who tried to scare her all the more. And then we remember what happened next—she pulled back the curtain and there was only a weak and pathetic little man." In terms of political satire, it is a story that has always resonated. Nothing particularly subtle, but for the Security goons, in the unlikely event that they thought there might have been a double entendre, could they really object to such a quintessential American story being told?

One day the band's MC called everyone up. "I know it is short notice, but instead of practicing tonight, one of my patients asked if we would play at a party at his villa, and each member of the band will be paid SR500 [around US$135]. Not bad for a practice night!"

We arrived at the villa, and around the pool was catered food for hundreds. The band set up in the disco room, equipped with strobe lights and dance floor. The bartender stood in the corner behind one of the best-stocked bars I've ever seen. When the band started playing no one else was there. Then a carload or two of nurses and medical technicians from the hospital arrived. They sat around enjoying the music. Then in came, usually one by one, Saudi men about twice their age. At some level you *knew* this sort of thing went on. It was another matter to watch it unfold before your eyes. Some of the female participants we knew, and we would have considered them the most unlikely to appear at such an event. But there they were. I was the ultimate fifth wheel, wishing I could at least get up and play an instrument.

Knowing I had to drive home, the best I could do was nurse, as it were, a couple of premium scotches and keep the bartender company. The band's gig ended at 10:30 p.m., as agreed on this weekday night, they were duly paid, and we packed up and left, as the real party was just commencing. The most optimistic interpretation of the band's participation in such an event could probably be rather pejoratively characterized as just another "business expense."

Papa Joe and Mama June finally decided to pack it in and return to the States. The British MC moved on; yet some gentle souls and a couple of new arrivals loved the C & W outlet, and a new band was formed with the almost prophetic name of Doin' Time. The band was invited to the newly opened National Guard hospital across town for a performance. The new MC had a heavy Texas twang, which just may have saved everyone in the band. It was a large audience, including a few scattered Saudis. The Texan decided to tell a joke:

"You know, we're from King Faisal Specialist Hospital and Research Centre, and over at our Research Centre we had some budget constraints. We could no longer buy all the rabbits we needed for our experiments, and so we now use Saudis—they breed just as fast, and you don't grow near as fond of them." There was utter disbelief on the face of everyone else in the band—he just couldn't have said it. But he did. Eyes discreetly turned to the few Saudis in the audience. There was no visible reaction. Maybe, just maybe, with that heavy twang of an accent, they didn't understand. Somehow the band played on until intermission when all the other members of the band told the MC that he was never to pull a stunt like that again. After the performance finished, the waiting game began—for the knock on the door and the announcement that "Your passports have been prepared," and like the Exit Visas before us, we'd be shipped out. The knock never came, and we'll never know whether the Saudis in the audience didn't understand or whether they understood perfectly well and it was one more insult that would be tucked away, left to fester and build the resentment against this invasion of their country by the "barbarians," as well as against the countries from which we came.

11

Other Shores, Other Diversions

When Thesiger traveled through Layla on his second crossing of the Empty Quarter in the winter of 1947–48, he never mentioned the existence of a lake there. But there it was, a natural formation in the middle of the desert, around two kilometers long and 750 meters wide, a natural target for anyone looking for water. The lake was located approximately 350 kilometers southwest of Riyadh. In 1976, 30 employees at KFSH chipped in and bought a motorboat in Dhahran and moved it to the lake for the purpose of water-skiing. And indeed we did. With relish.

Thesiger says that elements of the *Ikhwan*, the "Brotherhood," who had aided Abdul Aziz in unifying the peninsula and later became his enemy, had settled in the area. Given the supposed sentiment in the area and the later dominance of the *mutawaa* (religious police) throughout the country, it is hard to believe that Western men and women, wearing swimsuits, were able to water-ski there for years, in almost complete peace. On a couple of occasions I scuba dived in the lake, hoping to discover the bottom, but elected to surface after diving to a depth of 20 meters. The diving experience was different from any before, eerie even, because at that depth it was impossible to orient oneself visually as to the direction to the surface—the water was perfectly translucent in all directions.

Many years later, in the mid-90's, I walked on the dried lake's bottom, about 35 meters below the surrounding edge of the former lake. Where did all the water go? The standard quip was that it was shipped to Riyadh in the many watermelons that were grown in the region, a quip that contained a large element of truth. The entire water table in the area dramatically dropped over a period of fifteen years in order to support the regional agriculture. Among the problems the Kingdom now faces is the depletion of the aquifer in several regions of the country, all due to the profligate use of water in support of agriculture in the 80's and 90's.

A far longer and much more interesting shore ran along the entire western border of the country—the Red Sea—and one of the best places to scuba dive in the entire world. There was no diving resort in the Kingdom, making logistics a challenge, but corresponding to this challenge was the satisfaction of often being the first to dive in a given location. Although I enjoyed a few boat dives in the Kingdom, almost all were from the shore, which meant we needed to determine easy access to the beach in rental cars without four-wheel drive, as well as choosing a place where the reef itself did not involve a long walk through waist-high water with the heavy tank on one's back.

In the very early days there was only one dive shop in Jeddah which had the capability of providing the most essential ingredient—compressed air. Those capabilities were gradually expanded, but the most important expansion was the acquisition of our own very funky air compressor which we showered with so much care.

Of course one also had to know how to dive, and a British anesthesiology tech took on the task. He was certified in BSAC (British Sub-Aqua Club), so he set up a chapter in Riyadh and we underwent its more extensive training course, far more extensive than PADI, the American training course. Most of us were grateful for the additional rigor, because once under water, one was very much on one's own. It would be years later before the Kingdom acquired its first diving chamber for the treatment of the bends, the condition resulting from diving too deep, or ascending too fast, that could result in paralysis or death. Thus it was imperative that divers stayed well within the dive tables in terms of depth.

Our diving trips ranged along the coast to Wedj, seven hours north of Jeddah by car and to Shweiba, an hour south of the town. There were many great trips, but perhaps my favorite was driving the 1,200 kilometers from Riyadh to Yanbu in our own jeeps, fighting our way through the sand dunes, and camping in one spot for five days. Two jeeps, and four divers made this trip, along with the essential air compressor—we didn't see another soul for the entire period, save for the periodic visits from our friends in the Coast Guard.

Good relations with the Coast Guard were even more essential than compressed air. Outside the immediate Jeddah area, cinder block station houses were built all along the coast, spaced around 10 kilometers apart. We were never on the beach for long before the Coast Guard arrived to determine the nature of our activities, so it was generally best to visit them first. In that division of duties on a dive trip success begat success, and I was usually the person delegated to obtain the permission from the local blockhouse. Early on, I lucked into using *lau samaat*. It was a very polite form of *please*, more akin to "if you please," and certainly not as common as the more straightforward form of that expression, *min fadluck*. I saw the one Saudi Coast Guard officer look at the other, smile, and say, "He knows *lau samaat*." I didn't even have to play card number two, the bit about the specialist hospital in Riyadh. Instead it was, "How long do you want to be here?" I taught diving for a number of years, but before I got to the dive tables or how a regulator works, I always taught *lau samaat*, and how to use it. Those two simple words also worked in fields completely unrelated to diving. The Vietnamese equivalent of these words I never learned, nor did any of my buddies on that "winning the hearts and minds" mission.

Another story that became part of the teaching curriculum occurred at that lovely Al-Hasi inlet, 48 kilometers south of Umm Laj, the site of our honeymoon. A year after our honeymoon, we were sitting around our tent, drying off after a dive. Our jeep was about 20 meters away. An old Datsun pickup truck rattled down the nearby hill, and a scruffy looking Saudi got out, walked over to our jeep, and started rifling through the gear in the back. Not only was this most uncommon behavior, it really wasn't acceptable. But everything depends on how you approach things.

So I walked over to him, gave him my best *as Salaam Alaykoum,* and invited him over for tea. The hot water was already boiling, so he was quickly served. He asked about our activities, so in Arabic I gave our standard account of diving. No, we never ate the fish, and no, we didn't have a spear gun. We only took pictures. He was satisfied and left shortly after finishing his tea, telling us to have a good day. The next day the man returned in full uniform. He delighted in my recognition. He was in charge of the Coast Guard for the entire region. This led to another axiom in that diver training course: "Just remember, if the Saudi who approaches you at your campsite is not actually in the Coast Guard, his cousin is."

I normally did not relate in the diving course what occurred on his second visit. He wanted to show that he was a gracious host also; he invited Mary and me to have tea with him at his Coast Guard station. We talked of diving again, Riyadh, his home in Madinah, the hospital, and America. Perhaps I had passed character test number two, and I'll never really know if he had a twinkle in his eye when he did this, or if he really was serious, but he asked me if I would consider marrying his daughter, given the normal conversion requirements. After our experience, almost on the other side of the peninsula, in Al-Khunn, my wife had the routine down. She went into her *ragam wahead* routine, and he quickly assured her that yes, she would be the number one wife. She quickly cut him short with a *wa bas* (and only) delivered as well as any Saudi woman could. We were his amusement for the day—he chuckled heartily at Mary's feistiness and there were smiles all around when we left.

These were all the land-based side of the adventures, but the real thrills were underwater. The waters off Saudi Arabia remain one of the absolute best places in the world to dive, and the water is warm enough that a wet suit is not required. Groupers, eels, tuna, barracudas, sea turtles, the poisonous and distinctive lionfish, box and parrot fish, the even more deadly scorpion fish, crimson Spanish dancers, and spotted lagoon rays were only a few of the highlights to be enjoyed. There was the reef itself and sun-dappled grottos. Some of our best dives were at night when a fair number of the fish were asleep. The parrot fish were enveloped in their nighttime bubble, and it was possible to approach them closely for a portrait photo. A full moon provided plenty of visual orientation, and after such a dive, one could easily handle another week of committee meetings with the termites. In the dive classes many people expressed a bit of trepidation toward the "dangers of the deep." I assured them that, in general, the most dangerous thing they would be doing was driving to the beach. Underwater, as in geopolitics, if you leave dangerous things alone, more often than not, they will leave you alone. Playing with scorpion fish, just to see their colors change, is not too bright.

Experiencing the beauty of the Red Sea was not easy for individuals who did not work in the Kingdom. The Saudis did not issue tourist visas, the Sudan had very limited facilities, and at either end of the Red Sea, in Djibouti and Sharm Al-Sheikh, in Egypt only modest effort was made to cater to divers. Of the limited number of people who could document this underwater beauty via photography, none had a stranger life's story than Leni Riefenstahl. She had first achieved prominence as one of Adolph Hitler's propagandists, most notably directing the 1935 movie *Triumph of the Will*. She existed in a twilight zone after the war and for the rest of her life, claiming that she had only produced the film for its "artistic value" and was most naive when it came to the true political situation. She was held for four years in a French detention center after the end of the war before she was released. At the age of 71, lying about her age, she learned how to scuba dive and later published a remarkable coffee-table book on the Red Sea entitled *Coral Gardens*.

One of the very few boat dives I experienced came via contacts established by an American woman working at the US Embassy. She linked us with a Saudi who owned a boat and offered dive trips offshore, and she came along for the ride. The boat carried no communication gear or lights, but this was, after all, a simple day trip. All the necessary arrangements had been made with the Coast Guard to ensure the legality of her venture and our trip. We signed up, and she said they'd be taking us to "whiskey reef," about 15 kilometers offshore.

After a choppy run out to the reef, the coastline disappeared, and the anchor was thrown overboard. We "kitted up" for our dive and jumped in. The sea's floor was around ten meters deep here, and suddenly a frisson of excitement, as much as if we had touched an electric ray, raced through the divers. There were hundreds of bottles of real booze lying on the seabed. Almost all the labels had washed away, but the shape and the still-sealed caps often indicated the contents. Most disturbing though, coral was thriving inside the vast majority of these bottles in this most unlikely of environments. The water pressure itself must have been sufficient to force the coral around the sealed caps. We had a lot of hope for one bottle! It was Johnny Walker, the color was the original amber, and NO coral was growing inside. We surfaced with it and with many other bottles. On the boat we were going to try the JW, but the odor strongly indicated that it had gone off—something else you would not think would occur. So, we had just observed the results of one very large inadvertent experiment—Johnny Walker is not sealed well enough to keep in 10 meters of sea water.

How the booze came to be located here also became clear. It was the result of one of the numerous smuggling operations of real booze into the Kingdom. Apparently the Coast Guard was closing in on the smugglers—forcing them to dump their contraband. Though all the bottles were now useless, we were encouraged to surface with as many bottles up as we could. The Coast Guard paid a bounty for each bottle with a sealed cap—no doubt as proof to higher authorities that they were doing their job.

The very next weekend the same boat, same pilot, and same American woman hit the reef and sank. Other divers from KFSH were on the boat, so we were told the entire story—the boat was half underwater, much of their gear was permanently lost, and the top half of the boat was out of the water at a 45-degree angle. The passengers clung to the boat all night, sleep a virtual impossibility given the angle at which the boat rested, and the next morning, during its routine rounds, the Coast Guard rescued them.

The trip to "whiskey reef" was my last boat dive in the Red Sea. The next year we tried a boat dive on the other side of the Kingdom, in the Arabian Gulf out of the port of Jubail, to see the turtles on Jenin Island, maybe twenty kilometers out in the Gulf. Seasickness abounded, and I had a prime place on the stern. Ultimately we dove, but the most disturbing aspect of the whole trip was watching an enormous oil supertanker hugging the Saudi coastline as it crawled north, considerably landward of us in our little dhow. This was during one of those "forgotten" wars (at least in the West), the Iran-Iraq war, when up to half a million youths were slaughtered in World War One–type warfare, with similar results in terms of changing territorial boundaries. In the air and on the sea were the so-called tanker wars, when the air force of one side tried to blow up the tankers of the other. That same year an Iraqi jet attacked the USS *Stark*, a guided missile frigate, killing 29 American sailors. But Iraq was on "our side" at the time, so this was not cause for war. We blamed Iran. And the incident was quickly forgotten. All things considered, our boat trip into the Gulf was not a very bright thing to do and would be our last boat dive—period.

12

The Age of Respectability

We had other letters of recommendation with us, but we did not need them. The fact that we came with our children was enough to open doors. The people of Peyrane love children, and they assumed we were not up to mischief since we brought ours with us. . . . I was told that some of the Communists were skeptical at first. Their rumor was that we had come to prepare the next American landing, but before many weeks they, too, accepted our story. Indeed, the impression made by the American institutions of sabbatic leave and foundation fellowships was remarkable. In this village they increased respect for American Civilization more than any propaganda could have.

—Lawrence Wylie,
Village in the Vaucluse

Since my wife overcame her *kharbaan* status—and it is the wife who is broken, as in most cultures, but particularly in the Kingdom, it could never be the man—and pumped out those two little "Ramadan bundles," our lives dramatically changed, as all new parents learn. With one child, we felt that we were still able to accomplish 75 percent of what we had done previously. But two little ones cut that to 25 percent, even with the support of a "saint" living with us, an Eritrean au pair named Salma. The scuba diving door closed, but in a country that particularly loves its children, others were flung open.

With two little kids in tow, even the *mutawaa* (religious police) left us alone.

Lawrence Wylie and his family ventured to a small Provençal village, Roussillon, thoroughly undiscovered by tourists in the year 1950. In his account he changed the village's name to Peyrane. His two small children provided the same "respectability" that we found, and although he had no religious police to dodge, as he indicated, even the more doctrinaire communists overcame their suspicions that he was an agent for some nefarious American plot.

Why "wind, sand, and stars" never seemed to translate very well is that the Arab ideal of paradise is the lush green oasis: trees, grass, and a babbling brook. For years a prayer call alarm clock (naturally made in Taiwan) playing the most melodious voice and accompanied by running water was sold in the souks. This tape was also used at the airport to indicate *saleh* (prayer time). Many expats, and no doubt many Saudis themselves, would have strongly preferred that the local mosque also use this same tape for the morning prayer call—one hour before dawn—rather than the coughing and screeching to which the local imam often subjected us.

The municipality of Riyadh built numerous versions of paradise throughout the city. My favorite was Al Yamamah Park, located on a side street not much more than half a kilometer from our residence, so inconspicuous on the Riyadh landscape that most of the Saudis who worked at the hospital did not know where it was. The park was the size of a small city block and boasted a large, multifunctional fountain in the middle, displaying choreographed colored lights programmed for different displays. Two very large children's playgrounds dominated the park's corners. Mature palm trees lined the walking paths and dotted the numerous well-utilized, semi-secluded, grassy picnic areas. The adults spread their ground cloths and enjoyed their meals as the children ate and played. Sometimes we joined them with our *shwarmas* (the Middle East chicken or lamb sandwich) and at times my beer. Mary thought I might be pushing it a bit to imbibe so publicly, but that never stopped her from joining me! I told her, perhaps too many times, about my training in such public drinking displays, with concessions to the prohibitionist milieu. At Georgia Tech, the rule was that you were not allowed to be seen drinking on campus. Opaque paper cups had become de rigueur for drinking there—and here.

Occasionally Salma accompanied us to the park. We weren't very good at that master-servant hierarchical business, as surely the Emir of Yabrin could attest when I didn't serve him tea first. Salma was a part of the family and adapted to our traditions of sitting and eating with us in the park. Sometimes Mary and I took the kids to play, but most often it was I and the two kids. When I came home from work I often gave Mary and Salma a break from "kid duty," and let the kids run in the playground for an hour.

And that was the most interesting part. The park was enclosed by a fence and had one entrance. Admission was SR1 (28¢) per adult. And most importantly, you had to be a "family" to enter, that is, at least a husband and wife, and usually kids. A single man could not enter. Yet an exception was always made for me—the rule was not really aimed at Westerners, who probably would not use the park anyhow and would not be chasing a black *abaya* if they did enter. To the best of my knowledge, no one in the park ever complained to the authorities about this exception. It was one of the numerous accommodations that were made to our lifestyle.

During the three-year period that we so often frequented the park, we never saw another Westerner.

Another recreational area was a funky amusement park just off the King Fahd Expressway, a Coney Island sort of place with bumper cars, amusement rides, and a very long set of multiple, multicolored slides. The kids loved sliding down them on the provided carpets. The slides worked their way into our whimsical benchmarks on when it was time to leave, and although the slides were still there when we left in '89, they would finally be torn down in the winter of 2002–3.

Very, very rarely was I nailed by this "single man" business. For example, Mary told me that we were almost out of Huggies and would I mind running up to Al Azizia (the nearby local supermarket) and picking some up? Normally a 10-minute round trip, including purchase time. I got out on the road and the madness had already started. An important soccer match had been played that night, and fans were celebrating, which generally meant doing crazy things like hanging out the windows and sun roofs as they drove their autos at high speed. Perhaps not all that different from the madness that consumes an American city that wins the Super Bowl. It was not a time to be out on the road, but the Huggies wouldn't wait. The parking lot at Al Azizia was notoriously a major hangout for Riyadh's disaffected Saudi youth. The authorities had brought in several school buses full of police, ringing the parking lot. Cars were being admitted, so I turned to enter. The policeman stopped me.

"*Fayn zojhatak?*" (Where is your wife?)

"*Fil bayt, min waleds.*" (At home, with the kids.)

He shook his head, I couldn't enter. I shrugged and motioned like, "Do I look like a soccer hooligan?" He shrugged too, he had his orders: No wife, no entry.

Well, I knew another grocery store a bit further away that wasn't a hangout and still had Huggies. Off I drove into the madness again. Finally, I arrived back home, and the wife gave me one of these, "Where have you been?" looks. Well . . .

The countdown continued to the day when Huggies runs would no longer be necessary and the ending of an even larger phase in our lives would occur. Our son duly came through his toilet training before his second birthday, and now we were approaching his third birthday. We found ourselves on the sidewalk in front of our now former residence, the sardonically named "low-rise." Our 4-wheel drive vehicle was in the background, loaded absolutely to the roof and beyond, containing many of the necessary essentials for what we hoped would be two and a half years and, indeed, was. Two large, gaily painted Yemen trunks, along with two kids' bikes, firewood, and water were strapped on the roof rack. Our friends took suitable farewell pictures of the four of us. I wore my "It's not long now" T-shirt.

On the streets of Riyadh it is considered acceptable for men to kiss other men on the cheek but not for men to kiss women on the cheek. I already had my "Exit Only" visa in the passport and, feeling a little frisky, shook the hands of my two male friends and kissed their wives on the cheek. And then there was Salma. She had been part of our family for almost three years, and her life was changing also. In particular, she would be losing her dear little "John-John" and "P.T." whom she had treated as her own for this period. Tears were rolling down her cheeks. My wife cried, hugged and kissed her good-bye. It was now my turn, a very awkward time—should I treat her like the wives of the other two friends? I think she was relieved when I opted for a reasonable compromise of embracing her one hand with both of mine in a hearty handshake. Fortunately her future would be a happy one, avoiding perpetual servitude to the whims of another family—she got out, married, and is now an Australian citizen living in Melbourne. She was the exception, as she was exceptional.

Ten days later I was pouring the dregs of the last beer over the embers of the final Saudi campfire, anticipating a good day, and a much needed shower in the Holiday Inn in Aqaba, Jordan. It would turn out to be one of the toughest and worst days of the entire trip, a day when even my kids would "fail" me miserably.

I had decided to save about 250 kilometers of driving and at the same time see one of the more remote and lovely parts of the Kingdom, Wadi Zaytah. Instead of taking the main border crossing on the Tabuk–Maan highway and backtracking to Aqaba, I elected to drive this lovely, sinuous, lightly traveled road off the Hejaz plateau down to the warm Red Sea and cross at Haql, with Aqaba only 10 kilometers away. This border post had recently been opened for crossings by foreigners.

We arrived at the Saudi frontier post just after the noon *saleh* (prayer). It took a couple of hours, as expected, to out-process. The Exit Visas were stamped in our passports. We were OUT. Ominously, however, they insisted on taking the license plates, which I had been told I could keep. They said yes, if I was leaving on an Exit-Reentry Visa, but with Exit Only the plates would have to come off. And so they went. I drove across the one kilometer of no-man's-land and reached the Jordanian post. "No license plates, the only thing we can do is impound your car at the border; you are allowed to take nothing out of it; you must travel to Amman (at the other end of the country), apply for a temporary permit to cross the country, but are allowed no stops." Two little kids and substantial offers of baksheesh were not changing their minds. I turned around and drove back to the Saudi border post.

The first thing I did was erect two tents, a clear indication I was staying until this matter was resolved. We unpacked the stove, had some tea to steady my nerves, and I strode over to see the officials, telling them I HAD to have my license plates, insistent, but polite. Well, maybe the *mudeer* (director) who came at 7:00 p.m. would make an exception, given our circumstances. So, it was back to the tents, a brief nap, a meal, knowing a LOT would be resting on this meeting. Shameless child exploitation was about to follow. Paris dressed in her favorite Saudi dress, the black patent leather shoes, and the little white socks. She was cleaned up too, with a sponge bath, and ribbons tied in her hair. We met the *mudeer* at seven.

"What part of *la* (no) did you not understand?"

"I would therefore like to make one phone call—I worked here for ten years and think I'm entitled—even if I was a thief and arrested by the police, I would be entitled to one phone call to my sponsor."

"None of the phones are currently working at the border," replied the mudeer.

And so that was that. We were walking back to the tents, to break the truly bad news to Mary, and I was muttering darkly about what a hard-hearted muther the director was.

"But, Daddy, he can't be a mother, he is a man."

"Oh honey, someday you'll understand, but not now."

Deus ex machina is welcome in any form. A Saudi was following me. He was coal black, must have been from the southern Tihama, the African part of Saudi Arabia that I had visited 10 years earlier. He was the dog handler at this border post, the dogs trained to sniff for narcotics in in-coming vehicles. It wasn't a prestigious job, since most Saudis consider dogs unclean. He knew English, and the director had him in the office, if further elaborations on the part of "*la*" that I did not understand had to be made. He said: "I'm really sorry about all this; you can come to my apartment and use my personal phone."

Mary, Paris and John stayed at the tents and I followed my new friend. I was even more nervous—everything rested on one phone call, and it was Thursday night, the Saudi equivalent of Saturday night, when most people were involved in social obligations. I called the hospital switchboard. All the Sudanese and Egyptians who worked there knew me. I asked for a Western physician friend who had *wasta* and had contacts inside and outside the hospital.

"I'm sorry, Mr. Jones, he is on leave." How could I not have known that?

"Well you just have to find the hospital director for me."

Two minutes later he was on the line.

"John, I thought you had already left the country."

"Well, Dr. Fahd, that is exactly the problem."

I desperately explained our need to have our license plates returned, or else we would be stuck at the Saudi-Jordanian border.

I heard a laconic: "Well, John, I'll see what I can do." I asked him to please call me back in five to ten minutes and let me know what happened. In about five minutes the phone rang.

I picked it up: "Dr. Fahd?"

"No, this is Abdullah at the border post. You can come pick up your license plates now."

The magic phone call had been made, and had it worked! I tried to pay the Saudi dog handler for the long distance bill, a not inconsiderable bill knowing that he was not paid well. If I had insisted any more, it would have become insulting. He simply refused any payment.

Meanwhile, back at the border station house, it was nice to know that the phone service had been restored.

"Would I like some tea"?

Oh no, there was no need for me to put the plates on myself, they would be very happy to do it for me.

"Would I like anything to eat"?

Ah, the magic phone call and a little *wasta*. We packed up our tents and drove back to the Jordanian side of the border. We must have been the first people in the history of the border post to have arrived without license plates and then turned around, gone back, and returned with them seven hours later. I could tell that the Jordanian border agents definitely had the capacity to play games with us, but it was muted. If I had *wasta* somewhere in Saudi Arabia, who was to say that I didn't have it in Amman? An hour and a half later we were on our way to the Holiday Inn.

But the Thursday night of social events in Riyadh and the Arab world was also the Holy Thursday of my youth. Yes, it was Easter weekend and half of Europe had flown to Aqaba for the warm water and first tan of the season. From the most expensive to the very cheapest, there was not a hotel room to be had in Aqaba. We were told there was a campground down the south coast a bit, a cold freshwater shower on the beach, and the camping was only a dollar a night. Well, we could do that. It was about one in the morning, and we set up the tents again. Sleep came easily.

***

For a story about Saudi Arabia and the Saudis, crossing the border would logically end part one. However, to underscore what would have happened if I had not been helped by the magic phone call, a brief epilogue section might be useful.

Aqaba's hotels may have been packed, but we were the only campers in the campground. The kids played in the water. The sun was warm, and the cold-water shower wasn't very. That evening we could see the lights of four countries, their lumens roughly corresponding to the country's GNP. The wonderful folks in the dental clinic had given me a short-wave radio as a farewell present, and I had it tuned to a classical radio station in Elat. The stars were out, and all was indeed right with the world.

The next morning Mary gently suggested that I get back to dealing with things, and Exhibit A in that regard was an enormous bag of dirty clothes, the result of over a week of camping. She stayed on the beach with John, and Paris and I went into town to mail the thank you card to Dr. Fahd, purchase fresh provisions, and find laundry facilities. I came out of the laundry, glanced over at our vehicle, and there were two Western women looking at the back, in fact they were actually *feeling* the license plate. There were now few things of which I was more possessive!

"Er, ah, may I help you ladies?"

In an American accent I heard: "Oh, we were just wondering, are these license plates from Saudi Arabia? How did you get them?"

"I worked in Saudi Arabia for 10 years and just drove across the border."

"Well, we worked in Abha for eight years and just crossed the border ourselves." And so their story of woe tumbled out— impounded car, paying for the most expensive suite in the Holiday Inn, and they would hear at noon if they would be thrown out due to a prior booking. No place to stay and not even a toothbrush to their name, all their belongings were locked in the car. I volunteered one of our tents, but they swung the suite for another night. I even tried my own *wasta* on their behalf but, alas, no. They sent a nice thank you note to our stateside address, saying that they hired a taxi to take them to Amman and after a few days, they had all the necessary paperwork for a seventy-two-hour transit visa. They weren't even allowed to choose which country would be their destination and were forced to transit through Iraq, prior to reaching the relative sanity of Turkey. Starting from such a low baseline, I certainly hope that the Jordanian Tourism Authority has made significant progress in improving the country's "*Ahlan wa Sahlan*" hospitality.

13

Innocents Abroad

Stereotypes are draped on various nationalities in terms of their travel styles. Mark Twain shared a classic account of Americans traveling abroad in the 19th Century. The Japanese famously follow their pennant-carrying leader. The pushy people in the ski-lift lines are often labeled Germans. The Americans are not necessarily sure what country they are in ("if this is Tuesday, it must be Belgium"). Even more embarrassing, as one of my English friends pointed out, the Americans are notoriously the loudest diners in European restaurants, something to which I had previously been oblivious. But once this pink elephant was pointed out, that distinctive accent cascading across the restaurant always caused a wry smile to appear on my face. Mary, after numerous meals in such restaurants, admitted the accusation was true, but sought an explanation: "We grew up in a big country . . . large distances to one's neighbors . . . you know, etc."

Then there are the Saudis. Lubna Hussain wrote a markedly accurate column in the *Arab News* about the signs indicating the arrival of summer in the Kingdom. No, it wasn't the heat or the end of school. It was the large traffic jam in front of the Diplomatic Quarter as Saudis scrambled at the last minute to obtain the required visas for overseas trips. A Saudi colleague was taking a 45-day leave, and a couple of days before his departure, I asked where he was going. "We haven't made up our minds yet." When they did decide, the destinations were often narrowly defined—Harrods's in London, the George V in Paris, and certainly to see and be seen on Les Champs-Elysées, just one of the courtship rituals of upper-class

Saudi youth. At one time Saudia, the national airline, flew direct flights to the "other" Magic Kingdom, the one in Orlando, Fl. Egypt and Lebanon, when peace returned, became well-sought destinations also.

It was the period of our European trip, from 1989 to 1991. It was an opportunity to observe Saudis outside their native habitat. Khalid, our friend who visited Yabrin with us in 1988, knew our trip wouldn't be touching on normal Saudi destinations. His wife told us that he was a bit different, as I already knew. He'd even visited places like Portugal. I explained that one major facet of the trip's planning was to rent houses in the more rural areas and visit the large cities for a long day, but at all cost avoid staying in hotels in the cities and relying on restaurants. "A good plan, may we join you for parts of it?" And that was how the Danish *folkeferie*, a resort of free-standing independent chalets, in Gilleleje, about an hour north of Copenhagen, obtained almost certainly its first Saudi guest.

On the appointed morning of our rendezvous, my family and I left another *folkeferie* at the top of Jutland, figuring we had a six-hour or so drive, including the ferry ride. Khalid and his family had arrived in Switzerland the day before and had to drive the entire lengths of both Germany and Denmark. I thought they would be at least a day late, but when I signed in at the Gilleleje *folkeferie*, the receptionist told me that a man from Saudi Arabia was asking if I had arrived. The two weeks went by all too quickly, the kids played well together, and we used the heated swimming facilities, the kids took horseback riding lessons, and utilized the other recreational facilities. We also observed, but did not participate, when the Danes performed some of their "colorful native customs," like dipping in the frigid North Sea.

The following year Khalid joined us at our *gîte* (a house, usually in the rural areas, that may be rented for short-term vacations) for a couple of weeks in Brittany. I picked him up from the TGV (*Train à Grande Vitesse*—the French high-speed train) station in Rennes. He could roll with almost everything but, for example, preferred lamb chops to our pork chops. With some English friends who were also visiting us, the seven of us drove over to the coast to eat at a funky old restaurant, *Chez Jacky*, in the little village of Riec-sur-Bélon— the true heart of oyster country. The *fruits de mer* were the specialty, and they were piled high on our table—oysters, mussels, crab, winkles, and a few things we couldn't name. Mary squeezed lemon juice on one of the crustaceans, and it moved! Very fresh! As the rest of us tried to point out, it didn't move much. Maybe it just twitched a bit. At this point, my little daughter and Khalid became the non-participants in this meal. Saudis can be blunt on occasions, as Mary had experienced with questions about her *kharbaan* status, and Khalid simply said to me, "Don't you think this is a bit barbaric?" We made amends to him a few days later, taking him to an excellent seafood restaurant in Questembert, assuring him beforehand that everything would be cooked . . . no sushi, no fruits de mer. Six years later Khalid tested my own squeamishness.

14

What They Learned in School Today

What did you learn in school today,
Dear little child of mine?
What did you learn in school today,
Dear little child of mine?
I learned that war is not so bad;
I learned about the great ones we have had;
We fought in Germany and in France
And someday I might get my chance.

—Pete Seeger, folk song:
What Did They Learn in School Today?

Two and half years after we had camped on that beach just south
of Aqaba, I boarded a plane at Heathrow bound for Atlanta. My wife
and the kids had preceded me by a month, and I had the rather
difficult task of legally disposing of the vehicle that we had driven
out of the Kingdom. The date was September 1, 1991, and in three
days Paris and John would be in school.

Atlanta friends had lobbied us to place the kids in the public
school, with all the usual valid reasons. Was I growing more
conservative by making the safe choice for my kids—this wonderful
touchy-feely private school? Sure, it might be located in funky
clapboard houses, but the school seemed to have it all, especially, the
spirit of a fun-loving attitude: "love the kids and they'll love to
learn." In general, the parents were a good lot, too. They might have
been drawn primarily from the professional classes, but when the

school had a spring cleaning workday, they were there, shirtsleeves rolled up, washing windows, cleaning floors, installing a basketball hoop. The school had a wonderful playground structure on campus and a park nearby.

After thirteen years abroad, I experienced being a foreigner in my own country. For sure, this wasn't the Atlanta of the 70's. What happened to Rose's Cantina? We were back in "miles," and much else, but after six weeks or so, our social gaffs and stupid questions were noticeably fewer. Welcome home.

But what were the kids learning? The most stunning difference from my youth was the treatment of the American Indians. Gone were all the black and white images of the savages attacking wagon trains full of innocent white settlers. The Indians were the original environmentalists. The kids learned Indian songs. Sacagawea was almost a saint and certainly worthy of almost an entire hour's class for a first grader. It was a remarkable turnaround in perceptions in only 35 years. Come the holiday season, the kids brought home models of spinning dreidels they had made. So they learned about Hanukkah, Christmas, and Kwanzaa. More embarrassment—I had never heard of Kwanzaa. Discrete inquiries resulted in the information that it was a holiday created in the late 60's--early 70's to commemorate Black heritage. Living as we did in a city that was 70 percent Black, that seemed fair enough.

I found an honest effort to celebrate the cultural diversity and heritage of so many people. Bravo. And so it was only a greater surprise when I was sitting in the school's library and picked up a book entitled *Children of the World*. The kids were all in there— Japanese, African, Dutch, Israeli, and the Arabs—all portrayed in a very positive light, well almost. There were the flaxen-haired Dutch, living below sea level, but with their creativity and energy reclaiming the land from the sea. The Israelis were "Sabras," as the generation of Israelis who were born inside the country was called. As the page explained, they were named after a native plant, soft on the inside, but tough on the outside, because they had to be tough to live in such a hostile environment. The kids' jaws were square, their gaze uplifted, like a socialist realism portrait from the then disintegrating Soviet Union.

And then there was the Arab. He was riding a camel . . . well, barely riding a camel; he was shown unable to do even this competently; he was desperately hanging on as the camel bounced through sand dunes. He was grinning though, the amiable buffoon. This was a turning point for me, no less dramatic than the savage Indians being transformed into environmentalists. This *is* what the Arabs are complaining about. Their negative portrayal in the Western media. Here was a clear portrayal of the epithet that was so often used to describe them, "camel jockeys." But in the real world of rapid urbanization, it was increasingly difficult to find a Saudi riding a camel.

If you were taking one of those tests that asked you to identify the picture that did not belong in the group, this representation of the Arab would have been the correct answer. But did anyone else know the correct answer? I made a few inquiries among my friends.

"Well, they did ride camels, didn't they?"

"Maybe you are being overly sensitive and reading into it more than was meant."

Well, yeah, I guess some Blacks still ate watermelons and played banjos happily, but that isn't how you would portray them in a kid's book.

Don't just bitch, propose something constructive. So, I decided to go to the principal, tell her I was glad that the school was teaching about Hanukkah, Christmas, and Kwanzaa, but wouldn't it be enriching if we also added something about the Eids. I wasn't Muslim, and I made that quite clear, but I could put together a brief presentation about their religious holidays and say something positive about Saudi Arabia and its development. Muslims weren't exactly the Rosicrucians; there were over a billion of them on our planet. How could she say no?

So, I went to the principal's office. She was energetic, efficient, caring, and Black. All this business happened in HER lifetime. The negative portrayal of Blacks, the *Amos and Andy Show*, how Blacks were like *The Invisible Man* because they were never portrayed in the media. *Surely, she would understand.*

I gave my pitch. It got real quiet in her office, painfully quiet. Her head was lowered, she raised it and said: "Why don't you show some of your underwater pictures from Saudi Arabia? The kids would love to see the fish." And so I did.

During the 21 months we lived in Atlanta I also read the *Wall Street Journal* on a daily basis. There were numerous articles over this period printed about Saudi Arabia. I decided that I would save any article that was not totally negative, that had just *one sentence* which hinted at something positive in the country. I know, "if it bleeds, it leads." News by its very nature is negative. But still, the industry is sensitive to that charge and sometimes prints good news, or even balanced articles, with the key phrase, "but, on the other hand . . ."

In 21 months there was not even *one sentence*! And during this period, there were numerous articles about Scott Nelson, a former King Faisal Specialist Hospital employee who alleged that he had been tortured in Saudi Arabia. I knew him and the case, and I knew that his case was essentially untrue. I wrote to the reporter who had been handling the case—surely he would want to know evidence existed that much of this story was fabrication. No response. Shortly before I returned to the Kingdom, a friend in Inman Park showed me an article from the *Atlanta Journal-Constitution* on Scott Nelson, a safety engineer who was just trying to do his job when the nefarious Saudis arrested him, threw him in jail, tortured him . . . blah, blah. I told my friend that the story was grossly inaccurate and exaggerated. "But it is in the newspaper?"

Is it any wonder that "And someday I might get my chance" came true?

15

Customs of the Country

Missionaries will travel on crusades,
The word is given, the heathen souls are saved,
Conversions to our morality,
Sigh the Cannons of Christianity,

Come the wars, and turn the rules around,
To bend your soul on the battleground
And the Lord will march beside me
Drone the Cannons of Christianity.

—Phil Ochs, folk song:
The Cannons of Christianity

And so Beale Street quickly dissolved back into Olaya Street. It was May 1993, and I had arrived in Riyadh as the long hot summer months commenced. There had been a war, and fortunately I had missed this one. SCUD missiles had rained on Riyadh. It was possible to drive around and still see the devastation. A camping buddy who had remained in Riyadh throughout the war had done something I would never have considered at Polei Klang. When the sirens sounded, he raced to the roof of his villa, videotaping the incoming missiles. Sometimes the famed Patriot missiles rose to challenge them. My friend wasn't trying to make a film of political content. He simply filmed it as it occurred. And of the eleven SCUDS that he filmed, not a single one of them was knocked out in the sky by a Patriot. Occasionally Scuds were hit, but the warheads still came through, causing an explosion on the ground. Demonstrative proof that the Patriot missiles did not accomplish their goal, but not something reported on the American TV, and Raytheon's stock price grew on the hype.

American female soldiers had driven army trucks in Riyadh. Saudi women decided if it was good enough for the foreigners . . . The war might have turned the rules around. And in a famous demonstration, some 40 women dismissed their drivers and drove themselves. The reaction was swift and severe—their jobs and careers were damaged, and in some cases so were their families.

But much of the old life in Riyadh remained. One of the benchmarks I wanted to check was my safety when walking in the streets and alleys of downtown Riyadh at night, something one would have been mad to try in Atlanta. Sure enough, one could still walk about in perfect safety. It was the Riyadh of old. Furthermore, there was the friendship and camaraderie of the expat community—traveler's tales could begin anew. And there were the numerous sincere welcomes from the Saudis—and invitations into their homes.

But there were rumblings of more negative developments. The *mutawaa* (religious police) were said to be much more active and venomous. With so much of what passes for "expat grapevine intelligence," sorting fact from fiction was difficult. But it seemed to be true that there were such abuses of their power as an incident when a Western woman was beaten by *mutawaa* thugs, her jaw broken when her head was struck against the car. I decided to have a look for myself. I visited Al-Akariya mall one night, the upscale mall at the time in Riyadh. I witnessed a *mutawaa* in action, the scraggly beard, his brown *bisht* (the long Arabian formal cloak) trailing behind him as he strode purposefully through the mall, emanating power and hate. Two policemen trailed behind him. As an expat man there was very little he could admonish me for, but still, I felt nervous in the presence of such power—the power that says that God Himself is with me, and if you disagree, you oppose Him also.

There was a Saudi woman dressed absolutely as conservatively as one could be—black socks, black gloves, naturally the black abaya covering everything else, flat shoes (heels can be sinful), and a veil so thick that she could not see through it. She was in a bookstore, one of the very few in a shopping mall, and she had lifted the bottom of the veil ever so slightly so she could read the cover of a book. The *mutawaa* saw her and yelled, and she quickly dropped the veil, blind again. Within a couple of years, one of my official duties would be orienting various Western women on short-term visits to the Kingdom. They asked me if the *mutawaa* had a defined dress code. How does one dress so that one is not criticized? I explained that there was no such thing, it is all about power, and foremost in my thoughts was what happened that night at the mall.

More pleasantly, though, there was the feeling of truly being home again. I caught up on the changes, the impact of the war, but the overall sense was that life would return to the pleasant days of the 80's; that the shock of the war was an aberration. An expat friend loaned me his car until I could purchase one. Before my family returned to Riyadh, after the kids had finished the school year, I was invited into numerous homes. The expats served their homemade wine and beer. The Saudis usually served the expensive Scotch, priced at well over $100 on the black market. I was enjoying a drink with one Saudi, and he was also smoking, as we chatted about developments. Suddenly the front door opened, and in came a completely covered woman—his wife, whom I had never met. A look of panic crossed his face as he jumped up and attempted to hide the cigarettes! She walked by the room, but did not enter. He sheepishly said: "She allows me to drink, but I'm not supposed to smoke." Hum! Appearances again betray the true power arrangements.

I called Mary that night in the States. Yes, many things were fine, and I was happy to be back, but there were some changes for the worse, and we might have to adjust if we were to remain. Soon I would be picking my family up at the airport. It was the night that I lost my mule.

As with so much else in the Kingdom, the skills of the customs and police officials had experienced a remarkable transformation. Back in 1980, on one of our scuba diving trips during the Thanksgiving holiday weekend, we decided to prepare the Thanksgiving meal in Riyadh and then transport it with us on the plane to Jeddah. The question of our favorite beverages naturally had to be decided upon. The consensus was to make it an individual decision, with the strong advice that if you did transport an alcoholic beverage, pack it in check-in luggage, not carry-on. One of the guys must have been dyslexic or had fallen asleep during this part of the conversation. As we were proceeding through the line to board the airplane, and the carry-on bags were being checked, the official pulled our friend's wine clocked in the familiar Rauch grape juice bottle with its re-sealable ceramic top out of the bag, and uttered one word: "alcohol." As the friend later related, his whole time in the country passed before him, and his carelessness would probably lead to his deportation. A very savvy friend quickly countered that this was simply grape juice, but the official knew that alcohol burned, so he lit a match, and put it in the bottle, where it was promptly extinguished. We shrugged and smiled, with the look of, "See, we told you, it was grape juice." The official returned the bottle and our entourage was on its way.

Overall, the principal role of Saudi Customs was to curtail the flood of narcotics smuggling from the Indian subcontinent into the country. When a Pakistani could make 30 years of his normal salary on a successful run, the nightly battle was intense, and that was where the real Custom's mission lay. A physician friend of mine was also a good friend of the head of Customs and occasionally they shared scotches. One day the man had just received another reward from the King—he was rewarded not by the absolute volume of narcotics intercepted but when his forces detected a new method by which drugs were smuggled. Heroin had been dissolved and soaked into the imported shirts. One of his more astute Customs agents had felt them and realized the shirts were stiffer than normal. The proscribed penalty for drug smuggling was death. The man explained: "If we executed everyone that we should, Pakistan would accuse us of genocide."

Within this overall context, the interaction between Westerners and the Customs officials was just a sideshow, a parlor game for bored officials. The black and white rules applied to a Westerner also, and if someone was so stupid as to try to smuggle a pound of heroin or hash, there would be *real* serious consequences. Blatant efforts to bring in alcohol might lead to different results. A bottle of

Johnny Walker might just be seized, with the offender able to get off by saying: "I forgot what country I was flying to." On other nights a harsher verdict was rendered for such stupidity. One American female who worked at the hospital was deported after it was discovered that she had taped airline miniature alcohol bottles to her body.

In a country in which *Vogue* magazine could be considered "pornographic," there was a vast gray area where the rules could be tested, with minimal consequences. In the early 80's, Customs focused on the magazines and the pictures of too much female flesh. Import of the written word was absolutely safe, even if it was critical of the Kingdom. Around this time, Holden and Johns' excellent *The House of Saud* was published. Renowned as a realistic account of the consolidation of the Arabian peninsula under the Al-Saud family, it was critical in part, and consequently, banned in the Kingdom. With the word *Saud* on the cover, I figured additional safeguard measures might be required to bring the book in. Mary bought Dr. Benjamin Spock's *Baby and Child Care*, the one showing a cute grinning baby on the cover, removed the cover, and glued it over *The House of Saud*. The ruse worked—this time. Six months later, on our next trip in, the Customs official asked me one question, "Do you have any books?" I had 17, and for the first time none of the books were about the Middle East. Customs collected all of the books and his helper hauled them off for further scrutiny. Fifteen minutes later the books were returned to me with a, "Sorry that we have detained you." But the lesson was clear—the rules had changed somewhat, and the written word was being examined.

On another trip through Customs in the 80's I was carrying one videotape. All videos were examined as a matter of procedure for "pornography." Justice Potter Stewart on the U.S. Supreme Court famously said that he could not define pornography but knew it when he saw it; neither could the Saudis define it, yet they saw it all too frequently. One had two choices. Let Customs have the tape to preview, get a receipt, and return a few days later to hopefully retrieve the tape, or take your chances and go to the Custom's room with its vast array of equipment and monitors and wait for the tape to be reviewed.

I opted for the latter, figuring that I was carrying perhaps the ultimate "safe" movie, the one movie made in the West that best portrays the Muslim point of view in the face of Western efforts to dominate them, Gillo Pontecorvo's *The Battle of Algiers*. Edward Said described this movie along with *Burn!*, which was also produced by Pontecorvo, as "the two greatest political films ever made." In the room were banks of monitors, a Customs agent, and two other Saudis. The Customs man popped my tape into one of the VCRs. But the real action, as it were, was on the other monitor. Like Justice Stewart, I know it when I see it, and increasing amounts of bare female flesh were filling the screen. But it was unlike any porno movie I had ever seen. The sound was turned down, as it was on all of the VCR's, so I could only guess the country of origin and suspected it must be Egyptian. The movie had definitely passed even the loosest standards for a tolerant Customs man. Only one question remained—would this be actual XXX, hardcore? Sure enough, the relationship was fully consummated on screen. And the movie played on, as the two Saudis carried on a discussion with the Customs officer. Every other word was *khawaja*. I understood the gist of the conversation. A bad Westerner gave them the movie—they had no idea what it contained—and they had been asked to bring it back to the Kingdom. After ten more minutes of hardcore action, the official finally told them to get out and kept the tape. After the two Saudis left, he explained the whole thing to me again in English. I made all the right sympathetic noises about the West being a difficult and treacherous place, full of pitfalls for Innocent Saudis traveling abroad. We agreed. One had to be very careful. Then a puzzled look appeared on his face—why was I here? I pointed at the monitor: Colonel Mathieu was leading the troops of his 10th Parachute Division as they paraded in the streets of Algiers. The Customs man took a couple of double takes. Unmistakably this was about Muslims and war, but, what the hell, he wasn't into nuance tonight, popped the tape out of the VCR, and handed it to me. I smiled and assured him that Ali la Pointe still lived in the Casbah.

Within this overall context of the Customs parlor game came "my mule," my wife. She was in the safest possible category, a woman alone with her two small children. The opaque electronic doors opened and shut as the passengers left the Customs area and I could see them, and they me, and we waved. Just a couple more minutes. She had three enormous duffle bags, filled with kids' clothes, toys, etc., trying to bring in as much as possible. She also had two very small containers: one of hops pellets, to give the extra flavor to my beer, and another of wine starter yeast. She had tried to be respectful of the Customs routine and had thoughtfully repackaged the contraband in fish food containers. The containers worked well, since it looked like original seal was unbroken. As a nice extra touch, she had even purchased a book entitled *Your First Aquarium.*

As the doors opened and closed, I watched the Customs agent as he opened these enormous bags. The first thing he reached for was one of those fish food containers. He popped the lid off, wet the end of his little finger, stuck it in, and tasted it. As I was to learn in an hour or so, he then said: "This is for making wine." My wife's efforts to dissuade him otherwise were for naught. The government's efforts to educate and upgrade its Custom officials' skills were very impressive. He did have a dour sense of humor about the whole matter, and inquired: "Well, where are the fish?" After an hour or so, Mary signed an Arabic language forms document which allegedly said she would never do this again; was fined SR80 (US$22), which she had to send one of the kids out to obtain from me since she had no riyals, then she and the kids were "released." Through our own higher Customs contacts, we were able to verify that Mary's name had not been entered in the computer on a "special watch" list, but, nonetheless, she informed me that her "mule" days were over. The times they were a changin'.

16

Injecting American Expertise

He was impregnably armoured by his good intentions
and his ignorance.

—Graham Greene
The Quiet American

The Saudi-US University Project was the brainchild of the former
Saudi Ambassador to the United States, Prince Bandar bin Sultan bin
Abdul Aziz. The inspiration behind the project was the knowledge
that there is much more to the delivery of health care than fancy
buildings and equipment. The essential ingredient is the actual
medical expertise of the staff. Like a giant hypodermic syringe, the
project was going to inject into the medical staff at King Faisal
Specialist Hospital the expertise of the faculty of five leading
American universities. The five universities were Yale, Duke,
George Washington, the University of Virginia, and Baylor. Other
doctors also came from Columbia and Vanderbilt. It was a mega-
budget project that definitely encouraged the leadership of the
universities to urge full participation from their staff.

Did the project accomplish its objectives? No definite conclusion
was ever prepared, as with so many other mega-projects. There were
positive achievements—the hospital obtained access to the Internet
four years prior to its general introduction into the Kingdom. As a
spin-off of the project, certain Saudi nationals were trained in clinical
and allied medical areas, such as the pharmacy and physical therapy,
and eventually returned to the hospital to assume leadership

positions. And some of the American physicians who came were truly excellent physicians, well respected in their fields, possessing the willingness and ability to conduct meaningful training sessions. Others were still in training themselves and related that the experience at the hospital was the best they had ever had, given the richness and variety of the clinical experience (doctor talk for: there were a lot of weird diseases that took very strange courses in unusual patients).

As the sole American who worked in the medical administration, I was quickly assigned the task of ensuring that all these FNGs felt comfortable in Riyadh and were aware of the real rules. I was to work with my fellow countrymen because I understood them. It was another learning experience.

The project commenced during Ramadan, not the most auspicious month to initiate such a project, since many of the normal rules in the Kingdom were transformed. Ramadan is the fasting month, and no one—Muslim or non-Muslim—could be seen eating, drinking or smoking publicly from sunup to sundown. Day and night are reversed, and at 3:00 am the streets are crowded with shoppers. The Saudis offered their best *Ahlan wa Sahlan* hospitality and housed key members of the project in the hotel designated for foreign diplomats.

For five working days, 60 American physicians from these universities were oriented and feted. On the eastern side of Riyadh a new soccer stadium designed by the British architects, Ian Fraser and John Roberts had recently been completed and was a source of considerable pride to the Saudis. Its gleaming white, tent-like structure appeared to be suspended above the eastern horizon. A full tour of the stadium had been arranged especially for the 'visiting dignitaries.' The acting Head of the hospital's Public Relations Department was pleased that he had arranged the exclusive tour, considering the often-dysfunctional occurrences during the month. Special buses had been arranged to transport the visiting doctors.

Precisely six of the sixty said they would participate in the tour. The Public Relations representative was visibly distraught. The turnout would be most embarrassing after all his efforts. "Why won't the others go?" After inquiries, and even vain efforts to change a few minds, I returned with the answer: "They are all going shopping—the gold *souks*, the carpet *souks.*" I was confronted with "shop 'til you drop" most dramatically. I was able to recruit nine other people, hospital employees or their spouses, on half an hour's notice, helped to fill the ranks, slightly attenuating the disaster.

The now single bus drove out the Damman Highway where the illuminated stadium dominated the desert sky. It was a most impressive tour, conducted by one of the Saudi architects who had been involved in the design and construction of the structure, a project about which he was visibly proud. We were shown scale models and a film of the construction. We ambled onto the field and were filmed and displayed on the electronic scoreboard. The tour concluded with a catered meal prepared for 100 plus. I asked the architect at the end of the tour how many people had been called in to work—he said around 50. I tried to apologize for the poor turnout; I knew that normally at this time of the evening, during Ramadan, he and the staff would be at home dining with family and friends. But he would hear nothing of it: he said it was simply his job to conduct such tours, and he was happy to do it.

There were, of course, the six visitors that participated in the tour, and they would have numerous successors. They performed their jobs well and expressed an intrinsic interest in the surroundings. Given a chance to see the desert and life beyond Riyadh, they were the first to go. Others, though, felt they had been sent on a three-month assignment to hell, and only the money was good. They had read all about Saudi Arabia in the *Wall Street Journal*.

Graham Greene drew a classic portrait of an American who "was impregnably armoured by his good intentions and his ignorance." His fictional character was Alden Pyle. He had attended one of the best universities and his head was full of the theories of a professor named York Harding. The theories and the education blinded him to the reality before him. It was a devastating portrait. Pyle was a CIA operative in Vietnam, and most ironically, given the present circumstances, the character was based on Kermit Roosevelt, who was the CIA operative responsible for the 1953 coup that overthrew the democratically elected government in Iran. Graham Greene was denied entry to the United States for a number of years. US Immigration needed to state no reason why it denied him entry, but his unflattering description of Alden Pyle could be a leading contender.

Part of my job with the Saudi-US University Project was dealing with the new "Alden Pyle" characters. One might say that numerically they were no more than 10 % of the project, but it was that minority that so rankled not only the Saudis, but also myself. They knew that the most offensive thing one could do to "Arabs" was to show them the soles of one's feet. They knew that alcohol was absolutely forbidden, and therefore they eschewed it. One of the female American administrators wrapped up in an *abaya* before she exited the plane. But with all their pseudo-efforts to conform to the customs of the country, the central accomplishment of this 10% was to offend. First and foremost, it was that insufferable, smug attitude that measures another person, or another country, by the degree to which they conform to American norms. The attitude that says, "I can learn nothing from you or your culture or your life's work." All the other offenses seemed to derive from this basic attitude. Some of the grim particulars I witnessed firsthand, others were related by "normally reliable sources."

One of the physicians arrived for a year-long assignment. He had been assigned to a very nice, newly constructed villa. The Saudi coordinator for the project called me to his office. The physician and his wife were arriving in a few days, on the first day of *Eid* (basically, in terms of services available, it meant that he was arriving on Christmas Day, when everything would be closed.) "I'll be with my family, please visit him that day, and make sure everything is okay, and if he needs anything, just take care of it." I did as he requested.

Several months later, when I was returning from a leave, I heard what had happened the previous week. The Saudi coordinator of the project felt he was in an increasingly impossible position. Theoretically, each of the physicians had been promised a car and a driver during their stay. As their numbers mounted toward 60, this became a logistical and financial nightmare. The coordinator proposed that the physicians, all living in relatively common areas, take a hospital-provided bus to and from work. The vast majority of the physicians considered it a reasonable request. The latest "Alden

Pyle" did not. In fact he delivered a tirade against the Saudi coordinator on the Wednesday before I returned from leave. After the weekend, on Saturday, even the physician knew he had overreacted. He came to me to determine how best to make amends. I said that it was now impossible.

"Well, what should I do?"

"I'd recommend that you not buy any green bananas."

He didn't appreciate my attempts at humor, but he was deported before those green bananas would have ripened, in three days. The various Saudis involved in this action personally assured me that his departure had absolutely nothing to do with the screaming incident —there had simply been a change in the "vision" of the project, or some such jazz, and his services were now redundant.

Another example of rudeness occurred during the initial Ramadan visit, and the intense shopping spree that lasted until 3:00 a.m. Another of the physicians was in a meeting concerning the opening of the Children's Cancer Center, modeled on St. Jude's in Memphis. I was at a four-person meeting, and the American physician fell sound asleep. One glance from the Saudi coordinator said it all: "So this is your American expertise." Well, at least he didn't show you the soles of his feet, but neither of us had the sense of humor necessary for such a rebuke.

One of the worst incidents which angered the Saudi leadership involved a very senior prince who was on a European trip and required medical advice in Paris. A team was assembled at the George V hotel, including one of the senior American movers in this project. At the conference, in a show of machismo, and no doubt to prove that he "loved" the prince more than the other participants, he threatened to break the hands of one of the Saudi physicians present, whose father just happened to be the Deputy Minister of the Interior.

Is it any surprise that the "Alden Pyle's" make the biggest impression on foreigners while the good intentions of the majority of Americans are forgotten?

17

At Peace with Vietnam

Kathleen had just turned ten, and this trip was a kind of birthday present, showing her the world, offering a small piece of her father's history. For the most part she'd held up well—far better than I—and over the first two weeks she'd trooped along without complaint as we hit the obligatory tourists stops. Ho Chi Minh's mausoleum in Hanoi. A model farm outside Saigon. The tunnels in Cu Chi . . .

One morning in Saigon she'd asked what it was all about. "This whole war," she said, "why was everybody so mad at everybody else?" I shook my head. "They weren't mad, exactly. Some people wanted one thing, other people wanted another thing." "What did you want?" "Nothing," I said. "To stay alive." "That's all"? "Yes." Kathleen sighed. "Well, I don't get it. I mean, how come you were even here in the first place?" "I don't know," I said. "Because I had to be." "But why?" . . .

For the rest of the day she was very quiet. That night, though, just before bedtime, Kathleen put her hand on my shoulder and said, "You know something? Sometimes you're pretty weird, aren't you?" "Well, no," I said. "You are too." She pulled her hand away and frowned at me. "Like coming over here. Some dumb thing happens a long time ago and you can't ever forget it."

—Tim O'Brien,
The Things They Carried

In 1992, while I was still living in Inman Park in Atlanta, I had lunch with an old acquaintance from the 70's. He said that the impossible was now possible. He had been back to Vietnam, and it was a perfectly safe and prudent thing to do. It was difficult for me to believe, but he was a reliable source. In about 18 months I, too, would return, during my first leave from Saudi Arabia in early 1994. I returned twice more, once each in 1995 and 1996. Each trip was radically different, and it would be hard to say that I was returning to the same country each time. At the time, I would not have believed how many of the same mistakes of the American involvement in Southeast Asia would be repeated in Southwest Asia.

And so I returned to the place "where the story all began."

On my first trip, in 1994, through some true serendipity, I traveled with four other people, only one of whom I had known previously, a friend from Atlanta. Two of these companions had been journalists, and through good connections, we were actually traveling as guests of the Vietnamese Ministry of Information. We toured Hanoi on our own, and one day we went to the Army War Museum and saw it before it was "toned down" for American consumption. When we left the museum, an old woman sat in the corner, selling books. Only two of them were in English, one was *The Quiet American*.

When we left Hanoi, the Information Ministry interpreter accompanied us on our nine-day trip; her assignment was to facilitate our requests. These were the very early days of the opening of the doors in Vietnam, and she had not been to many of the places that we had requested to see. She was a Communist Party member, and her personal feelings aside, it was her duty to accompany these Americans, since the official position of the Party had changed. In the course of the trip she told us that when she was one year old her father had been killed in a B-52 strike against what the Americans called the "Ho Chi Minh Trail." Her mother had raised her alone. She also discussed the human effects of all "those leafless trees in Asia." The incidence of cleft palate deformities in the northern part of the country was .5%. The incidence in the south was ten times higher, 5% of live births.

Normally, she displayed the accommodating façade of the party official, fulfilling her duties, whilst quietly observing the quirkiness of these Americans, whose compatriots had killed the father she had never known. I remember well the two times that her officious mien was broken and she "lost it."

We were near Quang Tri, and the talk was about American MIAs (missing-in-action). Suddenly she just blurted out: "You know, it really is so unfair, you Americans going on about your MIAs all the time, maybe 2,000 people in total, scouring the countryside for any remains. We have over 300,000 MIAs and there is nothing we can do about it." No doubt one of them was her father. On the bridge across the Ben Hai River earlier in the day we had taken each other's pictures at the obelisk that proclaimed: "Temporary International Boundary, 20/07/1954–30/04/1975." Later, we drank tea in a rustic roadside café just north of the river. Two Vietnamese men, roughly our age, sat at another table and watched us. It was always one of my principal concerns—if there were troubled-Vietnam-War-veterans in America who would occasionally lose it, how much more likely that there would be troubled-American-War-veterans in Vietnam? The men finished their tea, and as they passed our table, they asked our guide one question. I heard the *My* in her answer and confirmed with her the question: "What was our nationality?" *My* is "American" in Vietnamese. But all they did was nod to us and leave.

It was at the very end of our trip that she "lost it" the second time. We were in Saigon and had been on the rooftop of the old Caravelle Hotel, where one of my traveling companions had dined with Walter Cronkite and Abe Rosenthal and had argued about the prospects of "winning" this latest of our wars. We were discussing the name of the street. It was now called Dong Khoi (meaning "popular uprising"), and in the days of the French, it was Rue Catinat, named after one of Louis XIV's marshals. The guide asked us what had the Americans called the street? We said it was called Tu Do Street. We were trying to pronounce the Vietnamese, but she still did not understand us—no doubt because we were oblivious to the tones. We struggled, she struggled. Finally it dawned on her that we were saying "Tu Do." Her reaction was swift and overwhelming. She shook her head saying, "You had your nerve, calling it 'Freedom Street.'" Seems like Americans still have a weakness for the word freedom when they name their military campaigns.

In 1995 I returned to Vietnam again but stayed in the north. My lunch partner acquaintance from Atlanta in 1992 was now living in Hanoi, heading up a project to complete a modern orthotics unit in one of the local hospitals. He had been living in the country for six months, so I brought up what might seem to be my obsession—in this entire country, had there ever been an incident in which a Vietnamese simply lost it and killed an American, solely due to his nationality? He related only one questionable case and indicated that there had probably been other factors at work.

Meanwhile, the rules governing tourists were rapidly changing during this era, and the Vietnamese authorities had recently opened up the overland route to Dien Bien Phu. The trip took over 20 hours, spread over two days, for the Russian jeep to cover the 320 kilometers. I was probably one of the first 1,000 Westerners to take such a trip since 1954. I arrived during the Vietnamese version of an *Eid*, and how could one forget its name, "Tet"? Many places were closed, even on the sixth day of the holidays, but through the driver's Vietnamese *wasta*, my traveling companions and I were well taken care of. The war museum was closed but opened for our visit. The bunker from which General Christian Ferdinand de Castries walked out of to surrender on May 7, 1954, remained preserved. Even more interesting was a monument to the French dead in the battle which was the result of the work of one man—Jules Roy, a *pied-noir* (Algerian of French extraction) novelist, historian, and soldier. He had met with the Vietnamese in 1963, nine years after the battle. While lobbying for this remembrance, the Vietnamese bluntly asked him a question: "What would you have done with our dead if we had lost?" He answered with blunt frankness: "Thrown them in a common grave." His honesty was rewarded—the monument was approved.

In an almost impossibly long 16-hour one-day trip, the jeep rattled over the old Piste Pave, a track built through the mountains by the French in the 1880s. The destination was the hill station at Sapa. While at Sapa one morning, I awoke early and walked down a long dirt track to the rice fields in the valley. Coming up the hill was a Vietnamese man, about my age, wearing a pith helmet, Red Army star, and carrying an old gun. Twenty-seven years earlier he would not have hesitated to kill me. Now he just nodded and smiled, wishing me a good day. That contagion of violence that infects men periodically had left and moved somewhere else. It was coming my way again, but I certainly did not realize it at the time, secure as I felt "in my little bunker, deep in the desert."

Back in Hanoi I again asked my American friend to tell me how this transformation had occurred. He said that the Vietnamese viewed the Americans, with their continued obsession about the war and their MIAs, as so many "dinosaurs." It was so very long ago. They had fought the French, then they had fought the Americans, then they had to fight the Chinese and the Cambodians, and then they endured an "invasion" of Russian advisors. They had missed 50 years of economic development. They looked at Singapore and realized what was possible. As with the two Vietnamese men at the Ben Hai River, they may not have forgotten, but any further urge toward violence had been encapsulated and neutralized in a hard shell. It wasn't allowed to manifest itself. It was time to play 50 years' worth of economic catch-up and to enjoy the fruits of their military successes. Magnanimous in victory.

***

Later that same year, 1995, I saw the first dramatic sign from my desert bunker that peace might be troubled. The explosion was heard and felt at the American school many kilometers away. It had occurred on Talateen Street, then one of the most upscale shopping streets in Riyadh. A pickup truck, loaded with explosives, had detonated in the parking lot of the Saudi Arabian National Guard (SANG) training mission, and the entire front of its building was gone. It blew out the windows of all the stores across the street. As part of the "collateral damage," it had devastated Riyadh's first real grocery store, the Panda, which had opened in 1981.

The mission was a US project involved with the training of the Saudi Arabian National Guard, one of the "power bases" of then Crown Prince Abdullah. We had long-term friends who worked at the mission—one worked there in a civilian capacity, handling the many contracts required. His wife is an American of Lebanese extraction, with wonderful insight and abilities relating to the Arab women's community in Riyadh. She was also an incredible hostess and each year they orchestrated a brilliant New Year's Eve party, an intimate, black-tie affair for six or so couples. It was the most coveted invitation of the year. Despite my own "rough-hewn edges," my wife managed to "carry me," and an invitation was always eagerly received. For a few magical hours once a year, they transformed their home into a glamorous private restaurant. One server was present, effortlessly meeting the guest's requirements from the first aperitif.

Fortunately, our friend had a meticulous sense of duty. On that fateful day, as he was leaving for lunch, the phone rang. He returned to answer it, thereby saving his life. The explosion that ripped the front off the building was blunted by his office walls, though a large piece of glass came flying through his open office door, spearing one of his law books, a souvenir he still displays in his home. Five Americans were killed and if the news services could bother to remember, so were two non-Americans. One of the two was the Indian man who had served us so well for those magical moments once a year.

From our current perspective, after fortunes have been made in supplying concrete barriers that surround so many significant buildings, it is hard to believe that there was absolutely nothing around this building and that the bombers were not committing suicide. They had simply driven the truck into the parking lot, jumped in another truck, and were gone when the explosion occurred. The suspects were apprehended, or as the more cynically inclined would say, *someone* was apprehended, and quickly "confessed to their crimes," as is the custom. They were slated for execution, a process with none of the years-long legal nuances of the United States justice system.

There were six weekends remaining prior to my annual summer leave. The camping season was over, so I decided to try to witness the execution, a very public affair that occurs on "chop-chop" square, near the clock tower, on Fridays after the noon prayer. Traditionally, the date of an execution is not announced in advance. One just has to be there, and by and large, despite the reputation of the Saudi government for holding frequent executions, nothing happens. For the first two or three Fridays there were 30 to 50 other Westerners present, including five to ten women, all dutifully covered in their *abayas*. The men wore short haircuts. These were obviously the military friends of the five who were killed and of the injured. They had come to witness justice dramatically delivered.

The first three Fridays, nothing happened. I had my routine of driving to "chop-chop square" and could be down and back in an hour—the most time I wanted to spend trying to be a witness.

On the fourth Friday I had again finished my morning tennis game with the "boys," was enjoying the weekly brunch, and mentioned my mission. The wife of a hospital physician was a secretary for the commanding general of the US training mission, and she told me that the general said I couldn't go. I asked her to clarify the statement:

"You mean, US military personnel can't go?"

"No, no one can."

"Well, it just doesn't quite work that way, with all due respect to the general—I've been 'retired' for over 25 years."

And that was how I was the only Westerner at the square that Friday morning. It was eerie, a sea of Third World nationals and I. Fortunately, I stand a head taller than they and could see, but I was leery of a stampede or even of the friends of those to be executed showing up to make a "statement." My position and my exit routes had been carefully considered. Again, nothing, and the same happened on the fifth Friday.

On the sixth Friday less than a week remained until our vacation, and we would again shake the dust and heat and start our six-week summer vacation in France. An American friend called me; as a retired 20-year Navy man he was a member of the U.S. Mission, a place where drinks were never available, but where one could enjoy a wonderful brunch, including real bacon. My pork deprivation meter was high, and when he and his wife suggested we join them for BLTs as their guests, and to discuss the summer's plans, watching an execution suddenly was not a priority. The brunch was excellent.

Back home, around 1:00 p.m., he called, said he was sorry, and hoped I had enjoyed the BLTs. The executions had just occurred.

***

From my perspective a decade later, I can appreciate the irony that in 1996 I felt it was finally safe enough to take my family from Saudi Arabia to Vietnam. I again hired the Russian jeep and driver who had so faithfully driven me to Dien Bien Phu the previous year. It was to be his first trip to the south, and though we would see the sights along the way, the focus was on what was once called northern II Corps, with a particular emphasis on the rural areas. We spent Christmas Day in the ultimate no-name hotel in An Khe. The town had once been considered "strategic," but now it did not even rate a mention in the *Lonely Planet Guide to Vietnam*. The food situation was also grim, and we ate four of the twelve freeze-dried meals that we had brought as a contingency for such occasions. The guest house, as it was called, was so bad that the kids openly revolted when we showed them the showers in the common bathing area.

The next day we found a particular hill that was located eleven kilometers to the west of An Khe. At one time it had been called LZ Schueller, named after one of the first American soldiers killed in the area, as was the custom. It had been my home for four months in the summer of '69. My family and I were walking over the hill, which seemed to have only those low-slung-bellied Vietnamese pigs rooting in the dirt, when a Vietnamese man, followed by two soldiers, slowly approached us, making no eye contact. His Vietnamese was incomprehensible, but the message was clear: our presence on this particular hill was not desired. Of course, this man knew why I was there, and I wish I could have learned about his relationship with that particular piece of land. We returned to the jeep, and like in Yabrin, our driver confirmed that "we had to have special government permission" to be there. The persistence of memory. It was, however, the only time during the three trips that I was negatively impacted by that memory.

We continued to other obscure landmarks. The beginning of *We Were Soldiers*, a Hollywood movie about the battle in the Ia Drang valley in 1965, commenced with the ambush of the French Groupe Mobile 100 precisely in this area. One of the French tanks lay on the side of the road during the entire period I was there, a ghost haunting those Americans who were not certain that we were any better than the French.

When the jeep reached the top of the Mang Yang pass, I asked the driver to stop. I wanted to climb the surrounding hills, since I understood that there was a French graveyard on top, containing the 2,000 dead of Groupe Mobile 100—the ultimate in futile deaths, since this ambush occurred after the fall of Dien Bien Phu, when the world thought the First Indochina War was over. One bit of a foreign land that would be forever French. The kids and I struggled up the hill with a self-appointed guide in tow. The elephant grass was high and sharp. The hill grew steeper, but I encouraged the kids along in classic adult fashion—"We're almost there, I think I can see the top." My daughter finally looked around at me and said: "Dad, I think you are just a bit crazy." On the plane back to Saudi Arabia, I was reading Tim O'Brien's *The Things They Carried*, which I had picked up in Bangkok, and smiled when I read that his daughter had said almost the same thing when she realized his strange attachment to this seemingly inconsequential piece of foreign real estate.

18

A Journey to Hail and the School Board

The Arabs do not speak of desert and wilderness as we do. Why should they? To them it is neither desert nor wilderness, but a land of which they know every feature, a mother country whose smallest product has a use sufficient for their needs. They know, or at least they knew in the days when their thoughts shaped themselves in deathless verse, how to rejoice in the great spaces and how to honour the rush of the storm. In many a couplet they extolled the beauty of the watered spots; . . . Imr ul Kais had seen the Pleiades caught like jewels in the net of a girdle, and with the wolf that howled in the dark he had claimed fellowship: "Thou and I are of one kindred, and lo, the furrow that thou ploughest and that I plough shall yield one harvest."

—Gertrude Bell,
The Desert and the Sown

It was a glorious late March day in the mid-90's. Clear cobalt blue sky. My family, along with two other families, was taking a three-day trip to Hail. One of the families I knew well as solid and reliable camping partners, which brings peace of mind. The other couple was an unknown variable but seemed willing to fit in. It was absolutely the best time for such a trip—the wildflowers would be blooming, and the temperature would still be cool in the Aja Mountains, just to the west of the town. We had previously found an idyllic campsite near a broad plateau, far up into one *wadi*, which provided good shade trees and was within hiking distance of the mountaintops.

Some of the trees in the *wadi* were so large that the extended arms of two people could not meet around the trunks. It had rained heavily the previous winter, and my son, gazing out at the passing countryside as we drove along the six-lane expressway to Qassim, exclaimed, "It is so green now!" And it was, in that relative Saudi way that was his own reference frame, but if he had ever seen western Pennsylvania—I felt that Allah was in his heaven, and all was right with the world.

Suddenly I was aware of a car driving alongside us, exactly even with my front bumper. I was in the middle of the three lanes; the other driver was in the far left. We were both driving at 120 kph (70 mph). I figured it was Saudi kids wanting to play with the foreigners, and I knew the solution—ignore them, and in a couple of minutes they'll lose interest. Five minutes later, he was still bumper to bumper with me. My wife finally decided to glance over. "I think we have a problem," she said. I looked over, and that damn wild beard said it all. He was motioning, a clear "cover your face." This, really, was three standard deviations outside acceptable behavior. I was absolutely dumbfounded. Mary had a far better sense of humor about it all and suggested that I get out the *ghutra* I carried with me and cover my own face, and then let's see what he does.

Events, now out of control, escalated further. The husband of the couple that I knew well was German. I knew he had a temper and a much lower threshold for dealing with this foolishness than I. He pulled around me to the right and took the lead. The fanatic accelerated and when immediately adjacent to his vehicle, offered him the same gratuitous advice on improving his wife's appearance. I knew that Richard was ready and fully capable of giving this hirsute character the pounding he so richly deserved. This whole business was going to end very badly. Now the third couple passed on the right and was in the lead. The fanatic pulled next to them and rendered the same beauty advice for the wife. The man was Irish, and I was doing some national stereotyping by speculating on his ability to control his temper. Then the Irishman did something absolutely brilliant—he signaled an exit, ensured that the fanatic was too far committed in the forward direction, and quickly peeled off, taking the expressway exit. Our German friend and I quickly followed. The sky might have been cobalt blue, but a major black cloud had descended upon our little group. We were out of the cars, comparing notes. The others were more optimistic than I, figuring this was the end of that drama. I remembered the look in the fanatic's eyes; our destination was further north, toward infamous Buraydah, where this character probably lived. I also knew there was a major police checkpoint before the town. He would be waiting for us.

We decided to continue north, hoping that if the fanatic was at the checkpoint, our major assets—the four children—could overcome our major liability, the beer in our coolers that we have always considered the essential complement to the desert campfire. We didn't have to wait for the Buraydah checkpoint. Ten minutes later we crested a hill, and there he sat with the highway patrol. When they saw us, the police turned on their lights indicating that we should stop. His mission accomplished, and no doubt not wanting to contaminate himself by directly confronting us, the coward sped away. I stopped, breathed deeply, grabbed the hospital-issued permission letter for our three-day trip, and told the kids, ages ten and eleven: "Okay, it's time to do your stuff." I got out of the jeep and quickly assessed the cops—one was neutral, the other openly hostile. Like "obedient wives," the women stayed in the cars, while the three men and the four children went to meet the cops. "*as salaam Alaykoum.*" The kids pulled it off perfectly, and I could already tell it was over before it started. I handed the permission papers to the patrolmen and told them of our three-day vacation among the wildflowers in the Aja Mountains. Wonderfully, one of the cops was actually from Hail and was amazed that I knew the area that well. They were now quite friendly, apologetic, and even embarrassed by the incident. Only Allah knows what the fanatic had told them—that we were going down the highway with women who were topless? And in a fashion, I suppose they were. Richard hammed it up even more than I, and I wondered if he was going to offer the cops a beer! They were smiling, wishing us a bon voyage, or certainly its equivalent in Arabic, and seeing the wistful look in their eyes; you just knew they wanted to join us.

"Oh, one more thing, please take the Buraydah bypass," they cautioned us.

"Don't worry, we will."

An hour or so later we approached the significant checkpoint before Buraydah, and we observed the cops thoroughly searching the vehicle of two Saudis with shaggy beards. The cops didn't even check our papers—they just waved us through. Just some *khawajas* with beer in their coolers. *Mafi mushkila.* No problem.

A large array of grain elevators just to the north of Buraydah served as a suitable punctuation mark—that one was about to enter a different country. The expressway ends, and one begins traveling on a two-lane road through an absolutely pancake flat countryside. Wheat grows on either side of the road, as far as the eye can see. At this time of year, after the winter growing season, huge International Harvester combines cut and collect the wheat before the serious heat sets in. Somehow, maybe I did get back to Kansas.

The "sown" finally dissipated, and the desert reasserted itself. Three hours after taking the Buraydah bypass we were swinging left around Hail. Gertrude Bell reached the town at almost exactly the same time of year, 82 springs before. The winter rains had been bountiful that year also. Of the various eccentrics who traveled the peninsula in the days of yore—Dougherty, Philby, Lawrence, Thesiger—Bell's writings are the most expressive in their admiration for the desert environment and its inhabitants. She had crossed from the north the vast sea of sand known as the Nafud. The knowledge that she gained of the great tribes of the northern peninsula, in particular the Shammar, led to an appointment in the British Foreign Office, and she was most instrumental in the creation of the modern state of Iraq, even unofficially dubbed its "Queen." She saw the wildflowers, the ones that smell of amber, but did not linger in the Aja Mountains, our destination.

Again we found the entrance to the *wadi* leading to our destination, about 10 kilometers west of town. We drove almost as far as a jeep can go before finding the small *wadi* coming in from the side, with enough space for three tents and our vehicles. The next day was the sweet spot of the trip. No driving, only hiking and climbing. On the very top of the mountain there were meadows, and horses were brought up there to graze. Climbing another hill that led to the top rim, John scrambled past a bush, frightening a large hawk into flight. We counted 30 different varieties of wildflowers, generously scattered around the area, but at times appealingly clustered to display their color. The campfire and sweaters were fully needed that evening, as the temperature approached 10°C, and the Pleiades were in full view.

Bewitched by the dazzling stars, I decided to undertake a project I would later regret. I decided to enter the political arena. No, certainly nothing as dramatic as Gertrude Bell, such as forming a new nation. And it certainly had nothing to do with trying to "reform" some aspect of the Saudi political system. No, my project was far more modest—I decided to run for the school board. And proving the infinite wisdom of that Chinese adage, I got what I wished for, and regret it I did.

The American School in Riyadh had almost 2,000 students at the time, composed of 50 different nationalities. The school was losing 300 of those students, the result of the attack on the US barracks in Dhahran and the decision of the US military to withdraw all dependents of US military personnel from the Kingdom. Overall, the school was an exciting, vibrant place for any child to be educated. Still, there were areas that I perceived as deficient: a weakness in foreign language education; poor integration of information technology into the curriculum; and isolation of the school from the community, with only the barest minimum of Arabic studies. Lured by that old siren song of "You can make a difference," I ran in the school board election, won a seat, and found it was my own education that would be most enhanced.

As with many large bureaucratic organizations, there seemed to be a great gulf between its performance and its potential. The school administration and board had a reasonably good operational relationship. There was a strong emphasis that the board's votes on issues should be unanimous. About 90 percent of the time I voted with the other six board members. It was the other 10 percent of the time that I found myself in "trouble." As part of my education, I developed the opinion that our hospital's Saudi administration was actually much more open and willing to adopt new ideas than the school was. So, yes, contrary to that generally held American perception, it was the Saudis who were much more open to change than the Americans.

As part of my not-so-sentimental education, I actually endured a day longer than the eight-hour block of instruction on bed making that the US Army had imposed on me. It was called a strategic retreat that utilized a beautiful weekend day in October, a day perfect for camping. The board members, along with administrators, teachers, and selected parents, gathered for what was billed as a review of the school's operation. We had a facilitator who said all the right things—every effort was made to convey an environment receptive to new ideas, a day begun with high hopes. But somehow a discussion of any actual weakness in the school's operation was always shunted aside.

Real progress would be made by examining the school's mission statement. There does seem to be a special group of people who can be enthralled by an organization's mission statement. The school had a proper mission statement, saying all the right, unsurprising things. But in the best scholastic traditions of discussing angels on a pinhead begun in the Middle Ages, soon 25 individuals were fervently dissecting it. Two main factions formed: those who thought the word *student* was implicitly understood in the statement, and those who wanted to explicitly include it. At the end of that very long day, the sole "achievement" was the addition of the word *student* to the mission statement.

This tedium could at least be considered comparable with some of my numbing committee meeting work at the hospital. But there would be worse.

Although our hospital was the largest single contributor of children to the student body, it had been a number of years since a board member who worked at the hospital had been elected. The delicate question of obtaining medical care at the hospital was bound to surface. The hospital's purpose was to serve Saudi nationals— fulfilling King Faisal's intention that his citizens would not have to travel abroad to obtain quality medical care. There was tremendous demand for the hospital services from Saudi nationals. Nonetheless, the hospital's policy was to treat foreigners if it involved a matter of life or death, or loss of limb or eye. It was a very large gray area.

I received three phone calls during the period I sat on the board, of varying degrees of urgency, at all times of the day or night, from school administrative personnel who were seeking those acclaimed medical services.

The first involved a newborn at another hospital who had inhaled meconium, which had not being treated correctly there. Could the baby be treated at our hospital? Our own neonatal ICU was full, but the hospital's medical director said yes, we'd work out accommodation. The baby really was at death's door, but made a full recovery over the next 30 days. Additional follow-up care was requested and granted. A second case involved a teacher experiencing decompression problems after scuba diving. Again, arrangements were made, the Saudi patient scheduled for the compression chamber was rescheduled, and the teacher was treated. The third case involved one of the school's principals and his recovery from a neurological problem. This case was dealt with under the table, on a weekend day, and involved three physician friends of mine who agreed to conduct tests on the patient. The results were quite positive for the patient, indicating much recovery potential, thereby sharply reducing the pressure from certain board members to "get rid of him."

Three cases, each in a sort of twilight zone. Treatment could have been given or refused. Valid arguments could buttress either course of action. Certain Saudi nationals working at the hospital naturally expressed resentment over the preferential treatment that these members of "our tribe" received. I thought one of the best ways to attenuate this resentment was for the board to formally thank the Saudi leadership of the hospital. I introduced a resolution to this effect. And I was astonished by the response! The board actually voted *against* a resolution that simply said, "Thank you." In the discussion, one of the most stunning comments made by one board member was: "All those doctors took the Hippocratic oath, and it is their *obligation* to treat us." (I wonder how successful he would be in receiving medical treatment in the United States using this argument.)

The teacher whose baby's life the hospital saved was in the room but did not speak up for the resolution either. I later learned that he and his wife were quite religious, had prayed over the matter, and in their eyes the people who helped in the baby's treatment were just pawns in God's plan. Only God had to be thanked. I later relayed this to a Danish physician friend, the one who had orchestrated the treatment for the principal; he could only shake his head in disgust. It was a very sad and tangible demonstration of one of the worst American traits—the attitude that "the rest of the world owes us something simply because we are Americans." In sharp contrast, every Saudi that I had ever helped in obtaining medical services at the hospital thanked me profusely for something that was actually my job—to facilitate medical treatment for Saudi nationals.

19

The Guides

There are very few tourist guide books to Saudi Arabia. The exceptions are mainly camping guides that were developed by expats living in the Kingdom, and a few slick guides for international businessmen visiting the three major cities. The reason is simple. Despite numerous promises made over the years by the Saudi government, tourist visas are generally not available.

The trip into the Aja mountains outside Hail each spring can be attributed to no one's prior knowledge but stems from that curiosity to see what is around the next corner. We laid out the large-scale Bartholomew map and used dead reckoning—essentially the position of the sun and a willingness to try to get from A to B, with various fall-back positions. Fog, night, and sandstorms can mess up the best dead reckoning. In the mid-90's our horizons were wonderfully expanded thanks to the availability of inexpensive GPS devices. Trips that previously had looked foolhardy could now be undertaken with assurance, and the swapping of GPS points was part of the Riyadh cocktail party chatter. Then there were the human guides, both Westerners and Saudis, those who had been there before. With the Saudi guides it was much more a leap into the unknown, a leap across that cultural barrier, as they tried to calibrate their tour to their perceptions of Western tastes.

In the mid-80's I had a Saudi physician boss. His life had been altered by one of those conflicts almost completely forgotten in the Western world. It was during the days of Gamal Abdul Nasser, the secular voice of pan-Arabism and defiance of the West. In the West he is best remembered for the Suez Canal "crisis" of 1956. But my boss's life had changed due to an event less well remembered in the West—Nasser's participation in the Yemen Civil War. Nasser's Egyptian troops intervened in the Yemen, on the side of the Republicans. Many of the same factors were at work as in the Spanish Civil War of the 1930's. The Saudis were supporting the other side, the Royalists. During the war the Saudi town of Najran was bombed by the Egyptian Air Force. My boss was originally an Egyptian, but somehow he was working for the Saudis as a physician, and his services were rewarded with the Saudi nationality at the conclusion of the war. Seventeen years later, the Emir of Najran still remembered my boss's services and extended an open invitation.

Omar fashioned himself as something of a "bon vivant." He had a large photo album, featuring mainly himself in various "watering spots" and restaurants in the West, looking debonair, with an assortment of women. Of course, things had to be more subdued now, but his album said that the spirit remained. He called me in to his office one day and launched his pitch:

"I understand you are a traveler of the desert, so how would you like to see Najran? I'm a friend of the Emir of Najran, and his desert retreat has been placed at our disposal. Why don't you get 10 to15 of your friends together; all of you would have to pay your own airfare there, but everything else will be gratis."

"What can we expect in terms of facilities and accommodations?" He was a bit embarrassed in not actually knowing. "Will there be a swimming pool?" I asked.

He again had to claim ignorance. "But the Emir IS a very prominent figure in the Royal family, and everyone should bring something nice to wear for dinner." Which is why a couple of the single women packed their pearls and high heels. I had one concern though—it was August. One never went to the desert in August. Omar assured me that Najran wasn't hot even in August because it is much higher than Riyadh. I checked the map. Riyadh is at 1,000 feet. Najran is at 3,000 feet. Didn't seem that much different to me, but still there was the lure of seeing one of the more remote corners of the Kingdom under "special circumstances." Najran, until even very recent times, contained small Christian and Jewish communities, and it was nestled within eyesight of the mountains of the Yemen. It was one of the main border crossing points and was a very different part of the Kingdom.

The Emir's bus met us at the airport. The desert retreat was, well, a desert retreat. Why would one expect a swimming pool or tennis courts? There were large canvas military-style tents and standard metal single beds. Carpets covered the floors, and each side table had its own tissue box. There were flush toilets and a couple of enclosures that served as showers. With the right expectations, all things considered, it was nice, *as a desert retreat*. But my expectations, as well as those of most of our party missed the mark on the most essential element—there was no air-conditioning, and it was as hot as anything a Riyadh summer could have offered. By 7:30 in the morning following the evening of our arrival, we knew we were in trouble. Omar had cited "family obligations" and slept with relatives in town the previous night, paid us a visit, cited more obligations (and I thought, yeah, like a need for air-conditioning!), and took his leave of us for the day. "But everything has been arranged with the Emir's guide," he assured.

The Queen of Sheba ranks up there with George Washington and Napoleon in the pantheon of the Tourism Commission's dreams. Far be it for me to say that she slept around, but it does seem that she slept (and lived!) in a lot of places, including many, many places in Ethiopia and the Yemen. With the mountains of the Yemen in the background, it was only natural that an archaeological site with large stones containing Amharic writing would lead a tour guide to say, "Scholars are not certain, but some believe that the Queen of Sheba...." Mainly I remember the heat.

As we traveled from one site to another, we stopped the Coaster bus in front of a store, went in, and bought two cases of bottled water, and within fifteen minutes, 12 liters—half the bottles—were gone. In the middle of the afternoon, we arrived in "Arab heaven," as exemplified by those various parks in Riyadh—a palm grove oasis. A refreshing lunch had been prepared, and hand-woven rugs held plates heaped with mounds of grapes, pomegranates, oranges, and other assorted fruits, all locally grown. Who had turned on the air-conditioning? It seemed to be at least 20 degrees cooler in the oasis.

In every aspect, the meal and the oasis were refreshing. Perhaps there was a fort or two that closed out the touring day, I don't remember. But we found ourselves back at the desert encampment as the sun disappeared, eating again, and the women didn't need their high heels. The army-style beds were fine for the night, especially if you pulled them outside, but our thoughts turned again to the following morning and how soon that monstrously hot disk would rise.

By 7:00 a.m. it was again too hot to do anything but hide in the shade. No more ruins, please! We convinced the guide that our greatest desire was to arrive at the airport in *plenty* of time for our flight. Three hours before flight time, during a period and in a place when 45 minutes would have been ample, we were savoring the terminal's air-conditioning, having survived our personal experience with what the Bedouin had endured for generations. Despite the heat, it was one of those wonderful experiences that serendipity could provide the willing in the Kingdom.

Soon after we returned to the hospital, Omar and I went our separate ways, one more reshuffle of the KFSH organizational deck. The hospital continued its growth, and I rarely saw him. One day I heard he was "vaporized," that is, his departure was quick and without explanation—or the traditional farewell party. The usual suspects were, well, suspected—women and booze—something the newer Saudi administration took a harder line about, at least for flagrant Saudi indulgence. It must have been over three years later when I saw Omar shopping one evening at Al-Akariya mall. He was his usual amiable self. We didn't linger over the circumstances of his departure, but I did inquire about his current duties. It seemed he was serving in another war and was on leave. He was a physician at one of the field hospitals with the *mujahadeen* in Afghanistan, fighting the Soviets. It was hard to imagine this beardless bon vivant working with the "holy warriors" every day, and the full implications of his duties only became apparent many years in the future.

Eleven years after the Najran trip, in 1995, one of the orthopedic surgeons put out the word to "the campers" that the Emir of Hafr Al-Batin was hosting a weekend if we wanted to join him. Hafr Al-Batin is in another tri-border area that surely is labeled "strategic" in more than one War College, just as Polei Klang once was. It is not all that far from the point where Iraq, Kuwait, and Saudi Arabia converge. No doubt its "strategic" value has led to substantial real estate development, mainly King Khalid Military City. To those who think that the desert is devoid of interest, Hafr Al-Batin would be their poster child. Flat, in its superlative form, and ditto that for dusty. But unlike the reserved Emir in Yabrin, here was an actual invitation, from someone with a Rotarian booster streak.

What should we expect? Vague descriptions of hospitality and a tour, similar to the descriptions we received so many years earlier about Najran. We only knew that we were going to another extreme—as Najran was in the far southwest, we were going to the far northeast, and some 1,200 kilometers separated them. The hospitality began in Riyadh. The Emir had sent one of his retainers—someone on his immediate personal staff, in a Toyota Land Cruiser, to lead us to Hafr. Not that it was very complicated—go an hour north to Majmaa, take a right, and another four hours later you would hopefully stop in Hafr Al-Batin; otherwise, you'd be in Iraq. When we stopped for more petrol, around halfway, the retainer paid for everyone's petrol with an insistence that we could not refuse.

Where would we be staying the night? (We had come fully prepared, as a contingency, with all our bedding). He didn't know the word in English. It would sort of be like staying in a hotel, but this hotel was not open for the general public. Ah, a "guest house." Indeed, it was, and it looked like we would be commissioning the guest house for the Emir. It was brand new, in simple good taste, perhaps 20 rooms in total. None of the motel-type rooms had a lock on the door, and they were arranged in a square, with a fountain in the middle. The whole structure was covered by a single roof.

The festivities began after breakfast the following morning. How would we like to go to a Bedouin encampment? Of course, we had been to numerous ones before and thus felt we knew what to expect. But this was the Disneyland version. Just on the outskirts of the town, the Emir had set up the encampment. There must have been fifty "Bedouin" dressed in full regalia, swords and all. It was all set up just for us. Anyone who wanted a camel ride was accommodated, a favorite with the kids, if not the adults who are normally too afraid of falling off. There were demonstrations of spinning wool into yarn that would be used to make their tents. The whole event culminated in a sword-drawn "charge" of the Bedouin. There was a similarity with the Civil War reenactments in the States, with older, overweight guys in costume playing out historical dramas. There were no casualties that day, and although one suspected it had been a couple of years since the men had ridden their camels, no one fell off—the balance of youth remained.

We leapt from the millennium-old ways of the Bedouin to the glories of consumer society in about six minutes. Our guides were taking us to the newly opened shopping mall in central Hafr Al-Batin. The mall was scaled to the proportions of Hafr, and the merchants presented us with a few token gifts. The noon prayer call signaled an end to the morning's festivities, and we were taken back to the Emir's for a sumptuous lunch.

The Emir asked us what we wanted to do next, and realizing we could not maintain this pace of eating without a little exercise, we proposed some. That's how we found ourselves in the large municipal stadium, playing soccer. It was the Western men against the Western women and three of the Emir's retainers who had suddenly shed their indolent image and with their wiry frames were soon running circles around us. By mutual agreement, we declared the final score a mercy killing and kept it in single digits.

Allah only knows how many other folks were stirred from their normal routines for the next event—a tour of the local high school. We dutifully noted artwork and science projects, and the whole event was filmed by the local TV station; since we were suddenly transformed into "visiting dignitaries," most of us were able to affect a correspondingly thoughtful expression.

We were driven to another nearby location on the edge of the desert for dinner. My son, nine years old at the time, noticed the two sheep that were tied up. He was petting their heads, telling them everything was going to be okay. "Well, I don't think so, my son," I thought, and contemplated the number of professions that could use his consoling expertise. Later in the evening, he did not indicate that he was cognizant of the relationship between his dinner and the missing sheep. The entertainment that evening was provided by yet another of the Emir's retainers who had a remarkable ability to use a simple *ghutra* and facial expressions to perform characterizations of Gaddafi, Khomeini, Arafat, and an assortment of other leaders throughout the Middle East.

The next morning was the first day of Ramadan. An enormous, delicious Arabic breakfast had been prepared for us, ensuring we would be content on our journey back to Riyadh. The Emir sat with us but did not partake himself, exemplifying the better strain of observing one's moral beliefs without imposing them on others. The Emir tried to send the retainer with us in his Toyota Land Cruiser to ensure we made it safely back to Riyadh, but on the outskirts of town we stopped and insisted that he remain in Hafr Al-Batin and not undertake what would have been a 10-12-hour round-trip journey.

***

Khalid, our friend from various European and Saudi adventures, as well as having worked at KFSH at one time, came through with his own trip proposal. One of his good friends was the colonel at the army base at Wadi Dewasir. "How would you like a trip into the Empty Quarter? Colonel Abdullah will lead the trip, and all will be taken care of. Although the trip won't really be dangerous, you know, going into the Empty Quarter, one never knows, so of course we'll be armed, and it is best not to bring the wives."

Hum! With an invitation like that, none of the "usual suspects" could say no. I wanted to caution them all about one issue: "Most of the Saudis think we do this for only one reason—the old canard about us being in the CIA—so please, no jokes about those Chinese missiles that are down there. I'm sure the good colonel will do his job and make sure that we don't inadvertently stumble upon the base."

In the mid-80's the Saudis had purchased long-range CSS-2 "East Wind" missiles and brought them into the country through the port at Dhahran. In yet another embarrassment to the American intelligence efforts, it was a full year later before the Americans became aware of their existence. Many years thereafter, when I had permanently returned to the United States, I was discussing this trip with an American woman who had been in the Kingdom for over a decade. I mentioned the Chinese missiles near Wadi Dewasir. She replied that the Saudis never had Chinese missiles and rather haughtily added: "My husband worked in the intelligence area, and if they had any, he would have known about it." I suggested that she merely "Google" "Chinese missiles in Saudi Arabia" and watch the pages of information tumble out.

We arrived and slept in a villa that night, with the promise of a 6:00 a.m. wake-up call. By 6:30 we had had a light breakfast and met Colonel Abdullah as he was checking the final preparations for the trip, including the pickup truck that would accompany us. One last fill-up at the petrol station, and we were off. The first surprise was that we were not actually traveling south, the direction most of us considered to be the Empty Quarter. We were heading due north. We lowered the tire pressure by half, from 40 psi to 20 psi, which was essential to drive through the sand dunes just to the north of the town. (The lower pressure significantly increased the tire's surface area, greatly decreasing the number of times one would bog down in the sand.) The sand dune belt was narrow, ranging between five and ten kilometers. Once on the other side we re-inflated the tires to 30 psi with our portable compressors.

Once through the dunes, the area to the north was flat, without intervening gullies, and we flew along at over 100 kph. In the distance, to the far right, stood the Tuwaiq escarpment, which extended in a broad loop from just outside Riyadh, swinging slightly east, and then due south the several hundred kilometers to Wadi Dewasir. It was a good visual reference point as none of us had brought our GPS devices, again to lessen security concerns about us.

The colonel understood his tour group well, probably because he shared some of the same delights—the sheer expansiveness of the desert, its topography, its infinite variety, how it transformed itself every 5-10 kilometers, particularly in that area. The areas changed from the escarpment to sand dunes to table-flat areas where small bushes in the distance could appear as large water towers given the mirage-like quality of the light (and the mind). But the colonel understood what would really hook us. He led us into an area of large stone monoliths, massive rock outcrops, similar to the Ayers Rock in Australia or Stone Mountain outside Atlanta, Georgia. Of course, these other geological formations had been turned into a substantial tourist attraction. Here, not only were there no tourists in this area, it was unknown by the vast majority of Saudis. Even 100 kilometers away when I was talking to a Bedouin and I used the proper place name as used by the locals, he had no idea what I was talking about.

At least 50 significant rock outcrops covered the expanse, but the crown jewel has to be Abu Kaab (father of the heel). The origins of the name were lost in those sandstorms of time. Perhaps the entire rock looked like an enormous heel protruding from the earth. Perhaps the massive indentation on the southern side of the monolith looked like a heel imprint. Nonetheless, the rock itself, and it appeared as a single piece, was impressive, almost two kilometers long and a couple hundred meters high. Prominent headstones sat on the southeast corner, a majestic final resting place. Through a passageway between two large monoliths an enormous well had been dug, roughly eight meters across. We were told it was built by a prince who liked the Bedus in the area.

The sun was dropping lower in the sky and our thoughts turned to dinner. A member of our party was sent to purchase a sheep from a Bedouin. It was going to be another up-close look at what you eat without the intervention of supermarket cellophane. All the Westerners were city boys who hadn't even gone hunting in their lives. The sheep was tied to the truck by its feet, its throat slit in the *halal*/kosher style, and the blood drained away. A slit was made and a search for the liver ended successfully, though we all turned down, as politely as possible, the honor of eating a piece of the still very warm organ. The cook placed a large pot on the portable gas stove and brought some water to a boil. He tossed hunks of meat, potatoes, and salt into the pot and in another pot cooked rice. Pita bread had also been brought along for dinner, and though the dinner provided sustenance, it lacked flavor and certainly "presentation." As we were finishing the meal, the cook kept carving on the sheep, and threw all sorts of assorted innards, far more than French "sweetbreads," including what appeared to be pieces of the intestines, into the still boiling pot. We were glad we had already had our portions and didn't return for seconds. We spent the evening around the campfire and were entertained with tales of old, as well as leg wrestling contests.

The next morning we awoke in that calm desert air. Time for breakfast, and guess what was on the menu? More of dinner! We cast glances at each other. None of us needed to communicate the solution to a healthy breakfast; we were all on the same wavelength. We'd use the bread to select pieces of potato out of the stew that had been placed on the bed of rice. Khalid came around, good-naturedly put his hand on my shoulder, looked at the others, and said: "Aren't you all going a little light on the meat this morning?" The point was well made. Chez Jacky and the moving crustaceans were six years in the past but still remembered, and the food score was evened out. I think he even promised me a very well-cooked meal the next time!

We knew that we were 100 or so kilometers north of Wadi Dewasir. It would make sense for the return to Riyadh to drive east, find a gap in the Tuwaiq escarpment, and hit the asphalt of the Riyadh–Wadi Dewasir road, saving perhaps 250 kilometers and the crossing of the dunes again. I pushed the idea as far as I thought was prudent. By the expression of the colonel and other members of his party, I think they thought I was talking about driving off the edge of the world. Starkly, this was terra incognita. Geoffrey Moorhouse tried to cross the Sahara from west to east and wrote about it in *The Fearful Void*. He raised the issue of whether the Bedouin had real navigational skills or whether they simply knew where they were because they had been there before. In this case, it seemed that the issue was that the area to the east was beyond their territory and thus something about which they had no knowledge. The map may read "Saudi Arabia" but this was another strong example that the country was carved into tribal fiefdoms and a Saudi would rarely travel in another's domain.

***

Some of the guides were not Saudis, they were expats who had poked around the country a bit and developed a deep attachment to it. Stanley was a banker by profession, but his uniform was off on the weekends, and he too enjoyed the wind, sand, and stars. In particular, he had also developed an attachment to the *Rub Al-Khali*. He had visited Yabrin, but his real attachments were to an area several hundred kilometers to the west. There he opened our eyes to what had always been there but we had not seen.

Halfway down the Riyadh–Wadi Dewasir road we pulled off and headed due south into "Stanley's territory," his own slice of the *Rub Al-Khali*. He shared with us the "petrified forest," the most tangible evidence that climatic conditions had been different, way back when. Maybe 100 kilometers along this route the sand grew softer, and we lowered the air pressure in the tires. The traveling became more difficult, dunes had to be crossed. At one of our stops, like a Pied Piper, he gathered the kids around him, and we adults also listened. This is what to look for. And he showed us what must have been a lake bed with a pre-historic village that had been on its shore, back in the time this had all been savannah and the lions roamed, maybe 50,000 years ago in the Stone Age. Just look down. And finally we saw. There were stone axes among the rocks, and arrowheads too, along the edge of the lake of old. "Notice how the edges of this rock have been evenly flaked at the end, this one has been worked better than that—this one was broken, and abandoned during its creation," Stanley taught. We learned.

And seeing this evidence I thought, with man's nudge, which might be occurring right now, telescoping climatic change, would it be possible for the monsoons that water India each year to be bumped further north and the *Rub Al-Khali* to become a place of human habitation again?

Stanley also proposed a six-day trip into another portion of the *Rub Al-Khali*, an area that he had never explored. It was east of the road that connected Wadi Dewasir to Najran. It was now the age of the Internet, and he downloaded a few aerial maps. The ridges of parallel sand dunes, some five to eight kilometers apart, were vividly apparent from space. The difficulty of the venture was its appeal, because it meant very few people had traveled in the area before and a much more pristine prehistoric village site might be discovered.

We were easily reeled in. And times had so changed since that first search for Taithlith. It was now possible to ship a fully loaded SUV to Najran for about $100, avoid the 12-hour-drive, and fly. One of the wonderful things about the Kingdom was that one-way air tickets really were half the price of a round-trip ticket, as logic demands. We flew, slept in the Holiday Inn, and awoke to find our vehicles in the parking lot as we had instructed. We were off the next morning, and only later would we read that once again we had just missed a manifestation of the "gathering storm." A week later Saudi tanks were in that same parking lot, as there was a disturbance between the Ismailis, a particular Islamic religious sect dominant in the area, and the more orthodox Wahabi Imams allied to the House of Saud. More dead in the name of religion.

We drove straight north, to an area where Stanley had previously explored, and he took pleasure in showing us even more graphic evidence of a different climatic period. There were enormous ostriches carved into the stone cliffs, along with gazelles and lions. But it was the beauty of the ostriches and how that prehistoric artist had depicted the sense of motion that captivated us. We were equally fascinated by the number of bullet holes around the heads of these rock carvings—fanatics wishing to obliterate representations of living forms that is part and parcel of the fundamentalist beliefs. Afterward we crossed the Wadi Dewasir–Najran road into the "true" Empty Quarter and the unknown land beyond.

The dunes were towering, and I was never into "dune-bashing" for the hell of it. But this seemed to have a purpose, and it was certainly a thrill to explore an area that had almost never been traveled. We estimated a very modest 50 kilometers a day for three days to penetrate the area of the highest dunes. We quickly learned new driving techniques, such as gaining enough speed to just crest the top of the dune, always taking it precisely perpendicular to the edge, so that one did not twist and roll sideways down the 35-degree slope on the other side. There was much digging of vehicles, particularly mine (which was one of the heaviest), out of the sand at the top of the dunes.

The Dark Earth Society would have been happy too—night after night with no artificial light visible, other than what we carried, which we extinguished after dinner. The Finnish ambassador was with us, and he supplied the refreshments that helped us wax even more eloquently about that star-studded hemisphere above us.

It was a tremendous effort, and we found no hint of that pristine prehistoric village. Nonetheless, we were amply rewarded. The Saudi authorities were reintroducing wildlife that had become extinct in the Kingdom. With the cooperation of the San Diego Zoo, there were now gazelle and even more beautiful, oryx, the "unicorn" of legend. The latter magically appeared before us when we crested one dune. To see that oryx stand there, and then suddenly vanish, was worth the whole trip.

20

Working with the Saudis

At the beginning of the hospital's history, in 1975–76, only a few Saudis worked in administrative capacities. One of the Saudi men had spent ten years in college in Orange County, California, and was, even until the final days, the most Americanized Saudi I ever knew— well, more accurately, half of him was. He knew American history and society well. In the early days of the hospital's operation, Talib shared a villa with a Western department head and co-habitated with a Western woman. He shot pool with the Westerners at the hospital's Amenities Center. He never wore the *thobe* and *ghutra*. In a reversal of the common suspicion that Americans were really in the CIA, many Westerners figured Talib really worked for the Ministry of the Interior, which sanctioned his lifestyle so he could report on our actions.

When the second Saudi administration took over the hospital in 1984, Talib was summoned to the executive director's office. One didn't have to be in the room to know what was asked: "Are you a Saudi or aren't you? Then why aren't you wearing the *thobe* and *ghutra*?" The next day Talib was in the regalia; his face conveyed a sense of embarrassment. It was a watershed for him. Like those who are bilingual, numerous individuals can move smoothly from one culture to another, making the appropriate adjustments. In that cultural divide between the Islamic and Western worlds, the balance is more difficult. Talib eventually lost his ability to straddle the cultures.

The very first Saudi women who worked outside the home were employed at the hospital. They were the pathfinders. Many of them had attended the American University in Beirut, had obviously enjoyed the more liberal social conditions there, and must have believed that would be the future in the Kingdom. One Saudi couple, children of prominent families, started working at the Hospital in 1976. The wife became the unofficial "sorority mother" for the Saudi women. It wasn't "Villager" dresses that became obligatory but the black headscarves. This would be their distinctive mark, one that would differentiate them from non-Saudi Arab women. More or less they were worn, though sometimes only around the neck like a scarf, as one might wear on Les Champs-Elysées.

***

In the early 80's, when I was the manager at the Medical Care Facility, a 150-bed unit that was part intermediate care and part hotel, nine Saudis worked at the front desk. The common prejudice was that Saudis don't work, just like the poor are poor because they are lazy. There are enough supporting examples to promote the prejudice, but it does remain just that. In this case, eight of the nine were excellent employees, doing what was required effectively and efficiently. Murdi was an older, wise man who could be counted on to solve any delicate social problem. Another had a bit more of an edge to him. He once challenged me about that favorite bugaboo: the CIA. "America is responsible for all the world's ills." He knew history, or at least one of the many versions out there. I agreed with about half his contentions, mostly concerning the number of countries in which the CIA had overthrown the legitimate government—Iran, Chile, Guatemala. The other half, including the CIA's complicity in the assassination of King Faisal and its instigation of the Iran-Iraq war, I disagreed with. "Believe me; we are less omniscient than you think." After the latest intelligence fiasco in Iraq, I would rest my case with him. Of course, times do change, and at least some people mellow. He now has three children who are American citizens.

But what of the ninth Saudi? He fit that stereotype—rarely came to work and when he did, he didn't. I knew at the time that despite the organization chart, I was not actually the boss. Fortunately, I had a Saudi boss, Abdullah, who backed me up in such "trans-cultural difficulties." The other eight Saudis started pushing me to do something about Yousef. The minimum course of action was to call him to my office, counsel him on his absenteeism, and insist that at the very least, if he couldn't make it to work, he had to call and state a reason. He went absolutely ballistic. Abdullah told him signing the counseling form was non-optional. Yousef signed the form, but then began the serious conflict. He hijacked his supervisor's office, a Muslim Palestinian-American, and began praying at nonstandard times, such as 10:30 in the morning, daring us to interfere. We left him alone, and he more or less came to work according to his assigned schedule.

In 1984 when the new Saudi administration took over, Yousef raced directly to the top, charging me with insulting Islam. In essence, I was the infidel, he the good Muslim, and I should be fired. Wisely, the administration interviewed the other eight Saudis (although not me), and I was eventually exonerated, and Yousef was transferred to another area. Upon my return to the hospital in 1993, I saw Yousef again, now wearing the uniform of the scraggly beard. He had some books on Islam if I was interested. I assured him I was. Like patriotism, religion may be the last refuge of the scoundrel. During the period prior to the lead up to the second Iraq war, the hospital's administration supported the Westerners when various Saudis alleged that the Westerner "defamed Islam."

***

In 1995 I was called into the office of a senior Saudi administrator. "We've been handed a new assignment—we have to open a clinic on the grounds of Crown Prince Abdullah's palace." The word *conceptual* is the most operative on this type of assignment because the specifications are fluid to nonexistent. Adding to the difficulty of satisfying the desires of the ultimate recipient is the fact that one receives those desires second—or third hand.

During a three-month period, I visited the clinic almost daily, which provided the opportunity to bask in the perfume and beauty of the enormous banks of petunias which permeated the palace grounds. The security at the palace was never too onerous, though the personnel and routines changed frequently, as is appropriate in such matters. The design of the clinic met well the routine medical needs of the family and the "inner court" of the Crown Prince.

My main role was coordinating the relevant hospital services with the clinic's requirements, including staffing. I met with a palace engineer concerning the acceptance procedures from the contractor. He emphasized that he was only in the number two position, and he preferred that status since four number ones had already come and gone. "When you get too close to the power, they get tired of you quickly, and you're gone." His comment resonated with me, often having been in that number two position myself. Still, I knew that I'd be the "fall guy" if this assignment did not pan out from the hospital's perspective.

The hospital administrator told me one day that we had to find a Saudi female interpreter to work at the palace. Particularly at this time, there were not that many individuals who met the requirements, so I researched some of the hospital's new hires, found and talked to one, who said that she would be willing to work at the palace. I carried her file to the Administrator's office. Mohammed briefly looked at it, shoved it back at me, and said: "She is not a Saudi." I gently remonstrated, "But Mohammed, it definitely says that her nationality is Saudi," and added, in my eyes, the clincher: "Place of birth: Makkah." He shoved her file a little more forcefully in my direction, with a: "She is not a Saudi." I knew the real answer, so there was no rolling of the eyes on my part, no wise-cracks like: "Guess her ancestors have only been here 600 years." The real answer was that she was from the wrong tribe for this assignment— and the concept of the "right" tribe was often a movable feast. So, I unearthed another translator.

***

Those five, six, seven, and eight-year scholarships to the United States and Canada eventually run their course, and each year brought a new crop of returnees to the hospital. I was assigned one returnee to orient and introduce to the Byzantine complexities of the hospital's bureaucracy and power structure, now that he was a full physician. He had all the top career stops dutifully punched on his "card": Harvard, Yale, and the Mayo Clinic. Abdul Hadi had the American lingo down, knew that the Saudis had to reach "Joe Six-Pack" in the propaganda wars, and filled his office with Minnesota Vikings memorabilia. His plans were to greatly expand the services of one of the medical departments. I was in the rather ironic position of explaining certain aspects of his country to him, both inside the hospital and out. But there were many things within the Kingdom that he could explain to me, for he definitely had the Saudi side of his career card punched as well: He had married one of the nieces of King Fahd.

Each Saudi administrator, including the hospital director, was quite concerned about this doctor and his curriculum vitae. Even terrified. And terrified colleagues are not collegial. We took excursions to the desert a few times; I showed him some of my favorite places. One time he invited some of his recently recruited friends from the Mayo Clinic. He was acquiring, or reacquiring, a deep attachment for his country, and he was the first person to describe to me the olive groves in the Al-Jawf basin. He claimed that it was there that the olive tree was first cultivated.

I felt I knew him well enough after a few months that I could offer some gratuitous advice. The hospital was filled with employees of St. Exupery's hardened clay. Their job description included blocking anything anyone else was doing. I put my arm on his shoulder and told him at the very most, he had "five bullets." "There *are* some extremely malicious, incompetent people working here. At best, though, you can eliminate only five. The rest must be tolerated, even 'won over' through much 'tea drinking,' that laborious social process that says 'you are important.' Part of the job description here is to suffer fools gladly." But I could tell it wasn't what he wanted to hear.

Then one day he was gone, not down, nor out, but up. Very up. King Fahd had a stroke at his farm in 1995. Several Western doctors from the hospital were there. It was the consensus among the medical staff, for those who would speak of it, sotto voce, that the King received poor medical care. At some level, it was an unremarkable observation because the medical care was rendered via committee, with so many egos bouncing around for a measure of advantage. A test result might be "too confidential" for everyone to know. Foreign experts were flown in, usually two or three teams. Inevitably there were conflicts among them, and then vis-à-vis the locals, who had their own divisions, and also between the foreigners and the Saudis—not to mention the tribal matters that caused yet more divisions.

Consequently Abdul Hadi was called upon to "manage" all this. He was transported to the very heart of power, and we never saw him again.

A physician tennis buddy had made routine calls at the palace. I asked him if he had seen my friend. He joked: "Oh, yes, but I had to go through the King to get permission." He was indeed at the very center of things. I remember thinking when I was in school, why would anyone really need to study ancient stuff like Greek mythology? Though technical aspects of stagecraft might have changed over the intervening centuries, the story remains the same. Like Icarus, Abdul Hadi flew too close to the sun, something the number two Saudi engineer at Crown Prince Abdullah's palace could have warned him about.

One didn't need to be an observer to know what happened. Abdul Hadi's intolerance of all that "hardened clay" and lack of care around the compost-heap of palace intrigues had melted the wax in his wings. One day when he was walking down the corridor to see the King, as was his daily routine, the stiff arm of security barred his way: "Sir, you no longer have access."

21

The Rise of the "Taliban"

In a period of six years, starting from 1995, there were five different medical administrations at King Faisal Specialist Hospital. Somehow, despite very long odds, I was the only person of any nationality to have worked in the last four of them. Few organizations have had such diversity in leadership within a comparable period. From an American medical perspective, it was doubly hard to imagine. It was never about making money, though we paid homage to the budget like one would to a talisman in a religious ceremony. A constant in the funhouse world of budgetary allocation was that we were always a month or two over budget by the end of the year, and our friends in the government always stepped forward with an annual "one-time emergency" appropriation. They must have studied how the US Congress works!

Fortuitously, no one on the staff evaluated the insurance coverage, and then tailored the medical treatment to conform to that coverage. In that aspect, working at KFSH was most liberating. But what replaced normal money-grubbing was not necessarily Dr. Marcus Welby-style dedication to the patients. All too often it involved puffed egos bouncing around the hospital like so many bumper cars, emulating the random Brownian motion of particles. Occasionally I detected a vague pattern to the activity, the odd alliance, but as soon as I was willing to commit to even a hypothesis about who was who and their motivation, sufficient countervailing facts presented themselves, and thus I had to drop back to the random Brownian motion explanation. Despite all this heat, all this purposeless activity, the hospital somehow expanded and enhanced its ability to treat patients.

In 1995 the first of these five medical administrations had been in place for over 10 years, and if there was a single impetus for change, it was simply the perennial organizational call for new blood, new leadership. One of the leaders of the "new blood" movement was selected, a Palestinian who had acquired the Saudi nationality. He was coupled with a Saudi from the heartland, near Dawadmi, a Richard Nixon type of vice president, the "hatchet man," but without even Nixon's limited political skills.

Strong Saudi opposition mounted against this administration. In an amazing volte-face for the Saudiazation program, an American was recruited to replace them. He was a man with substantial international experience, and proved to be a quick study of the nuances of conducting a medical administration, Saudi-style. Not much more than a boy, he was wounded in that "forgotten war" of the early '50's, at Inchon, in Korea. That early reminder of one's mortality was a contributing influence to his no-nonsense management style. When his time came, and a decision was required, he gave an unequivocal "Yes." His behind-the-desk action lacked the dramatics of a filmed EMT rescue, but was just as effective in saving the life of a baby whose parents were teachers at the American school. Improvements in hospital process and procedures which he initiated unquestionably contributed to numerous other patients retaining their "mortal coil," in ways that no analysis would ever be able to determine.

But he personified the irresistible force against the immovable object. To achieve Mayo Clinic status in the Middle East, he implemented a major organizational change. The fatigue of "future shock" dominated the Saudi thinking, not to mention a certain revulsion from taking directions from an infidel. He resigned after a year, to be replaced, more remarkably still, by another American.

This one was the previous American's antithesis—he would have had difficulty coping with the foreignness of London. He was an extreme technophobe and culturally maladroit. Somehow he lasted two years, a reign in which the hospital's Head of Public Relations was openly mocking him in his column in a Saudi newspaper. His imprint on the hospital's operation was disappointing to non-existent. In the wings the "Taliban," had been waiting and in a remarkable swing of the pendulum, they were the fifth administration in this six year period. It was the spring of 2001.

"Get them out of here, now"!

From their bearded appearance, the "Taliban" may have seemed to be in that long tradition of the *Ikhwan* (the brotherhood) that had opposed both the introduction of radio and TV into the Kingdom. But when the "Taliban" administration took over, they gave a reasonable, politically sensitive presentation at their first General Staff meeting—the usual reassuring rhetoric about the need for good workers, etc. It was crafted to convey assurances of continuity and to allay the fears of the numerous secular Saudis on the staff. But these "Taliban" wanted to differentiate themselves, in particular, from the previous technophobic American administration. For this, their first meeting with the staff, they handed out 100 electronic voting devices. Various multiple choice questions were projected on the auditorium's screen, soliciting the staff's concerns about the current status and the future direction of the Hospital. The last question concerned themselves, and how pleased the staff was with their appointment. It was a gutsy sort of thing to do, to ask the employees for an anonymous vote of confidence at the beginning, with the results being immediately displayed publicly, when they knew there had to be strong opposition, and even fear, to their ascendancy. There was a range of possible answers, with the answer receiving the most votes being, as was no doubt intended by the structure of the question: "I'm willing to give them a chance for 30 days." The last answer, "Get them out of here, now!" received five of the 100 votes. They had stressed the anonymous nature of the voting system, but joked that of course they would be able to tell by the fingerprints on the devices who the five people were. A hearty laugh all around, and the "Taliban" were off to a good start.

It was the beardless, more fun-loving, and 'not-in-the-club' Saudis who had quickly dubbed the new administration "the Taliban." Justifiably almost all the Saudi women were concerned. In varying ways, they expressed their displeasure, even going so far as to break "tribal protocol," to express their concern to me.

It was comforting to know that my family and I were leaving. Once again, the age of my children reflected the predominate factor in that decision—in June, 2003, Paris would graduate from high school, and the issue of both her and my son's college education would be the tipping point in deciding our departure from the Kingdom and our return to the States. Unlike the Saudis, whose career fortunes were on the line, I could be more dispassionate in my assessment of "the beards."

There were the normal aspects of a change of administration—the desire to "change the wallpaper in the lobby," which in this case meant that once again this new administration moved their offices, and once again the hospital's construction team were working overtime. Naturally, they had to put their team in place, with the obligatory beards. Having a much better understanding than the previous American administration of the political and medical issues facing the hospital, they moved on a broad range of substantive issues. Without the normal economic incentive that dominates the issue in the United States, they tried to increase the throughput of the operating rooms by improving the scheduling of patients and staff. Knowing the fundamental health problems in the Kingdom resulting from consanguinity, they established a separate department of medical genetics. To address the issue of optimizing the medical expertise in Riyadh and delivering it to the remote areas of the country, they were enthusiastic supporters of telemedicine and "medical outreach." The programs allowed the physicians at KFSH to visit other areas of the country for a few days, presented medical lectures to the medical staff, and conducted clinics at other government hospitals. The administration wanted to improve communications within the hospital, and initiated an electronic newsletter. In order to minimize the bureaucratic nightmare for new patients, they completely re-designed the admission process, under the rubric of "one-stop" shopping—the patients were received in a new, well-designed building, and in one place all matters related to their admission was determined in a brief period of time.

Perhaps the most impressive change was the more collaborative and participative managerial style that was adopted. It was the antithesis of that stereotypical "oriental potentate," and much more akin to the Japanese lengthy collaborative style of evolving managerial direction. Day long managerial retreats were held in which a particularly thorny issue facing the hospital— for example, the operation of the emergency department, was examined by the top hospital leadership. Problems were identified and prioritized, and proposed solutions were similarly identified and prioritized. Overall, substantive, positive changes were initiated on a broad range of administrative issues.

Probably the most impressive event occurred outside the normal administrative matters. "The Beard" called me to his office and handed me a movie, telling me I might enjoy it. It was Bernt Capra's *Mind Walk*. The entire movie is filmed at Mont St. Michel, on France's Brittany coast, and involves philosophical discussions on the meaning of life among a physicist, a poet and a politician. One of the stars is Liv Ullmann. It is definitely not the sort of movie for someone comfortable inside his narrow ideological box. Very few of my Western friends would have the inclination and patience to sit through this movie, yet this Beard not only knew the movie, but actually recommended it. How is it possible that he could understand even half the movie, a man from the very heartland of Arabia, raised in such a different culture? Might it have been a reflection of my own prejudice? Yes, he had a beard, and short trousers, but had he not mastered two cultures? Even to this day I am not convinced that he understood one bit of the movie, but if it is just assumed that he felt it important to project a trans-cultural, intellectual image, it was most impressive.

The glass was definitely more than half-full, and all things considered, it looked like a substantial upgrade from the last American administration. But there were also troubling signs from the beginning. The newly appointed Saudi office manager was blatantly having an affair with a Western secretary in the office. Nothing subtle here, they were in the "drooling stage," and thus inseparable. In flashbacks to the days of the first Saudi Director, she started to strut with the same, "I can have anyone fired in this hospital I want" attitude, and she did have a couple of her secretarial enemies publicly humiliated and another terminated.

From *"Mind Walk"* to the oldest and most common of human peccadilloes, there was this dream-like quality to the summer of 2001. In the background, the "Taliban" are busily covering the walls with pictures of Islamic holy sites, and arranging to have prayer call piped throughout the hospital. Yet here is an all-too-public affair so emphatically out of sync with the image this conservative religious administration aspired to convey. I had come to the conclusion that the Beard was simply naïve; too busy improving the medical direction of the hospital and hanging those pictures of Makkah to realize what was going on right under his nose.

So when the Beard next solicited my opinion on how well his administrative initiatives were being received by the staff, I felt I owed this situation a frank discussion. After all, he was the man who had promoted *"Mind Walk"* to me—effectively proclaiming a willingness to address information outside an ideological straightjacket. Irony lay heavy over this meeting. It wasn't my morals that were being offended. But it turned out that I was the naïve one, unwilling to consider that the same hypocrisy that permeated the televangelists in the United States would be equally operative in the Kingdom with this particular Beard.

He listened quietly, acted surprised and expressed disbelief by noting that the woman was so much older than the man. I knew it would be improper for me as a non-Muslim to remind him that the Prophet's first wife, Khadijah, was substantially older than the Prophet. Therefore I simple said that even in the "godless West,"— and I did use that expression—around 70% of US corporations would not tolerate such an open affair, with the subsidiary power-tripping events. "Why don't you at least advise them to be more discreet, and protect yourself," I counseled. He thanked me for bringing the matter to his attention, and promptly told the Saudi office manager of my concerns. Naturally the guy was furious, and openly threatened me. I suspected the guy was unstable, and could easily bring a gun to work one day. Matters of honor were now involved.

At numerous levels, it was a serious blunder on my part. I had expected that the Beard would reciprocate my discretion, but he was currying the favor of his own office manager, placed in that position because he was related through marriage to the overall hospital director. Similar to events of 20 years earlier involving the mistresses of the first Saudi executive director, this affair was one of the perks of his position, a way of saying: "I have *wasta*, and the normal rules do not apply to me."

I had stuck my nose in a "tribal matter," even if done obliquely and with discretion, behind closed doors. It was the personal relationship that was paramount, and ideology was a distant second. The Beard's priority was to ensure that all the "backdoor communication" between his nominal subordinate and the overall Hospital director, was positive and flattering. The Beard papered over the affair by a showier and stricter adherence to the times of prayer call. All the Saudis had understood this from the beginning; once again it was I who was still learning.

My beardless Saudi friends pushed me from time to time on the activities of the "Taliban." Double or triple that from my Western friends. I knew I had to be circumspect in my conversations. One of the administrative innovations the Taliban instituted was an electronic newsletter for which I was responsible. There were some solid, informative articles but within the context of an internal corporate "everything is good, and only getting better" newsletter. One of my Western friends, wanting to underscore my new dubious position as "propaganda minister," starting calling me the "Leni Riefenstahl of the administration." Taking what was hopefully a joke to the next level, I replied with Leni's standard defense: "Well, I don't get involved in the politics; it is all just an art form for me."

However, with a very few close friends I had serious discussions of what I saw, trying to bend over backwards to underscore some of the positive developments created by those whose appearance so openly proclaimed their different values. After one such discussion, one of the longer-term physicians said to me: "I hear what you are saying, but I don't trust the man because I remember him from his days as a resident at the hospital. It is all about one matter—he *needs* to have the power."

And there was that nagging fashion statement—his short pants. How far I had come from that Atlanta social scene of the '70's, when it was *women's* hemlines that I noticed. Now I carried knowledge and instincts for a radically different fashion statement. The knowledge was the often told, and perhaps even true tale, of King Abdul Aziz's trip to Qassim in the '30's. The *Ikhwan* cut his long thobe to a shorter mid-calf range, because wearing a thobe that flowed to the ground boasted of one's wealth—in that one could afford so much cloth. It became instinctive. Whenever I'd see a beard, I immediately looked at the length of his thobe. The shortest thobe I observed was just at the top of a regular pair of dress socks. My boss, the Beard, normally wore trousers to work, as opposed to a *thobe*, like other Saudi physicians. It was telling that he kept them short too—perhaps 4-5 centimeters above the top of his shoes. In this fashion statement game, the shortness of the pants or *thobe* carefully corresponded to the degree of fundamentalism. For the beards, more consideration was given to this hemline length than a woman might give to the amount of cleavage she would reveal at a formal social event.

***

There was a 10-day period in every late September that contained the "magical day." The first morning when you awoke and sensed that it was finally slightly cooler outside. The heat seemed eternal, commencing in early May. But that magical day contained the promise of the beautiful months of winter in Riyadh and the inauguration of the camping season.

So that day, which has been repeatedly described as a beautiful early fall day in the northeastern part of the United States— September 11, 2001—in Saudi Arabia it was at the end of the smothering heat. It was around 4:00 in the afternoon when someone told me a plane had hit the North Tower of the World Trade Center. A few minutes later, the second plane conveyed something far more ominous, slamming into the South Tower. Like so many others, over the next couple of days I watched the Twin Towers collapse at least 100 times. Long gone were the days of no phones, no television, and simpler days on Olaya Street. No longer could the Kingdom sever all communications with the outside world, as they had done in 1979 when the fanatics stormed the Grand Mosque in. Arabia was as much plugged into the news as Amarillo. Numerous Saudis expressed their condolences over the event—it was part of their hard-wiring. When someone dies, everything stops, you console the family, and you try to get the body into the ground before sunset. The condolences were sincere. On the other hand, there were also those at the hospital who openly celebrated when the Towers collapsed.

Schadenfreude, the happiness at another's misfortune, is a most human characteristic, and one of the least noble. It seems to be most operative when the other is perceived to be rich, powerful, or arrogant. There were those elements in the populations of Mexico, Canada, Britain and France, to name only a few countries, who thought that America finally got what it deserved. The percentage of the population, and how open in their glee, will never be known. Even a few American fundamentalist preachers proclaimed the attack as an act of God, as punishment for "our sins." The same forces were operative in Saudi Arabia, compounded by their resentment over the negative, even crudely racist, portrayal of themselves in the media and Hollywood. I was an observer, one intrigued by estimating the percentage of the population engaged in some activity, or holding some belief, and one who is still amazed how often a carefully crafted poll of 1,000 well-selected people can predict the election results in a country of 300 million. I can't even hazard a wild estimate, but it is sickening to remember that there was even one joyful soul. Definitely there was more than one individual in a self-selected group of individuals dedicated to the care of humans. There were those in this group who were merely gleeful, but others with whom I had worked for years, who pumped their fists into the air, and yelled, "Yes."

But in the "Taliban administration" there were *none.* At least not openly, and I would never pretend to know their ultimate true feelings, the feelings they might discuss with intimate friends. They knew there was a real problem within the 60 nationalities at the hospital. It was not their job to sort out world politics, but rather to continue to provide quality medical care. I could only judge them by their actions, and these were mature, proper, and correct. The Beard called me to his office, offered me his own condolences, asked me to convey any concerns from the Western expat community, and wanted to know the names of any Saudi "celebrators." He would talk with each one individually. A number of steps were taken to calm emotions at the hospital, including a general staff meeting conducted within days of 9/11. I was given carte blanche to write the script, which was delivered without change. The Power Point presentation started with the cover of the *New York Times* magazine, appropriately attributed. The picture was two ghostly beams of light where the World Trade Center had once been, against the skyline of Manhattan. Anti-Muslim sentiment was strongest in the States in those days immediately after 9/11, leading to the hate-crime killings of at least three American residents, two of whom, a Sikh, and an Egyptian Coptic Christian, only "looked" Muslim. The meeting stressed President Bush's visit to a mosque in Washington, DC, as a show of support to the Muslim community, as well as pictures of the diverse number of Americans who were Muslim. Many of the Saudis and other Muslims in the audience received part of their graduate level education in the United States or Canada, and the hope was that the presentation would resonate with their positive experiences there. In addition, temporary changes were made to the Hospital's Personnel policies, removing any penalties for giving insufficient notice of termination of service on the part of the employee. Any employee who wanted to leave was free to do so, and every effort was made to ensure that they could do so expeditiously.

The Beard and I made the rounds of the hospital, listening to employee concerns. Most disturbing to me was listening to an American nurse from Utah who worked in the Pediatric ICU. He related to me how a number of Saudi physicians in the unit had openly celebrated on 9/11. "I've taken care of their children for two years, and they are openly cheering as thousands are dying." He and his wife left the Kingdom within a few days.

While there was much that was positive in the handling of these events, there was one aspect that was unsettling, an indicator of differences, even among long-term friends, of those who feel they have "tribal" obligations, and those who don't. This difference is certainly not limited to the Saudis. As the days passed, it became increasingly apparent that there was a very heavy participation of

Saudi nationals in the hijacking of those four planes. "15 of the 19" is one of those facts that more Americans know than, say, the circumstances and events of the Korean War. Yet almost every Saudi I knew would not accept this as fact. Attribute it to shame, attribute it to tribal instincts, whatever, the beards, and more importantly, the non-beards, my friends even, raised the issue in one way or the other. Mossad, the CIA, stolen passports, "America is too powerful and all-knowing," "Bush has gained an immense advantage, and therefore….," "You know that Arabs aren't organized enough to coordinate such an attack…." I received them all, mainstream conspiracy theories and those from the truly wilder shores.

I listened, I read, and I basically believed that the events occurred as portrayed in the mainstream media. I read with fascination an in-depth portrait of Mohammed Atta in the *Los Angeles Times*. A very small group of individuals, willing to die, and motivated by shame, injustice, inferiority or very skillful handlers, who will ever really know, maybe all of the above, set into motion the events that would affect the vast majority of people on this planet. "No, I'm afraid that 15 of the 19 were Saudis…… but that doesn't mean that all Saudis are guilty, I don't believe in collective guilt," I replied.

"We are all Americans," was the invariable refrain from every European capital, as well as almost everywhere else in the world. Trans-Atlantic solidarity, in the best tradition of Kennedy's *"Ich bin ein Berliner,"* and Pershing's "Lafayette, we are here." Even my tennis buddies, the Canadians, and those from the moral superpower—Sweden, were also Americans.

It was the fall of 2001, and even the Saudis themselves who thought Mossad was behind 9/11 realized that an immense good might occur if the Americans did invade Afghanistan and captured Osama bin Laden, because the man was much more a threat to their way of life than the American way of life. His avowed intentions were to overthrow the Kingdom's Royal Family, already in an uneasy alliance with religious fundamentalists, and to install a full fundamentalist theocracy. This would have been a true disaster to the numerous Saudis, even a number of the beards, who had experienced the broadening aspects of a wider world.

***

The B-52's were no longer based on Guam; this time they flew long distances from Diego Garcia, an island off the coast of India. Once again, from impossible heights, they rained death on the earth. What a different world it might be if the orders had been given not to 'outsource' this most vital of projects, but to have the 10th Mountain Division, and whoever else was needed, stay in Tora Bora until Osama was found, and if necessary, cross an invisible line in the mountains, and actually get their man. Imagine a war that would actually have been *successfully concluded* in 2001. Indeed, what a different world it might be.

But instead, another hijacking and other purposes were served. The minority who saw the advantages of war without end seized their chance.

22

All the News That's Fit to Print

Out of this style has grown the eye-witness, seemingly opinion-less politics—along with its strength and weakness—of contemporary Western journalism. When they are on the rampage, you show Asiatic and African mobs rampaging; an obviously disturbing scene presented by an obviously concerned reporter who is beyond Left piety or right-wing cant. But are such events events only when they are shown through the eyes of the decent reporter? Must we inevitably forget the complex reality that produced the event just so that we can experience concern at mob violence? Is there to be no remarking of the power that put the reporter or analyst there in the first place and made it possible to represent the world as a function of comfortable concern? Is it not intrinsically the case that such a style is far more insidiously unfair, so much more subtly dissembling of its affiliations with power, than any avowedly political rhetoric?

- Edward Said,
Reflections on Exile

A little more than five months after that beautiful autumn day in the United States, the American Embassy hosted a St. Valentine's Day party on February 14, 2002. Dinner, dancing, real wine: a real party.

There is pettiness, then there is real pettiness, and of the various offenses of decadent western civilization that the *mutawaa* try to sweep out, one is the vestiges of that pagan feast day, Valentine's Day. The pettiness best exemplifies itself in the assault on the color red, as well as on roses, red or white. The powers-that-be turned a blind eye as the fanatics raided shops, looking for offending items, seizing them if found, without any financial compensation to the shop owner. How on earth can a rose be offensive? The same way that an evergreen tree can be offensive in December. And why is it permitted, with dissent limited to an occasional grumble from the middle class, and a rare newspaper column by a courageous local reporter?

So the Embassy party is more than just a party, it is a positive affirmation of the power of roses. The Embassy can drift into its own craziness from time to time, but this event is looking positively normal. With not much more than a year left in the Kingdom, I was intent on simply enjoying the evening and was pleasantly surprised to learn that New York Times columnist Thomas Friedman was attending the event—his first visit to the Kingdom. I found him and introduced myself. I told him that I was impressed with the balance in his first book, *From Beirut to Jerusalem.* Furthermore, I told him that I hoped his insights might provide a different perspective from the always negative reporting about the Kingdom.

I was not only surprised but definitely saddened to find myself misquoted in one of his columns. Technically, I suppose I was not misquoted, but when only the part of our conversation which reconfirms preconceived opinions is used, the meaning of the interviewee statements is completely distorted. In his column I become an anonymous "US hospital worker" who was "appalled to see Saudi doctors and nurses around him celebrating on 9/11." Had I said that? Yes, but it was an oh-so-carefully parsed section of my overall statement about the number who had offered their condolences, the positive reaction of the Saudi hospital administration, and the number of Saudis who were far more concerned about Osama bin Laden changing their lives than the Americans' lives. Once again, the negative about the Kingdom was accentuated. That *is* the news business, the bleeding on the news leads, particularly profuse and inescapable concerning the Kingdom, as my article search in the *Wall Street Journal* in the early 90's proved to me.

Mr. Friedman and I exchanged a number of e-mails after he returned to the States. I wrote that I was disappointed in how he had quoted only the negative portion of my statement, and I pushed him on two specific issues:

First, had he found anything, anything at all positive to report about his visit, if only for contrast sake? The specific question was never answered directly. It would have been ridiculous to point-blank say that everything in the Kingdom was bad. It was conveyed indirectly, by ensuring that his columns were negative while he dispensed gratuitous advice about reforming the education system, liberating their women, urging them to become more democratic, in short, to become better people by emulating Americans.

The second issue concerned two parallel media events. In a local Saudi paper, a religious zealot had written an article that repeated the old anti-Semitic slur about Jews using human blood of non-Jews in their Purim cookies. It was such an appalling piece of racist clap-trap that the Arabic newspaper, and even the English *Arab News,* which did not print the original article, issued sincere apologies. Friedman denounced the article at least twice—he has my full support. Racial slurs can easily lead to more serious consequences, as the history of anti-Jewish pogroms readily attests.

But at the same time the editor of the *National Review,* in his blog, was openly discussing the use of nuclear bombs in the event of another terrorist attack in the United States. He didn't even specify that a second attack would be perpetrated by a Muslim—that was assumed. The nuclear bombs would be dropped on Algiers, Baghdad and Riyadh. Rich Lowry, the editor, also listed Mecca on his target list, with the logic that, "it wouldn't kill many people, but it would send a message," as well as on Ramallah, "if it's clean enough." His statement was much more than a racial slur. It was a clear advocacy of the murder of millions of people, almost all, if not absolutely all of whom, would have had nothing to do with such a terrorist incident. Yes, it would send a message! Where was Mr. Friedman's righteous indignation over Lowry's blog? His reply stated that the *National*

Review had apologized, and challenged me to come up with an apology from the Arabic newspaper. Furthermore, he said that I had been living in Saudi Arabia "way too long," as though a quick trip back to the States would make me a better person! I immediately sent him a copy of the published apology from the Arabic paper, *as well as* the article in the *National Review* in which they said they would not apologize. The facts were there, but they did not fit his story. The respective attitudes of the two Arab newspapers, and the *National Review,* could have been a quintessential "man bites dog" story, but Mr. Friedman did not find it newsworthy. Not surprisingly, I never heard back from him.

Another *New York Times* columnist who conducted a Riyadh "fact-finding" tour was Maureen Dowd. As she often does in other arenas, she highlights the women's perspective. And with Saudi Arabia, we know that means the tale of the "oppressed Saudi women," and our efforts to raise them to the freedom they have in the United States, where it is not even possible to pass the Equal Rights Amendment. In fact, even all discussion of the ERA has vanished, which may have been the whole idea, since we have been showing our concern for the fate of Saudi women.

Ms. Dowd had the opportunity to write a "woman bites dog" story. Various women who worked in the Diplomatic Corps had arranged for her to meet a number of very accomplished Saudi professional women. One could imagine a profile of three of them: how their families had encouraged them in their education and career, and the various adjustments they had made to achieve professional objectives vis-à-vis American women. She could have asked them if driving a car is their most burning issue. For whatever reason, she never met them. Instead she focused on one of the more visible incongruities of Riyadh life—the prominent lingerie stores, with their very skimpy wares prominently displayed in the windows and the completely covered women who enter to make their purchases.

She entitled her article "Frederick's of Riyadh." She was in the very upscale Faisaliyah mall, and was escorted by none other than Adel Al-Jubeir, then spokesman for Crown Price Abdullah. Al-Qaeda has denounced Al-Jubeir for his "silver, Americanized tongue," and he is indeed smooth and articulate. But even with such a tongue, it was everything Mr. Jubeir could do to keep the *mutawaa,* who were insisting that she, too, should be wrapped in an *abaya,* off Ms. Dowd. So, it made an "interesting" column, the contrast between the negligees and the black bags, the precipitated incident with the religious police, the "strange natives," and their "colorful folkways," in the best spirit of Said's *Orientalism.*

But the "bookmarks measure what we've lost," which was an understanding of how Saudi professional women work, what their personal aspirations are, not to mention the aspirations and workings of the vast number of Saudi stay-at-home middle class mothers. What part of their lives did the Saudi women want changed, and with what parts were they happy? And most importantly, how does this contrast with the aspirations of American women?

23

Spray, No Spray

Tash, ma Tash, which roughly translates as "Spray, No Spray," is a Saudi TV show. The show is named after a Saudi kids' game, played when Coca Cola was introduced into the Kingdom in the 50's. The streets were dirt, dust coated everything, and air-conditioning was non-existent, but it was a happy time, at least in memory, with Saudi youths playing carefree in the streets. It was also a time of polio and smallpox—the imprints of both diseases were discernible on various Saudi adults who worked at the hospital. The show's name referenced this simpler time of youth, before the complexity of the modern world manifested itself, which included vaccines, electricity and terrorism. Complexities brought alienation and angst to a society released from the exigencies of survival.

Coca-Cola arrived, housed in those famous green bottles, in a wooden crate of twenty-four. In preparation for the game, the caps were loosened on some of the bottles, releasing the carbonation, thereby making them flat. The caps were re-tightened so that it was impossible to tell which bottles were flat and which were fizzy. The object of the game was to select the fizzy bottles instead of the flat ones.

Tash ma Tash is a specific reference that practically all Saudis understand, like Americans understand references to *The Wizard of Oz.* The show is one-of-a-kind, 30 minutes long, broadcast only 20 times a year (the first 20 nights of the month of Ramadan), just after the evening "break fast" when the sun has set but before the more opulent evening meal. It is broadcast in Arabic, with no sub-titles. Watching the show is *de rigueur,* since viewers discuss the previous evening's episode at work the next day, in the supermarket, at the gas station or wherever one or more individuals were gathered. The percentage of Saudis (and other Arabs) who watch the show is almost higher than those who watch the Super Bowl in the United States. A Saudi once explained that the reason the show is so popular is that the principal actors (who write the scripts also) "understand us so well." Abdullah Al Sadhan and Nasser Kasabi are the "Jon Stewarts" of the Kingdom, with social satire the predominant theme. The foibles of Saudi society are addressed in one form or another, with two topics usually skirted—the Royal Family and Islam—but even these subjects enjoyed an occasional nibble at the edges. The scripts included the inept, time-consuming government bureaucracy, the treatment of foreign workers, maid abuse, the position of women in society, the health care system, the prospects for tourism in the country, the disastrous showing of the national soccer team in the World Cup of 2002, and the influence of the religious establishment on the educational system (the latter produced death threats for the show's creators).

I had the good fortune of seeing an episode of the show on a Saudi Arabian Airlines flight from Riyadh to Jeddah to which sub-titles had been added. The show concerned Saudi men picking up Saudi women in Riyadh—or at least attempting to. The Saudi "city slicker" was showing his Bedouin cousin the ways of the big city. The city slicker had bought a jeep, which would supposedly impress the women. The technique in the show, as in real life, involved tossing telephone numbers at a covered woman through the open car window, and if she was interested, she would call. A very heavily tinted window means that there might be women in the back seat, so the young men pulled up next to a car, preened by adjusting the crease in their head dresses, the *ghutras,* and motioning for the window to be rolled down. The episode's humor was that the car's occupant was none other than an officer in the Ministry of the Interior!

A more obvious drawback to tossing telephone numbers at someone who is covered in black from head to toe is that person's looks are unknown. This disadvantage was captured in another scene when a geriatric Saudi lady exited on crutches and literally hundreds of phone numbers flooded to the ground like confetti.

Through that great provider of opportunities, serendipity herself, I was approached about appearing in an episode of *Tash ma Tash*. It was one of those "friend of a friend" deals. A distinct lack of acting skills was to be no impediment to my participation. I was qualified by being a "real American," with a "real American family." I tentatively agreed after talking it over with Mary and John. Paris was in boarding school, so the friend's daughter was cast as our daughter.

"What is the show about?" I inquired.

"September 11th."

Gulp! The Saudis doing a show on September 11th? Perhaps a few more details would be in order.

Those details were provided, and we again said "Yes."

For it was really a love story. A tale of love and loss that had applied to so many Saudis. The Saudis who had been schooled in America, or regularly vacationed there, and maintained a deep affection for the country. America had become their ideal, but after 9/11 they were experiencing a very cold shoulder. Certainly, they were of a tribal society, and understood "tribal thinking," but America, with its pretenses towards equality, should not be caught up in "collective reprisals," right?

Not until the episode was actually aired did I realize how the entire show played out, since it was shot out of sequence, as is commonly done in films, but a new concept to this neophyte actor. The script was in Arabic, so I could only speculate as to how one scene might fit with another, and not all the lines were entirely apparent, but I remained comfortable with the overall theme.

The initial scenes were filmed in black and white, to denote the ancient past. For these segments the make-up team had darkened my mustache and fitted me with a black wig. I bore a striking resemblance to the person who had walked off the airplane and arrived on Olaya Street 25 years earlier, hair and all. In the art of the cinema, the director must use an economy of shots to capture the essence of an attitude and experience. To depict a traditional expat photo-op I climbed on a camel and Nasser, one of the principal Saudi actors, said "cheese" (in English) as he shot the pictures. He indicated that I should have one hand waving free. The sweet irony was that unknown to them, a very similar photo was taken by Mary in the village of Yabrin almost 25 years earlier.

The first scenes were shot on the farm of Prince Abdul Aziz bin Fahd. "Farm" is the English word the Saudis used, and it bore the same relationship to reality as when the English use "country cottage" to describe one of the palaces of an aristocrat. The farm best resembled a Saudi "Williamsburg," an array of buildings built to celebrate the Saudi heritage, a perfect movie set for old Riyadh. There is a complete, full-scale replica of the *Musmak* fort, the fort which was seized in the 1902 battle, which launched the formation of the Kingdom, and the *Marabah* palace, from which Prince Abdul Aziz's grandfather later governed. There were numerous other replicas of buildings and a *souk* area. I was cast as an Aramco employee who had come to attend the wedding of my Saudi friend, Nasser. One of the scenes required my participation in the traditional Saudi sword dance.

"But, Abdullah, I don't have the slightest idea what to do."

"Don't worry about it, you're an expat, you're not supposed to know. Just get out there, and wave the sword around."

The dance was accomplished without lethal consequences!

The next scene was shot in color, depicting the characters after a lapse of 20 years. Abdullah and Nasser now have gray in their hair and are browsing through old photographs, pausing when they run across the picture of me on the camel. "Ah, Mr. John."

Nasser's son, Fahd, is morbidly obese. Fahd's medical problem is increasingly prevalent in the Kingdom—thanks to the change to a more sedentary life style and the introduction of fast food. The solution: Why not take Fahd to America, where their good American friend, "Mr. John," would help with the arrangements after they arrived. A mishmash of scenes follow: a fun-house mirror reflection of America's misconceptions of the Middle East, where, for example, Persians are called Arabs and the pyramids are located outside Riyadh. The footage shows the Saudia plane landing in Chicago, but shortly thereafter, the background shows a street in Manhattan, with me at the wheel and telling my friends I have rented them a house; we soon turned into a housing area scattered with palm trees that looked like we were in Arizona (and indeed, we were in the "Arizona compound" in Riyadh). Throughout this photomontage of that wonderful place they called America, they deliberately hang out the windows gawking at all that is new and marvelous. Once inside their rental house, Nasser makes a big point of adjusting his trousers, "This damned western underwear," he mutters. Both men wear very tacky sport coats and pants, capturing what so many Saudis did on their first visit to the West, when they had bought their western-style clothes somewhere down on Tumari Street. Inside the house there was more deliberate gawking, as they exaggerate their role as "country bumpkins." But it is more than the physical surroundings that have changed.

Illustrating this change, there was a scene of the three Saudis in shorts, even fat son Fahd, jogging down a street. Western men, women and children were recruited to shoot an "American street scene." As they jog, each person they meet nods and says, "Good Morning," or "Hello." The purpose of the scene was to convey one real difference between the two cultures, as Abdullah later said to Nasser, when exiting a store: "You see, here in America everyone speaks to you, not like in our own country." It is a tribute to the openness and welcoming attitude of the American people.

A later shot shows Mary and me in our living room, (the scene was actually shot in our hospital-provided villa in the Al Marooj section of Riyadh), serving coffee to our guests. Nasser sips his coffee loudly, and Abdullah elbows him, "You must have your best manners now, you are in America." They go on to inquire about treating Fahd for his obesity.

I persuaded them to shoot me reading Huntington's *The Clash of Civilizations*, which they did. Our guests had left and the family is seated on the sofa watching TV, and there it is: the planes hitting the World Trade Center. Cut.

Nineteen people willing to end their lives, and a few thousand of their supporters, were able to dramatically change the lives of millions throughout the world, almost entirely in negative ways. As was so often reported in the media, "15 of the 19" were Saudi nationals, to the extent that almost no one knows the nationality of the other four hijackers. And does it matter? Consequently, the lives of everyone in the Saudi tribe changed, particularly for those who had an established relationship with their "second home," America. That was the focus of the second part of the episode. How all Saudis had suddenly become suspected of terrorism.

The next scene shows me giving three ridiculous wigs to the Saudis to wear as a disguise. I advise them to stay off the streets until the situation becomes calmer and order them a pizza. John, who plays the part of a pizza delivery boy, hears some Arabic when he is making his delivery and promptly informs the FBI, who detain my friends for questioning. Departing from their rigid rule of allowing only self-deprecating humor, they poke fun at America's inability to cope with the Arabic names, which underscores our deeper lack of knowledge of their culture or customs. I was allowed to *ad lib* a couple of political statements, mild by comparison with, for example, the editorials in the *New York Times,* but still radical in a country where criticism of governmental policy is not expressed publicly. One statement addressed the central issue in the so-called "war on terror." Instead of moving quickly and actually capturing the persons responsible for the 9/11 attack, the attack was co-opted for other agendas, and predictions were openly made that this war might last decades. Imagine if Franklin Roosevelt had proclaimed the same after the attack on Pearl Harbor? Are Osama and his scraggly followers really so much stronger than Nazi Germany and Imperial Japan?

The key part of the script which I changed concerned the departure of my Saudi friends from the USA. After their ordeal with the FBI, they were leaving and never coming back. I told them about General Douglas MacArthur and the quote that every American school child learns: "I shall return." They liked it, and with my encouragement that we need not let 9/11 divide old friends, they agreed they would return, and broke into English to render the MacArthur quote, though I realized that few of the Saudi audience would understand the reference. But the point was made: We, my Saudi friends and I, would remain on the same side, and "the enemy" would remain the fanatics who exploit religion for their own political purposes—and those who benefit from endless conflict.

Rarely could one's experience so dramatically illustrate the parallel universes that the Saudis and expats inhabited in the same country. The majority of Arab language speakers had seen the episode, and the novice actors were suddenly recognizable on the street, in the malls, and in the desert, having appeared in what the Saudi newspaper *Al-Eqtisadiah* would later bill as the most watched episode *of Tash ma Tash*. The Arabic speaking kids at the American school, perhaps 30% of the students, immediately proclaimed John's new status: the pizza delivery boy. None of our Western friends had seen the show. When I entered the hospital the day after the show aired, the old Sudanese man who had worked in the laundry since the Hospital's opening hailed and congratulated me. One Saudi asked if I had "cleared" what I had said with the US Embassy. Another standing next to him answered for me. "Of course not," he said, "I had my son with me, and I told him this is what makes America such a great country, you can say what you want."

A prominent Saudi at the hospital, and one with an eye for the nuances of the show, told me someone had altered the Arabic translation of my English statement about John Ashcroft and the American Bill of Rights. He said it must have been deemed too radical, even though the same theme has been outlined in stronger words in *New York Times* editorials. He told me that someone had cautiously decided to re-run the translation to a statement I had made earlier, concerning the American need to conduct wars to justify the procurement of the products of its large "defense" industry.

My family and I tasted celebrity status, those Warholian "15 minutes of fame." Once, when Mary and I were in a mall, from behind the veil we heard two Saudi women simply say: *"Tash ma Tash."* There was even a modest cash value to that status. I was stopped at a police roadblock where they were checking car registrations—mine was not current. I had adhered to the "unofficial rule" of simply renewing the registration at the time of sale; the police were trying to change this attitude by reminding, via a fine, that it had to be renewed every three years. They were writing a ticket when one of the policemen recognized me and immediately told me to drive on, they were sorry to detain me, and they all shook my hand. I told them this wasn't Hollywood, this was Riyadh, and the correct thing to do was give me a ticket. The five policemen were divided on this matter, reached a compromise, and went through the motion of issuing a ticket, but they never actually filed it with the higher authorities.

24

The Long Good-Bye

Christopher Rodway was killed by a bomb placed in his car on November 17, 2000. The explosion occurred just off Olaya Street, on Arbayeen Street (40th St.), in one of the more prominent shopping areas of north Riyadh. His wife was seriously injured. The Saudi authorities quickly concluded that the bombing was the result of an "alcohol turf war" among Westerners. It was a story that I believed. There was more than a certain plausibility to the story. Significant fortunes could be made, (US$ 30,000—50,000 a month) by taking the risks of supplying alcohol to those in need, reminiscent of Prohibition in the 1930's in the United States. Perhaps standard monthly pay for a corporate CEO, but very real money for someone earning that amount over a 12-month period. It was another version of the financial incentives that led Pakistanis to attempt to run the gauntlet of Saudi customs every night with significant quantities of hash or heroin.

Believing that good and evil are fairly evenly distributed among the world's people, I thought there was a very good possibility that the recent bombings may have been the result of crazed Westerners dazzled by $50 k a month.

The innocence of imprisoned Westerners, whether in Turkey or Singapore, but particularly in Saudi Arabia, makes excellent copy in the Western media. Even when they are quite guilty, as they were in the movie *Midnight Express,* their plight makes a good story, one that would rarely be told if someone was locked up under similar circumstances in a US prison. During my stay in the Kingdom, I became personally involved in two different cases regarding Westerners and a Saudi prison. In both cases I eventually concluded that the Westerner was guilty. A long-term friend of mine who worked for the US military once told me that he was almost certain that one of the men on the base had killed his wife. He said: "Riyadh really is the perfect place for a Westerner to commit such a crime. Fundamentally, the Saudis don't want to get involved, and they don't have the experience or skills required to investigate a crime involving only Westerners." Even if there is strong suspicion that a Westerner is guilty of a crime against another Westerner, they will deport the person, dreading the howls in the Western media about their "medieval criminal justice system."

One case that underscored this preference to avoid treating Western criminal cases in a judicial manner was the murder of Australian nurse, Yvonne Gilford, in the Eastern Province in 1996. My only source of information was the news media. Piecing events together, it seemed that two female nurses had murdered a third over money and jilted lesbian love. Several of my Western friends, in an instinctive reflexive action—no doubt reflecting their own tribal bonds— assumed that the two nurses were innocent.

"But they were filmed using the bank card of the murdered woman," I said.

"Well, I can't explain that, but would one woman really murder another?"

"Yes," I retorted, "why not? There really are bad Westerners here."

It was a tough situation for the Saudi authorities. The Australian brother of the murdered woman, under *Sharia* law, could either accept substantial monetary compensation and the imprisonment of the accused, or he could demand their execution. However, as yet another "exception" the Saudis made for Westerners, one had never been beheaded/executed. And certainly executing a woman would have been a terrible precedent, no matter how guilty. Eventually, in order to avoid doing so, the Saudi authorities kept raising the ante, and eventually found the right dollar amount for the brother to decide that forgiveness was the better course of action. The women were simply deported, but some portions of the Western media were wising up to the game of Western innocence and ran stories about the nurses' possible involvement in crimes in England prior to working in Saudi Arabia, and after returning to the U.K.

I was on leave on June 20, 2002, when I read about the car bombing death of a British banker, Simon John Veness. For the first time, the "alcohol turf wars" story rang hollow for me, as well as for the Western embassies, which openly disputed the Saudi version of events. The "one hand waving free..." Dylan lyric of happiness and joy was no longer the first one that leaped into my mind. Rather, it was: "Because something is happenin' here, and you don't know what it is, do you, Mr. Jones"?

But it was my daughter, with her odd affection for the songs of the '60's, who would morph these lyrics into the even more appropriate ones from the Buffalo Springfield:

There is somethin' happenin' here.
What it is ain't exactly clear.
There's a man with a gun over there.
A-tellin' me I've got to beware.
...

There's battle lines bein' drawn.
Nobody's right if everybody is wrong.
...

Paranoia strikes deep.
Into your life it will creep.
It starts when you are always afraid.
Step out of line and the man come and take you away.

For the first time since my arrival, the Kingdom was taking on a more sinister tone. The place that had simply been safe—had provided the refuge envisioned by Gary so long ago at Polei Klang— was no longer. The danger extended beyond the normal military targets, those that were attacked in 1995 and 1996, and now involved all Westerners, regardless of their nationality, regardless of their outlook or politics.

Western eyes were moving toward the exits. Some, of course, had already departed in the wake of September 11th. If that original mission, to capture Osama, when everyone was an "American," had been successfully concluded in the fall of 2001, perhaps the events to come would have been avoided. The constant concatenation of Saddam Hussein and 9/11 seemed to work with the majority of the American people, though it played out much less well in the rest of the world, including in Saudi Arabia. It was, as one of my more astute Saudi friends remarked, as though after Pearl Harbor the United States decided to attack China and not Japan.

I had the pre-established timetable of a departure in June, 2003, and I adopted assorted rationales and actions on how it would be safe for the remaining 10 months or so. I'd be more careful, watch where I parked my car, actually check under it, as the embassies were advising, if I felt it was warranted. Of course, there was the problem of the hospital itself and what I considered to be only one or two real unstable nut cases who might come to work one day and "go postal" as the expression has it. Riyadh might have its problems, but at least the desert was still safe; it was where I felt the most comfortable.

The accelerated departure of long-term friends was also disconcerting. A bit of one's life was constantly draining away. Fred was a physician friend of 10 years or so when he announced his departure. In his upbringing he was a witness to the face of adversity personified by the workers in the coal fields of eastern Kentucky. He was a man who was proud of his Jesuit education, which was reflected in his sound judgment. I thought my departure more imminent than his, but he said now was the right time to leave. It was early 2002 and he had had enough. Fred said that 90% of his patients respected him for his professional ability and that 50% of them actually liked him. It was the other 10%... I wrestled with the percentages myself on various issues, and thought his percentages were right on the money. I said: "But Fred, that 10% has always been here—do you think the number is higher now, has it changed?" "No" he replied, "the number has not changed, but I have. I can no longer stand the 10%, and might do something unwise in the heat of the moment." His reasoning was sound. He exemplified the changing mood in Riyadh: positions were hardening, and tribal forces were ascendant.

Departures were also a time of confidences. Latent questions could finally be asked. There was that old canard that various Saudis would espouse. What else could be the motive for an American to remain in the Kingdom for a long-term period other than his 'real' job, working for the CIA?"

Carter had been in the Kingdom much longer than Fred. A physician who gave excellent advice on almost any medical condition one might have—including the perfect sleeping pill to take on the 12-hour flight from Riyadh to New York City. He was also a good personal friend who kept confidences. You knew he would never talk about one of his patient's medical conditions. However, politically, there was a gulf between us. He described himself as "to the right of Attila the Hun."

But he was leaving, so I decided to pop the question. Here was a man who had treated many of the top Saudi leadership. He had been in practically every palace. He also went to the "happy hour(s)" at Uncle Sam's, the US Embassy's bar. I think it very unlikely that he would betray his medical ethics, but mainly I wanted to know if he had ever actually been *approached* by a CIA agent—which could have been so easy in the pub's convivial atmosphere. At most, I hoped for maybe a nod or a wink for an answer. But the response was a blunt sledgehammer. It was a clear-cut "No." I asked him why he thought they might not be trying to gain some insight in this manner. He said, "Because they are too fuckin' stupid." A telling comment that continues to unfold in the numerous "intelligence failures" that are now openly conceded.

On the theme of departures and the correct timing, I tried a little "gallows humor" myself and told a story that I entitled "Xuan Loc" at a few expat gatherings. The story was about knowing when it is time to leave. How was it that people were scrambling to flee Saigon at the last minute, as depicted in the pictures that are burned into our national consciousness of the last Americans being evacuated by helicopter from the roof of the Embassy? Couldn't they see the end coming? What does it take before one decides to leave?

Like the long-term expat community in Riyadh, there were expats in Saigon who had a comfortable lifestyle, even with a war being fought, mainly in the countryside. In fact, the villas in both cities were usually graced with bougainvillea, a point I stressed among the admitted dissimilarities. Pleiku, Quang Tri, Hue and Danang had all fallen to the Communist forces, but a few in Saigon still clung to any rumor of a possible halt in the coming tide. Even the NVA generals admitted that, in retrospect, they did not expect the end to come so quickly as they rolled down Highway 1. Individuals subjected to this apocryphal tale had never heard of Xuan Loc, which I explained was a small town 60 km northeast of Saigon, and the site of the last stand of the ARVN (Army of the Republic of Vietnam). Then I asked how long the ARVN held the NVA. No one really remembered: they had actually held out for all of two weeks.

The point was made. Were we just as blind to the gathering storm as we planned our next camping trip?

But plan them we did, with a renewed sense that this was truly the Last Hurrah. Yabrin certainly merited one last visit. I had more than 20 years of pictures of the area and its people. The road was finally paved. The trip was now 45 minutes from Harrad, as opposed to the laborious five-hour struggle in 1980. I asked a Saudi friend from the hospital to call the Emir so that we would be formally "announced" prior to our arrival.

The Emir was cordial and correct, as expected. We sat on carpets near the camel pens. The prepared CD's which covered almost a quarter century of the people and landscape of Yabrin were shown to the Emir via a friend's laptop. Some Saudis are into their heritage and history. Others are not. Occasionally he would muster a *maut* (dead) with a philosophical shrug. It was obvious that the Emir was not a fan of Faulkner. The past was definitely dead, and it was certainly in the past.

The next day Mary and the other women in our party were hustled off to the women's quarters. A remarkable transformation from the small dark room of previous years. The villa was large, spacious and airy, and the Emir's wife wore no veil this time. Her Bedouin dress of many colors had been replaced by a dress more sedate, but equally covering. A few of the younger women wore make-up and were well turned-out in designer blue jeans. The Emir's sons were now young men, tall and handsome, and as friendly as when they were boys. The guests were served tea, coffee, dates and soft drinks. After an hour or so of socializing, in Arabic and in English on both sides, lunch was served in another large room. The food was abundant and was placed on carpets around which all of the women sat. There was much laughter, but Mary later commented that she sensed a change in attitude, one that must go with the more expansive position. Noura was cordial, gracious and generous with her Western visitors, but now there was a certain aloofness that she had not noticed before. They still were unsure how to respond to us since they did not know where we fit in the social structure. The truth, of course, was that we were fitting in less with each passing day.

We also saw Rashid, who had hosted us back in 1984. He still had his camels and his sheep, but Sudanese shepherds now tended them. He smiled when he said that his Bedouin days were over; he lived in a house, and was the "night watchman" at the government clinic.

Of the many amazing physical developments, the people of Yabrin boasted a paved, four-lane street lined by a long row of street lights. The street did not actually go anywhere, three km or so of asphalt laying arrow-straight in the middle of the village—it was one more symbol, like an American city getting a pro-football franchise. Arrival in the big times. In 1980 there may have been two to five foreigners in the town, the Sudanese school teacher, the Yemeni at the gas pump, perhaps a Pakistani running a little shop. Now there were literally hundreds, and these included that ubiquitous crutch of Saudi domestic life, the Indonesian maid. Others were employed picking up the garbage along that four-lane street every day.

All around the town there were more signs of progress. Kilometers of wire lay on the ground, part of a seismic program—the Saudis were conducting surveys searching for natural gas. Of course the Emir was pleased to hear that we had not changed, and that we were very happy to sleep on our favorite butte, four km to the northwest of the town. So we did, one last opportunity to look south over that infinitude of sand that reached to the Indian Ocean. Thesiger had come through this way roughly a half century before and found no one, since they were all out herding their flocks. He thought the introduction of the motor car to the peninsula would be a disaster for his beloved Bedouin. He had died in a nursing home in England only a couple years previously, and I'm sure he would have been glad never to have seen the Yabrin of today. All things considered, though, their life was substantially better on many fronts. Why and what we lose when we gain will remain an eternal question.

Another return-to-old-haunts was the trip to Abu Kaab. I had shown pictures of the mountain to numerous Saudis; they were amazed that this massive expanse of stone existed in their country. They, too, saw the attraction, and expressed a desire to visit the area. The desire of the Beard to visit the mountain was sincere, but he wanted to make the trip in one day. I told him it was impossible; there was just too much cross-desert traveling. I wanted to prove myself wrong on that statement and make the trip in one very long day. As the hawk flies, the distance was around 450 km from Riyadh, a little more than the three-hour drive to Damman on the expressway. The desert tracks we must traverse might add another 100 kilometers to the distance. If we left at 5:00 a.m., and drove in the dark the first hour and a half on the expressway before turning south, it just might be possible to reach the campsite by sunset.

It was early December; the Kingdom would be celebrating *Eid Al Fitr*, the holiday at the end of Ramadan. Our convoy of campers would be celebrating and performing a pilgrimage of sorts. One might speculate that this massive stone monolith probably had religious significance in pre-Islamic times. Each vehicle carried two spare wheels and an extra 120 liters of petrol. The weather was ideal, highs around 28° C, lows around 15° C. And it was a reliable and compatible group of tested campers who were as enthusiastic for the trip as I, with the majority knowing it would definitely be their last desert trip, and the remainder considering that to be quite possible for them also.

Departure time and we were moving; two hours later we were beyond Quawayiya on the expressway, at the exit almost exactly aligned with the 45th meridian, one-eighth of the way around the world, if you keep track from London. It was then another 40 minutes or so down a two-lane asphalt road before jumping off onto dirt tracks. Even with a GPS, there is still a considerable element of dead-reckoning to such a trip, for the obvious reason that one is not on water and thus cannot steer a direct course. The key decision always related to which desert track was the best choice. Overall, the further east we swung, the flatter the terrain, which meant making better time. The more eastern course would take us further away from the "hawk's path." Our goal was to find petrol at one of the desert stations, preserving our 120-liter reserves. Sometimes those desert stations ran dry, necessitating a change in course. Mechanical problems, certainly including tires flattened by sharp rocks, could throw the entire plan off.

On this trip people and machines worked amazingly well together. With about ten minutes of sun lingering in the sky, Abu Kaab appeared in the distance. We established camp in an idyllic spot where acacia trees dotted the landscape, and we were surrounded by other monoliths that offered a sense of privacy. The campsite was to the east of Abu Kaab so we would awake with the dawn's light reflecting off of it. The tents were raised and a campfire started before full dark. The advantages of reaching Abu Kaab in one day were significant, since we would have the same campsite for three days, optimizing our opportunities to explore the area.

Though it was now my fourth trip to the mountain, it was the first time I realized how many monoliths were in the area. From the top of one that was climbable, we could see at least another twenty in the vicinity. The *Hijerian* calendar allows one to easily know the phase of the moon and the *Eid al Fitr* heralded a new month, a new moon, a dark sky. Light pollution was non-existent as we extinguished our lights; the thrill of seeing the stars, actually feeling their presence as they were felt by man 50,000 years ago, was an additional bonus of this trip. Our DNA was "hard-wired" to resonate with those people of pre-history; we enjoyed the warmth of the campfire as they must have.

Three days at Abu Kaab was not sufficient, but it was most satisfying. We had agreed to push due west and fulfill another almost quarter century desire of mine. One of the principal road networks in the Kingdom is in the shape of a large triangle, from Riyadh to Abha, then along the mountain road to Taif, and back to Riyadh on the expressway. Al-Bisha bisects the Abha-Taif road, and from the first trip back in 1979, I had wanted to cross that large blank area on the map between Al-Bisha and Riyadh. This trip would cover a large part of the middle of that triangle, and would include an increase in elevation as we ascended back into those "mountains of the Yemen" that Lawrence had once fantasized about. The area to the immediate west of Abu Kaab turns perfectly level, with a light covering of sand and no dry watercourses of any size. In short, it acted as an expressway where the vehicles ran abreast, at 120 kph. After 20 or so kilometers we encountered a large *wadi* with sand dunes and shrubs, making the passage difficult. Eventually though, we completed our climb of the westward, gentle-sloping side of the Asir mountains. We found another excellent campsite nestled on the western side of low hills with dramatic vistas of extinct volcanoes.

The next day we spent hours trying to find a way to the top of one of these volcanic mountains, but the petrified lava flows, with cinder balls the size of bowling balls, tightly clustered, meant that both driving and walking them was impossible. We met a Bedouin who wondered what we were doing in the area. We went through our *ijhaza* routine. He ventured that the area was dangerous and that other Bedouin in the area did not like strangers wandering in their territory—and might kill them. The "dangers of the desert" was a story that we heard somewhat often, but only from urbanized Saudis. Eventually, I was able to reconcile this attitude—since the desert was actually safe for us—as one of those "hard-wired" throwbacks to the days when the desert actually was dangerous for the Saudis, and travel in it could mean death. But this was the first time that a Bedouin himself had spoken of it. The death was not to come from a lack of water, but people.

We were in the area of the "Al-Ghamdis," one of the large tribal names of the peninsula, and I later reflected on this chance meeting when reading the names of the various individuals in what the Saudi authorities referred to as "deviant" groups (read: Al-Qaeda terrorists). With over half the group realizing that we most likely would never travel this way again, a decision was made to push on. In full dark we eventually set up our tents at the Wahba Crater, 100 kilometers or so east of Taif. It is a large crater, three kilometers across and has the appearance of being created by a meteor, but it is actually an extinct volcano. The following morning we hiked to the bottom of the crater and played along the salt floor, before undertaking our six-hour drive back to Riyadh.

Approximately 70 days after our final trip to Abu Kaab, the second major Islamic holiday occurred, *Eid Al-Hada*, after *Hajj*, the annual pilgrimage to Makkah. The core days are from the 9th to the 15th of the *Hijerian* month of *Dhu Al Hijjah*, and thus the evenings are blessed with a full moon. The light is so strong on the evenings of the full moon that a flashlight is not needed around the campsite; I would throw a blanket over my head to block the moon's light in order to sleep.

It was during the *Eid Al-Hada* holidays that we embarked on our very last significant camping trip and it involved all new territory. At some level it was embarrassing to have lived in a country for 20 years and never seen its far northern parts. It is only a limited consolation to know that the vast majority of Saudis have never seen it either. We knew of no other expat, and certainly no Saudi, who had undertaken such a trip. Our travels would take us so far north that we would be within a degree of latitude of Jerusalem. There were a number of major draws to such a trip—seeing the Al-Jawf basin, where more than a million olive trees were cultivated, returning to the sand stone cliffs of Wadi Zaytah, which Mary, the kids and I had so enjoyed 14 years earlier when we left the Kingdom in 1989. I also wanted to break through the mountains of the northern Hejaz, from the Red Sea coast to the area around Madain Salah. On the downside, tensions continued to rise as the US prepared for the invasion of Iraq, which commenced five weeks after our scheduled return to Riyadh. A large part of the trip involved driving the Tapline (Trans-Arabian Pipe Line) Road. This road paralleled the large pipeline that had at one time carried Saudi crude oil to awaiting tankers at the port of Sidon, in Lebanon. At its peak, the pipeline carried 30% of all Saudi oil production, but was no longer in operation. The road also paralleled the Iraq border, between 30-50 kilometers away.

Once again, we would have solid traveling companions, veteran campers who knew all the required rules of such a trip. As a major extra, our friend's son-in-law, a German citizen fluent in Arabic, having done his doctorial dissertation on the Shammar tribe of northern Arabia, accompanied us. Our own little "certificates of respectability" were now grown; our friend's daughter and son-in-law had their own certificate: a one-year old daughter.

Considerable excitement built up in anticipation of what was definitively marked as the final major camping trip in the Kingdom for any of the participants. We might all camp again, in another country, but the camping would never be the same. Lost would be the ability to camp anywhere, with aesthetics being the major criteria. We had acquired the permits from the Ministry of Antiquities to visit the historical sites at Al-Jawf and Madain Salah. Concerns about our safety had increased, and in the interval between the Eids, a British citizen had been murdered at a stoplight in Riyadh, solely because he was a Westerner. A Saudi had pulled next to him, used an AK-47, and simply "blown him away." We continued to hope that "other people's agendas" would remain on hold long enough for the completion of this final trip, and continued to rely on our impression that the desert was safer than the city.

As with so many previous trips, we drove north on the Qassim expressway. We turned off, before reaching infamous Buraydah, and headed northeast, towards the Tapline Road. The first stop was Ar-Artayiah. Only our German traveling companion realized why it was important for us to stop there. It is a flat, dusty, non-descript town. An American might conjure up images of a town in west Texas where *The Last Picture Show* was filmed. The adjective "Allah-forsaken" would be appropriate. So, should it be a surprise that the inhabitants of such a place would develop an especially close and intimate relationship with Him and be certain that only they understood His will? Ar-Artayiah was the birthplace of the Ikhwan, the "Brotherhood," the religious fundamentalists whose extremism had bedeviled the more moderate Saudi leadership since the days of Abdul Aziz ibn Saud. I didn't feel the Ikhwan ghosts so there was not much more to do there than take the appropriate photos under the street sign proclaiming the city's name.

Rain and more rain had converted to green the area along the Tapline road, far to the horizon and beyond. In another sign of the change of the times, 18-wheelers with triple-decker trailers hauled hundreds of sheep to these greener pastures. A sizable portion of the remaining Bedouin population had become "part-timers," and established their tents as temporary accommodations several kilometers off the road. With the greenery and the rain it was a festive time, and people were in a joyous mood. We stopped at a recently-formed lake near Rahfa and a policeman, who had driven all the way from Hail to enjoy the greenery, recognized me from the *Tash ma Tash* show, pumping my hand in thanks. We stopped along the Tapline road for lunch. Camels wandered by, and true to that expat axiom that you can never have too many camel pictures, I ambled over for yet a few more with the green background. An old Toyota pick-up truck, its occupants a couple of scruffy-looking Saudis, was "herding" the camels, as I had seen done many times before. Always aware of the photography prohibition observed by some Saudis, which even encompassed camels ("all living things"), I questioned with my hands if it would be alright to take the pictures. In perfect American-accented English I heard: "what are ya'll doin' up here"?

I didn't need to go through my Arabic *ijhaza* routine with this guy. After a brief explanation in English, the much more relevant question, at least for me, was, what was *he* doing up here? He explained that he was an engineer at Aramco, toiling away to make sure all those American SUV's had enough gas. He had been educated at an American university and had the lingo down. His father wanted him to stay in touch with his roots, so some weekends he drove to the countryside to take care of the family's camels. His scruffy unshaven appearance simply matched our own. There was an invisible line, somewhat to the north and east. We were on the safer side, which gave us peace and tranquility, and hopefully an absence of bombs for now. The Saudi and I both knew what was coming on the other side of that line. In parting, there was mutual agreement that Saddam Hussein and George W. Bush were both *maajnoun* (crazy).

That evening our little caravan camped on the west side of the road. The next day we arrived in Ar'ar, the major Saudi crossing point into Iraq, now closed. At the time, unbeknown to us, and with mutual denials from the Americans and the Saudis, the airport at Ar'ar was being prepared for American use in the attack on Iraq. From the town we turned west, heading out on the long northern arc that would take us through the Al-Jawf basin, on to Tabuk, down through Wadi Zaytah, and finally to the Red Sea. It had grown noticeably colder. We couldn't wait to see the olive trees, and there was a certain oblique symmetry to the objective. I had previously visited Nyons, France, famous for their wrinkled olives, the result of a deliberate harvest after the first frost. Nyons is generally considered the northern-most point in the Mediterranean basin where the olive tree can thrive. The Al-Jawf basin is the southern-most region where the olive trees are actively cultivated, though they do grow in a wild state much further south in the Asir Mountains.

The Bedouin, with their quirky sense of humor, had a well-known nickname for the Al-Jawf basin, which meant the Valley of Flatulence. The nickname was derived from the idea that the people who lived there had an excessive sense of hospitality, piling the meal plates high with the attendant consequences.

With our antiquities permit, we were intent on seeing the Za'bal fort in Sakaka. We spotted it perched high on the hill, within the town, and drove up to the locked gate. Eventually, the Saudi caretakers, in a very, very expansive use of that term, sauntered up, examined our permits, and opened the gates. The view from the fort was impressive, but the fort itself, dating back to the days when the Emperor Hadrian incorporated the area into the Roman Empire in 106 AD, had seen better days, despite recent attempts to restore it. The walls were covered in graffiti, and all the light bulbs had been smashed. In fact, despite the fort's locked gate, most of the fort appeared vandalized. The caretakers later deemed to show us the one well outside the enclosed area. All in all, it was a depressing place, particularly in light of the attempts to bring tourism to the Kingdom. But worse, yet, was to come.

We left the fort as the sun was sinking to search for a suitable campsite, preferably with stunning views of olive groves. Within five minutes, while still in the heart of the town, a Mercedes with four men sped up next to us, screaming at us, yelling the dreaded "*ameeriki,*" flashing the bird, and spitting at our vehicles. Foremost in our minds was that although they actually had not shot at us, that possibility remained. By quick common agreement, the olive groves were forsaken. We weren't all American passport holders, (since our party included a German and a Canadian) but once again, we were "all Americans." We fled into the desert, putting as much territory between us and Al-Jawf as possible. Around 100 kilometers later we pulled off into the desert, setting up camp in darkness. It was a bitter cold night, and our souls, too, had been chilled. Five days later, the Deputy Governor of Al-Jawf, Hamid ibn Abdul Rahman Al-Wardi, was gunned down in an execution-type slaying. The discontent in the region extended beyond Westerners.

Driving through Tabuk the next day, we bought extra blankets to supplement our sleeping bags. Our spirits were lifted in Wadi Zaytah. The shifting cumulus clouds scattered patches of sun and shade over the sand stone cliffs and sentry-looking hoodoos. Even the desert wildflowers, now in bloom, contributed to uplift the mood. The following day we had regrets leaving such a lovely, unspoiled area, but it had been cold for a number of days, and the warmth of the Red Sea was beckoning as we weaved our way off the high plateau. Soaking in the warm sea, and sponging off with some of our fresh water, we were once again warm and clean. Down the lightly traveled coastal highway we sped through Duba and Al Wedj. We even found a derelict old Ottoman fort, another neglected part of the Saudi heritage.

Our route ran through the town of Manjur, where we left the asphalt and climbed into the mountains again. Our destination was the famous archeological ruins at Madain Salah, the site of a Nabatean civilization that stretched up to Petra, in Jordan. The GPS helped us immensely, but one had to pick the right path, since these devices were not tied to land maps, as they so often are now in the United States. At one particularly confusing juncture in the paths we decided to disprove an old axiom—men actually do ask for directions. In this case we asked directions from two young bedu in a pick-up truck. The answer didn't seem right, but they were "locals," and must know. About ten kilometers later we came to the conclusion that we were intentionally given the wrong directions and were heading back to the Red Sea. What a difference from 1979, when a Bedouin guided us for 40 kilometers to help us find Taithlith.

We eventually picked our way through the mountains and east of Madain Salah found an excellent, but again cold campsite. The following morning we drove to the historic site. At best, the guards were "correct" as we showed them our permission slips, containing that dreaded word in the nationality blank. Improvements had been made since my family's visit in 1989. These included steps, platforms, and handrails so that one could see the empty holes in the rocks which had once been tombs. Far more remarkable, though, we actually saw Saudi tourists. They were there for no other reason than an interest in their own heritage, which included the *jahaliya*. They studied the uses of some of the ancient stones.

"Well, where are you from," I asked.

"Buraydah."

Still, it was most refreshing.

It was too late in the afternoon to reach my preferred campsite in the Aja Mountains outside Hail. We pushed as far as we could, and found a mountainous area to the south of the road—rocks, trees, and sand in the right proportions for a final night. Despite the unpleasant incidents, each unprecedented in our travels, we felt great satisfaction in a solid accomplishment. It was a fitting way to say "Good Bye." We wanted to update the old scientific saw: once a hypothesis, twice a theory, and three times a law. Culturally, we decided that twice would become a "ritual," since there would never be a third time. Thus, we poured the dregs of the last of the beer over the embers of our final Saudi campfire. Departure from the Kingdom, for the pourer as well as the photographer, was a little more than three months away.

25

War and Remembrance

Beneath our eyes violence was being done, but we were as detached from it almost as from history. Space, like time, anaesthetizes the imagination. One could understand what an aid to untroubled killing the bombing plane must be.
It was a highly symbolic introduction to South-East Asia.

—Norman Lewis,
A Dragon Apparent

There is the war, and then there is the struggle on how it is to be remembered, as well as forgotten, and passed on to the next generation. The victors write the history books, as it is so often said. But even the victor's tales take some unusual twists and turns, with points emphasized and others omitted, often the result of present day political considerations.

There were over 30,000,000 dead as a result of the war between Germany and Russia during World War II. In terms of savagery and scope, it was the most devastating war in all of history. In July, 1990, my family and I were driving across the Russian steppes, where the wheat was growing tall. One of our designated stops was the town of Kursk. In the same month, 47 years earlier, the largest tank battle in history had taken place here. Over 3,000 Soviet and German tanks had slugged it out. Having spent a year living on and with tanks, I was strongly motivated to determine how this battle was remembered.

There was one low-slung memorial along the side of the road with a grainy old black and white film showing snippets from the battle. An old house in the town had been converted into a museum. The battle descriptions were in Russian only. During the hour we looked at the pictures and maps, not another tourist was seen.

Similarly, on the American side, various aspects of wars are also emphasized and others forgotten. One can travel into every nook and cranny of Provence, in France, and never sense that 86,000 Americans of the Seventh Army marched through the area starting on August 15, 1944, quickly pushing north towards the German border. Simone, the woman who owns the *gîte* that we rented annually, had once shared with me how, as a girl, she had watched American tanks enter her village of Pernes-les-Fontaines. Simone was on the receiving end of the chewing gum the American soldiers were famous for giving to the children.

The real remembrance "industry" is north, on the Normandy coast. Every town, or so it seems, has a war museum. And there are all the movies, books, and TV shows that focus on the D-Day invasion. As with all wars, much did not go according to plan. It took the Americans almost seven weeks to accumulate sufficient manpower and materiel to break out of the St. Lo salient and commence their rapid approach to Paris. Progress was even slower for the British and Canadian forces. The town of Caen, ten kilometers inland, was a first day objective but it was over a month later on July 7th that the town finally fell to the Allied Forces, and was largely destroyed in the process.

It is most fitting that Caen now has one of the most impressive war museums anywhere in the world, *Le Mémorial de Caen*. One enters, directly from the parking lot, what appears to be a one-level building. The entry level is light and airy, containing a bookstore and a restaurant. There are two timelines of man's development —two and only two--that dominate the lobby. One is Christian, the other is Jewish. All other possibilities are omitted. One enters the museum proper by walking down a long spiral, and as one walks, it grows darker, and the noise, the shouting crescendos. The sensation is of being sucked into a vortex, no doubt correctly reflecting the feeling of so many Europeans in the late '30's. Reaching the lower level, one sees the actual war exhibits.

The metaphor of a vortex was operative in Riyadh in the spring of 2003. "Shock and awe" was on the lips of the insufferable Rumsfeld. Wolfowitz was predicting a flower-strewn path for American troops. Bush goaded his opponents with his famous "Bring 'em on" challenge. The short, quick, decisive war, as wars have always been sold, would result in a truly remarkable transformation of the opponents to the American way of thinking. Then it is on to the next country on the "transformation list." All this bravado by men whose only war time experiences had been watching war movies.

Saddam had rained Scud missiles on Riyadh 11 years earlier, and it was extremely rare to find a Saudi with a kind word for him. They understood that he was a megalomaniac tyrant. Still, they seemed to have an instinctive understanding that something was seriously amiss in the selling of the Second Iraq war, something the American population would come to understand, in bits and pieces, over the coming years. The elements of the Saudi population with the most black and white views of the world, and with real or imagined resentments, became increasingly open in their hostility to any Westerner in their vicinity. The emotions of group loyalty and of war-time hatred were ascendant. A Saudi woman who worked at the hospital, and identified by many as a prominent celebrator of 9/11, stated quite bluntly: "If the United States invades Iraq, I will bring a machine gun to work and shoot any American I can." A long-term bearded Saudi physician on the administrative staff openly threatened me. Tensions were rising, and the darkness was increasing, as was the noise in that vortex.

Unlike the response of the hospital's administration to the events of 9/11, in that month or so when the entire world sympathized with the Americans, their response now was far more tepid. The official line concerning the machine-gun toting Saudi woman was that she was just "joking," and I was the one who should be *more understanding*. With this woman's attitude, it was not surprising that she had a conflict with another Westerner, this time a Canadian physician. I watched as she came to the administrative offices, sobbing over his harsh words in response to her "death to all

Americans" gibes. One of the prominent Saudi beards on the medical staff stopped what he was doing and went to comfort her. I thought: "If only she had tried to drive a car, as had those other Saudi women in 1990, she would have been in serious trouble, but threatening Americans was no big deal." Still, at least some effort was made to temper emotions.

I was asked to ghost write for the hospital's executive director a memo to reduce trans-cultural tensions. It was a formal directive prohibiting threats against Westerners, *even if conveyed as a joke.* That phrase was left as originally written in the signed directive. Perhaps more telling was the language that was deleted. It concerned Al-Qaeda, *or their passive supporters.* The *passive supporters* phrase was deleted. Within a couple of months, then Crown Prince Abdullah repeatedly used exactly the same phrase, *their passive supporters* in the context that indicated they were as bad as Al-Qaeda members.

There were people who tried to apply the brakes to this downward spiral. And it was not something necessitated by political considerations, with phrases carefully deleted or retained. It genuinely sprang from character and fundamental moral beliefs. Most prominently in that category was Abdullah Al Sadhan, one of the two stars of *Tash ma Tash.* "Why don't you come up to my farm in Shaqra for the weekend, bring your family and friends?" So as the war was raging in Iraq, Mary, I and eight Western friends spent a wonderful weekend on Abdullah's farm. It was a nice country retreat, where he patently took delight in growing his own food and raising a few sheep.

As with the political climate, the weather was growing warmer, but the evenings were a delight. A few other Saudis dropped by, the stars were just above us as we sat outside, and we delved into our own version of *Mindwalk,* kicking the philosophical ball around for much of the evening. I saw an opportunity to push a future *Tash ma Tash* script idea or two, and advocated the idea of taping an episode at Abu Kaab—showing the Saudis some of their country, the tourism angle, etc. Of course, the logistics of just getting there, not to mention bringing and operating an entire filming crew, would be formidable. Abdullah interjected that there were similar monoliths just to the north of Dawadmi, about an hour and a half west of his farm. I told him that seven of us would swing by and check out the area the next morning when we were driving back to Riyadh. Abdullah apologized for not accompanying us, citing family obligations, but strongly urged us to visit the old part of Shaqra town before we looped over towards Dawadmi.

The morning was still reasonably cool as we wandered in the old part of Shaqra, amazed by its extent. Efforts had been made to restore a few of the old mud buildings, but the vast majority of the area was dilapidated. We freely wandered around. A Saudi drove by, observed what we were doing and stopped. He introduced himself as Fahd, said that he had lived in the old village as a child, was glad we were interested, and that he would be happy to show us around. It was necessary to drive our vehicles to the other side of the old area, where the really interesting sights were: the old mosque where Abdul Aziz ibn Saud himself had once prayed, the well where camels had trod, continually drawing the water, and the old market area. Fahd was generous in his explanations and the morning was serene, until everything turned upside down as the *mutawaa* struck. I was to experience my first personal encounter with them.

A recap of my family's interactions, over the previous few years, with this evil element might be a suitable antecedent. The *mutawaa* is the informal name for the Society for the Preservation of Virtue and Prevention of Vice. Working for such an organization aligns you directly with God's will here on earth. Well, at least one interpretation. The *mutawaa* are hardly unique in this regard. God is dragged into many terrestrial events, certainly wars, real estate claims, football games and even sex, and the appropriate way that it is to be conducted. Invariably, God's human advocates seem to know His will, and merely act on His behalf.

It is appropriate to begin by saying a *good* word about the *mutawaa*, and I hope that various Saudi friends, who claim that there is no such thing, will forgive me. On rare occasions, they do something important and useful. They might have saved my daughter's life. One day Paris had walked a half block to the local convenience store alone and was stopped by a civil policeman. He told her to get into the police car, which she did (despite being warned never to do this). There was zero justification for his actions. Fortunately, a GMC Suburban full of *mutawaa* had observed this, intervened, and placed Paris in their vehicle They drove her to the housing compound, with suitable admonitions, including warning the Bangladeshi gate guard to never let her go out alone again.

Mary knew how to play the *mutawaa* game well, and not until the events of 9/11 did she wear the *abaya*, or, at least carry it with her, "for emergency use." One of the cardinal rules for a woman in Saudi Arabia was a variation of one from Vietnam—during the daytime, the Americans held the countryside, at night it belonged to the Viet Cong. In Saudi Arabia, the *mutawaa* prowled at night, and generally the daytime was safe, particularly the mornings. It seemed a useful modus vivendi—if you don't want to be harassed by the *mutawaa*, then shop in the morning. Mary was operating under these informal rules when the "sneak attack" occurred.

She had hailed a cab and was leaving the Al Azizia grocery store, where so many expats shopped, at 10:30 in the morning, on a cold winter day. Her first thoughts were: "How can the vermin be up so early in the morning?" They were coming right for her. She was conservatively dressed, of course. Black dress, stockings and shoes, all covered by a three-quarter length dark green Gortex rain jacket. She was unmistakably within the rules of the three passages in the Koran which address a woman's dress, [7:26], [24:31], and [33:59], though the Gortex rain jacket might not have been envisioned. Most importantly, she had "righteousness," it is what is in the heart that really matters. But this *mutawaa* business has never been about enforcing a defined, conservative dress code. It is all about power, and in so many cases, no matter what a woman does, they want to take it to the next level. He started yelling that she needed to have an *abaya* on. Feigning astonishment, she pointed at the overcast sky, and said: "*Mumkin mataar,*" and touched her jacket. He did a double take; there was a fleeting upward curl at the corners of his mouth. She had broken through that officious exterior, and touched the soul of that little boy who had played in Riyadh's streets seeing if Coke bottles would spray or not, so many years before Saint-Exupery's clay would harden his face into a permanent scowl. The thought must have flickered through his mind, this woman really was right, maybe it would rain, and so shouldn't she have a rain coat on? It made perfect sense. He quickly recovered his scowl, his officiousness, and muttered something about "letting her go this time, but she had to wear an *abaya* the next time or face the consequences." I asked her that evening how her day went. "Pretty good, I almost made a *mutawaa* laugh."

My son's situation was quite a bit different. He had a "Maureen Dowd moment," but he had no intentions of writing a column about it. At the time, John was a sixteen year old with a passion for baseball and roller blade hockey. In that regard, Riyadh had been good to him since there was an excellent sports program in the expat community. Unlike many teenagers, he was not ashamed to be seen with his mother and sister in one of the most impressive malls in town, the Faisaliyah, where Ms. Dowd experienced her *mutawaa* encounter. Paris was home from boarding school for the Christmas break, known euphemistically in the Kingdom as the "winter break." It was a festive time, and the three of them were enjoying themselves while I was at work. Suddenly, a man two to three times John's age, with his own signature reddish, ragged beard and short *thobe*, was pointing and screaming at him: "Women! Hair!" In the "*mutawaa* game," this is their preferred tactic. The accompanying man is responsible for the "good behavior" of "his" women. John was being told to "get his women under control." They were both wearing *abayas*, a novelty in itself, reflecting the changing times, so that was why the *mutawaa* took it to the next level —they had to cover their hair!

That evening, as we were having dinner, Mary and Paris were relating this latest *mutawaa* incident. I needled John a bit, asking what was it like to be responsible for his mother's "good behavior," a rather unique position for an American teenager. He just shrugged. I asked him for his take on the whole matter. "Whatever god that man thinks he represents, I don't think I want any part of him."

So let's go back to that Friday in old Shaqra. It is reasonably cool, seven Westerners being shown around the old ruins by their self-appointed guide, Fahd, when the *mutawaa* unleashed their wrath. Their target: the only person in the family who, so far, had missed the *mutawaa* experience. Now it would be my turn to enjoy the spotlight. Our vehicles had obviously attracted the *mutawaa*'s attention.

I was the first man he approached. He demanded my *iqama* (my government residency card). The brown cover denoted that I was non-Muslim, which of course he had suspected. He was interested in only one line on the document, found it, and spat out: *ameeriki*. He jammed my *iqama* in the breast pocket of his *thobe*—an unprecedented act. The Saudi authorities had a right to request one's identity card, and in the 20 years I had been in country, through airports and highway police checkpoints, I must have shown the card 500 times or so, but it was *always* immediately returned. The rules were changing, a most ominous sign. The two other men, a Canadian and a Dane, seeing his refusal to return my *iqama*, refused in turn to give him their *iqamas*, which infuriated him. I had slipped my digital camera into the side pocket of my cargo pants, but he saw the bulge and grabbed it, violating yet another rule of "the *mutawaa* game." He demanded the film. I showed him that it had no film—he didn't understand why I would have such a useless camera, but he decided to keep it anyway—it could be just one more infidel trick.

The Canadian, a long time physician at the hospital, had become almost fluent in Arabic through his clinical practice. He helped me with some of the nuances when the "charges" were being made against me. They were:

1. Making a sex movie
2. Smoking near a mosque
3. Disrespecting *saleh* (prayer call)
4. Trying to hit him.

I had remained perfectly calm during the whole process. Of course every charge was a complete fabrication, and among other matters, none of us had ever smoked. The first three charges, though, were just "boilerplate." The real charge was the attempted assault charge, serious, just as it would have been in the United States if I had tried to assault a policeman. As emphasis, the *mutawaa* drew his fist back, pointing at me, indicating this is what I had done to him. He had an "apprentice" with him, some eighteen-year-old kid attempting to grow his own scraggly beard. To me, the key was looking over at him—he knew everything was a complete fabrication, would he agree? He nodded in agreement, yes; this is what I had attempted to do. Yes, the future.

We were taken into custody, and commenced the 50-meter walk back to the vehicles. One of the docs had a cell phone; we were desperately trying to reach Abdullah, our host of the previous evening. The *mutawaa* mocked me—"call anyone you want—I am the boss here." Furthermore, he said, "*I* can call people too," specifically the civil police, to deal with your two recalcitrant friends. Abdullah wasn't answering his cell phone. It was looking grim, and I anticipated seeing more of Shaqra than I had wanted, with visions of a *mutawaa* jail coming into focus. Since I was dealing with these evil-minded government functionaries, I gave the cell phone to Mary and asked her to keep trying. Finally, success! And she explained our predicament. The *mutawaa* asked why we were in Shaqra. I explain the *Tash ma Tash* connection which was even worse than being American. They absolutely *despise* the show since various episodes ridicule them in particular. After we left the Kingdom, we learned that the leading actors had received death threats following an episode, no doubt inspired by what had occurred in Shaqra.

The civil police at last arrived. Both were clean shaven— promising. Their countenance was grim, the "we are only doing what we have to do" look. We knew the next move in this game. The civil police requested the *iqamas* from the two other men. They were legally compelled to give the documents, and they did. The policemen delivered the *iqamas* to the *mutawaa*, who pocketed them with a grin that said: "You see, I really am the power here."

The two policemen were talking to me along the lines of, "There is nothing you or I can do, *they* have the power. It is best to comply. If you fight it, you'll lose." They said that we had done nothing wrong as far as they were concerned, and that they were leaving. The policeman's personal cell phone rang; he answered it, gave me a surprised look, and said: "It's for you." Certainly, I was as astonished as he. It was Abdullah. Now how did he do that, I wondered, even here in what we call the "Magic Kingdom"? It was again the magic phone call, like many years before, at Haql, when we needed help obtaining the license plates so we could cross into Jordan. "John, I am so ashamed and embarrassed. I should have come with you. This is absolutely the worst thing... but don't worry, I've called.... and he went on with a Who's Who of Saudi society, including Prince Salman, the Governor of Riyadh. Everything will be alright. But I can't come down there myself.... I'd lose my temper, and that wouldn't be good for any of us. Please, please, understand, and make sure you call me when you are outside Shaqra and when you reach Riyadh." Most comforting.

There remained a little hitch to our freedom—the *mutawaa* had possession of our three *iqamas*, my camera and the power.

On this quiet Friday morning, we stood on the side street as the day's heat increased, waiting for the next move. In about five minutes an old Toyota pick-up truck rattled down the street, stopped, and a very dark complexioned Saudi (denoting that he was originally from the southern Tihama, or the son of a former slave,) climbed out. The *mutawaa* who attacked us was driving a brand new, government-issued GMC (known by expats as the mutawaamobile). The visual cues were not conveying the power arrangements here. What, indeed, would James Baldwin have thought about this? The color-blindness of Saudi society is, as they used to say in college, beyond the scope of this current discourse. Suffice it to say, the most recent arrival was in charge, as he placed his hand on the other *mutawaa*'s shoulder and led him off for a few minute's conversation about "the facts of life," or, more precisely, the actual power arrangements of this street.

I felt I knew how the denouement would unfold. I would have to swallow my pride, this was not about "right or wrong," or "truth or lies," it was about saving the first *mutawaa's* face by saying that we were sorry, would never do it again (yes, my porno movie making days in Shaqra were over), and we'd get our *iqamas* back, I would have my camera returned, and we'd be on our way to Riyadh in maximum half an hour. That was how it worked out, with minor variations of interest.

The boss *mutawaa* in this event came back to us with his now more subdued colleague in tow. He spoke English, and the first thing he said to me was: "You're diplomats." I knew immediately what had occurred, Abdullah had decided to take no chances about all of this, and had played the "ace in the hole" with the Saudi senior leadership. For a couple of reasons, one of which was simple curiosity to determine if they could figure it out, I decided to stonewall it. No, I replied, we are not diplomats. Again he pressed the matter. I simply shrugged, and said, "Look, he has all our *iqamas*, please look for yourself. We are all employees of King Faisal Specialist Hospital, these two are physicians, and I work in the administration." He took the *iqamas*, and verified the information himself. I had been telling the truth, we weren't diplomats. He might have been puzzled on why his superior had told him that, but it didn't really matter, he had his orders to resolve this matter and let us depart.

Prior to receiving the *iqamas*, though, we had to complete the paperwork. He had to list all my "crimes," all in Arabic of course, and though I could not read it, I'm sure the Arabic equivalent of "alleged" was not one of them. I promised never to do it again, with the emphasis on again. I signed the document with my own Arabic signature.

But before the *iqamas* were returned, the boss *mutawaa* wanted to have his own philosophical discourse on the dusty streets of Shaqra. He voiced that he knew all Westerners hated the *mutawaa*. Also, about 80% of the Saudi population, I thought. "But I had been in the country for a long time now—Why?" he asked. It was a good tactic, and forced me to list the many good things that I liked about the country. Then, in the best tradition of taking credit for making the sun rise, he said all those good things are the result of their work. Under other circumstances, the conversation might have proved interesting, but with the heat of the sun increasing by the minute, my traveling companions simply wanted to get those *iqamas* and get the show on the road. I would love to have asked if all this goodness was the result of harassing innocent people and fabricating crimes for them to confess to. Even more importantly, I would love to have asked him if women had souls. But I didn't; we retrieved our *iqamas*, and the three of us returned to our vehicles and the four sweltering women in them and drove off.

In spite of their obsession about documents, identities, and copying *iqama* numbers, they simply had not done the math, unless, of course, they thought they were adding up a "zero." For, the seventh person was the reason the boss *mutawaa* had been sent to release us, pronto even. She was the wife of the American ambassador.

And although the *mutawaa* in Shaqra failed to grasp all the implications, the Saudi leadership that Abdullah called understood—because they had *insisted* on that implication. They were not interested in having an American ambassador who was an "Arabist," who understood their culture or spoke Arabic. In fact, almost certainly, they preferred that he did *not* speak Arabic. Prioritized was a single qualification for the position—that he had an established personal relationship with the President so that the ambassador could pick up the phone and immediately speak personally with the President, with no intermediaries. Democrat or Republican administration, it didn't matter. Thus, during the '90's, the ambassador was a former Democratic Congressman from Atlanta, and certified "FOB" (friend of Bill), Wyche Fowler. With the new administration, the ambassadorship was given to a long time Bush family lawyer, Robert Jordan.

The Saudi decision-makers knew that a phone call to the President could be made, but now that would not be necessary. The pathological fun of one of Allah's self-proclaimed servants, as well as his tutelage of the next generation, must be placed in abeyance. Would Fahd, our kindly guide, or some other unfortunate Saudi in Shaqra pay for our early release when this fanatic sought new prey so that he would feel he "earned" his monthly governmental paycheck?

We had driven about 500 meters when the next surprise occurred. The ratty old pick-up truck stopped, the *mutawaa* alighted (the fancy mutawaamobile had retreated in the other direction). The man said, "Look, I really am sorry about everything that happened back there, that other *mutawaa* is a little crazy. We would like for you to stay, please feel free to wander in the old parts of Shaqra as long as you wish. You are very welcome here." Yes, we were now getting the *Ahlan wa Sahlan* treatment. We thanked him profusely but cited pressing duties in Riyadh and took our leave, gladly widening the distance between us and the dusty town of Shaqra.

We cleared the city limits and called Abdullah, who wished us *bonne route*. Ann Jordan had traveled with us before, specifically on our last trip to Abu Kaab. She knew that traveling anonymously with us was much safer than riding around in an armored car with the American flag waving, surrounded by four Secret Service personnel. She had a deep, intrinsic interest in the country, as well as its people, in sharp contrast with many in the Diplomatic Corps who were content to sit out their tour within the bubble of the Diplomatic Quarter. Ann knew she had only one opportunity to see many sights in the Kingdom and she was a prime factor behind the side trip to the Wahba Crater at the end of the Abu Kaab trip. In coordination with other diplomatic women, Ann had set up the interviews with important Saudi professional women for Maureen Dowd, who preferred to write an article about the lingerie shops in Faisaliyah mall. So, because Ann was somebody, really wasn't a "zero," my life, and that of my traveling companions, was a bit easier. For sure, even without her presence, Abdullah would have stayed on the matter, and probably before sunset we would have been released. But Abdullah knew what would resolve the matter the soonest; he played his "best cards" first.

I shared this story with several of my Saudi buddies in Riyadh. I remember how one in particular chortled after I had only gotten past Offense #1. He said, "Those dirty bastards, the first charge is *always* about sex. That is the only thing on their minds." They urged me to file a formal complaint about the incident. "We live here, if we complain they may retaliate. You are the foreigner, there is a better chance they will listen to you, and besides, you are leaving anyway."

My first draft included a "there was a good *mutawaa* and a bad *mutawaa*" tactic. When my buddies read this, they acted as though I had slapped them in the face. I knew they were *really* hostile to these fanatics, but I still underestimated how hostile. One said to me all too prophetically, "There is no such thing as a good *mutawaa*—make no mistake about it, they would kill you if they could."

The revised complaint was submitted to Prince Salman, the Governor of Riyadh. I gave a copy to my boss, the Beard. In the U.S. one's employer would normally not be concerned about minor police matters involving employees if they have no impact on work performance. However, in Saudi Arabia, the employer is officially one's sponsor, and ultimately responsible for an employee's behavior and well-being. If we had not had friends in high places, our sponsor would have had to send someone to Shaqra to negotiate our release.

The month following the Shaqra incident, I had a personal meeting with Prince Sultan bin Salman, the Director of the Supreme Council of Tourism. His office had arranged this meeting, probably because few people had traveled as extensively in the Kingdom as my family and I. Furthermore, I had brought in three sets of tourists, including my mother, using the acceptable ruses of the time, for no other purpose than to tour the Kingdom. I had considerable enthusiasm for the Director's new project of developing tourism within the Kingdom, but I gently suggested that he would have to do something about the religious police. "They are not like street hooligans that might attack a tourist in a western country. These people are on the government's payroll." I then gave him a copy of my formal complaint.

I never heard back from the Governor of Riyadh, the Director of Tourism, or the Chief Beard, so I suspect my file with the government still has me down as a smoker, along with other more serious charges. In the coming days, Westerners experienced far worse than our group did in Shaqra, and that would include kidnapping and execution.

The Ramadan after we left the country, there was a *Tash ma Tash* episode which played out the numerous problems that could be anticipated when the Kingdom opened its doors to tourism. In the show, after several difficulties in their scheduled tour, the Japanese tour group is eventually taken back to their hotel, and they are shown the Kingdom via large, coffee-table picture books.

Meanwhile, out in the still more sinister world, "shock and awe" was wreaking havoc. For so many viewers watching from afar, the carnage was like one glorious video game. A few of us with personal, up-close views and experiences of war knew that it was not glorious or a game. One can witness the linguistic slight of hand that ossifies thought processes. If a bomb is placed in a car, explodes, and kills civilians, that is terrorism, and we can show suitable moral outrage. But if bombs fall from our airplanes, vaporizing men, women and children, that is termed mere collateral damage, and "sorry 'bout that" is the retort. When Al-Jazeera news airs the pictures of the carnage which has been so carefully censored by the Western media in order to spare their viewer's "sensibilities," it is immediately charged with "incitement," and the Al-Jazeera offices are bombed.

26

Beard, No Beard

"I see you've confused what you're learning in school with actual education," he said in his thick voice...

"..Do you want to know what your father thinks about sin?"

"Yes."

Then I'll tell you," Baba said, "but first understand this and understand it now, Amir: You'll never learn anything of value from those bearded idiots."

"You mean Mullah Fatiullah Khan?"

Baba gestured with his glass. The ice clinked. "I mean all of them. Piss on the beards of all those self-righteous monkeys."

— Khaled Hosseini
The Kite Runner

Each day I shuffled off to the hospital was like taking another step into that Caen vortex, the darkness and noise increased. Should I have been more worried about the stoplights in Riyadh, or should the concern have been about one of my fellow employees bringing a machine gun to work one day—as a joke, of course? In the background, though, somehow the central mission of the hospital continued to be fulfilled. Saudis with illnesses came each day, were treated, and in many cases their lives actually improved. One of them was our old friend Ali Salem, from Yabrin, whose baby was on death's door but was brought back to full health after a lengthy stay at the hospital.

One morning I received a phone call from the Western secretary in HOBA, the "Health Outreach and Business Affairs" part of the hospital. In some ways it was a progressive force within the hospital and within the Kingdom's health care system. HOBA had taken a number of positive steps to facilitate the treatment of patients throughout the country by improving the dissemination of the medical expertise at KFSH.

It was also the true heartland of the "Taliban" in the hospital, the guys with the beards. HOBA was a place of extremes. In the Western media, pictures of dead babies killed by bombings are carefully censored. In HOBA, a Saudi had a picture of a dead child as his computer screen saver.

This Western secretary had settled on "the wilder shores of love," married a Saudi and converted to Islam. At work she wore a headscarf, which was pulled very tightly around her face, in the style of Catholic nuns in the 1950's. She was always cheerful, and more importantly, she was competent. We had had a few professional interactions, but I certainly did not know her well. She asked me if I was attending the awards ceremony.

"Sorry, I don't know anything about it."

"It's at 11:00 am today, in the auditorium, didn't you get the invitation?"

"No."

She knew she had sent me an invitation, and she probably had her suspicions. She also knew what to do—check the "control." She had sent two other invitations to Westerners, one a Canadian, the other an American. She was in my office fifteen minutes later. They hadn't received invitations either, but she personally handed me another invitation and urged me to attend, as she would do with them.

It was one of those insincere, corporate "maybe-it-will-raise-morale-if-we-pat-the-employees-on-the-back-and-give-them-a-certificate" type of ceremony. I had a zillion things to finish prior to leaving, and I would gladly have skipped the whole thing. It was obvious what was going on. Some of the "Taliban" would choke if they had to say thank you to a Westerner. These newer "Taliban" were emulating the position of the American School Board so many years earlier. Both to honor the secretary's efforts at defusing those tribal forces, as well as to just see what would happen, I attended.

The event was to honor all those hospital employees who had worked on KFSH's presentation at the January 2003 Arab Health Conference in Dubai. The three of us, as well as numerous Saudis, had performed our assignments properly and professionally. Overall, the hospital's presentation was a success. Real teamwork had been involved. Even though this was just May, the previous January seemed like a decade ago, manifestly on the other side of "shock and awe."

My name was eventually called, as were the names of my two Western colleagues. I walked up to receive my photocopied "Certificate of Appreciation" which was in an attractive leather folder. My name was actually spelled correctly (Jones, and not the so-often Johns). The presenter shook my hand tepidly, not making eye contact. One more step down into the vortex. But I was too busy focusing on the multitude of tasks remaining prior to final departure—those at work, as well as all those personal issues including what to take, what to sell, what to give away—to give eye contact much further thought.

I went to bed around 10:30 on the evening of May 12, knowing three weeks remained of Kingdom life. Mary continued to pack downstairs. The freight forwarders were coming in about ten days. About 11:30 the front door rattled so much that she thought someone was trying to get in. She was going to awaken me, but looked out the window instead. No one. She went to bed shortly thereafter, double-checking to make sure the door was locked.

The first phone call came around 3:00 am. "Yes, we are okay, why"?

"No, we hadn't heard. We were asleep."

But no longer. I logged on to our slow dial-up internet connection. The confusing initial reports were being posted regarding four upscale compounds in Riyadh having been attacked by suicide bombers. The "visitor" at the front door earlier that night was the shock wave of the explosion at the Al Hamra compound, eight kilometers away. In reality, three compounds were targeted: the other two were Jadawal and Vinnell. One of the more poignant e-mails I received was from a Canadian friend who had recently left the Kingdom: "Dare I ask, were any of your friends killed or wounded, or was it 'just' other people's friends"?

When the dust settled, literally, we were able to reply that it was the latter. One more bullet was dodged. But this was not something on the other side of the world, with confusing and mispronounced place names. It was only on the other side of our front door. It was up tight and personal. Paris's good friend is Samah, the daughter of the Palestinian-American manager of the Al Hamra compound. Paris occasionally slept over at their compound. Fortunately, Paris was finishing high school in France at the time of the bombing. John sometimes stayed with friends at Jadawal, but this school night he was in his own bed. We had just given two cats away to a man who lived at Jadawal, and one of John's baseball buddies lived at Vinnell.

As is the habit of national news media, each would highlight the number killed of their country's nationalities, and the rest were, well, the rest. Death was even-handed this time: eight Americans and eight Saudis, the remaining 18 were scattered across other nationalities, just so much "collateral damage." As always, there were the larger number of wounded—some who would never fully recover. There were tales of miraculous escapes. Of the eight Saudis (which excludes the suicide bombers), one was the son of the Deputy Governor of Riyadh, who lived at the Al Hamra compound. He had had more than eye contact with the infidels. Most were those "hapless common foot soldiers," the compound guards who had endured seemingly endless boredom to have their lives obliterated in a few quick seconds of adrenaline-pumping terror.

The "Taliban" administration didn't know what to do; they stood frozen in those headlights of a serious terrorist attack on their own soil. Would anyone celebrate this one? There was resentment by individuals at the hospital against those who lived in those "oasis" upscale housing compounds, knowing they were exempt from many of the normal street rules of the Kingdom. But if there was any celebration, it was *very* muted, behind closed doors. Finally, I decided to try to shake their immobility and entered the Beard's office:

"You should do something about this, just like you did after 9/11. Someone at this hospital knows who is responsible for this. There are too many Saudis here, and these terrorists did not drop in from Mars. They live among us."

The eyes were lowered, the hands fiddled. "Riyadh is such a large city now. We don't know who our neighbors are anymore. We are just trying to run a hospital—the Security Forces will handle this."

All evasion and no action.

Mary and I had to make one of the hardest decisions of our lives. Should our daughter return to the Kingdom to say goodbye to her friends? Would lightening strike twice in the same place, or much more relevantly, would it strike in the next three weeks? Each of the four members of our family had developed strong attachments to the Kingdom, and each would strongly miss it. But Mary, John, and I all saw a downside, too. Perhaps Paris's attachments were stronger, due to her three-year absence in France. We decided to take the gamble, hoping never to regret it, with one purpose: visit the three bombed compounds, show her the damage, to let her know that, "Whatever our feelings about the Kingdom, we have to realize that a few people here want to kill us, simply because of our nationality." We drove to the compounds together. Ironically, it was at the "American compound," Vinnell, that an American came out and told us to leave. The damage there had been the most visible, with the entire front of a high-rise building sheared off.

The farewells intensified: there were numerous going-away parties, some exquisite dinners, the last tennis tournament arranged by the "WBTC." Mary was particularly fortunate. After her forced departure from hospital employment during the dark days of the first Saudi administrator, she had worked on and off for about fifteen years, with a law firm in Riyadh. Technically, like much else in Riyadh, her employment was illegal. But as so often, there was the "nod and the wink." Her work colleagues, including the Saudis, were gracious and sincere in their "best wishes" at the end.

***

"Dad, there is a tank sitting outside our compound."

"No, son, remember that a real tank has treads. That is only an armored car, you can tell by the wheels. And there is not a 'main gun'; it is only a 50 cal. machine gun on top." Along with the requisite platoon of soldiers. That was the lesson from today's "school" as the world was offering him the same "chance" his father had.

So, it had finally come to this. That far off, impossibly remote valley near the tri-border area of Vietnam, Cambodia, and Laos, Polei Klang, is now living in peace and tranquility. I had gone off to live in my little oasis, deep in the desert, and the contagion of violence had finally turned it into a bunker. Those old evasive maneuvers in the event of attack might again come in handy: "Always maintain a moving target...."

Mary called me at work. "A soldier has just looked into the back window of our villa. He had a beard. For the first time since I came to the Kingdom, I am frightened." I knew she was quite right to be concerned. What could possibly be this person's motive? Certainly the leading answer would be: Determine in which villas the Westerners lived. I reported my concerns immediately to the head of the "Taliban" administration, and was brushed off with a remark that maybe I was getting a little paranoid. "Yes, but maybe I have a reason to get paranoid!"

A Saudi engineer friend who lived in the compound was even more paranoid than I. He told me that he had pulled his mattress into the hallway, in the center of the villa, and slept there each night, figuring that would give him the maximum protection in the event of an attack. Together we discussed this matter with the Head of Hospital Security (and 'card carrying' member of the Ministry of the Interior), who fortunately also found this totally improper. "I'll take care of it today." He did; no soldier entered the compound thereafter. The infiltration of Al-Qaeda elements or sympathizers into the Saudi security forces would be a serious impediment to their efforts to eliminate this scourge from their society.

The remaining days rapidly blurred into one another. Finally, our last day in the Kingdom arrived. Our plane was leaving at 8:30 that night. I was still at work, finishing those inevitable last minute duties.

I knew what to expect. It had been foreshadowed by the incident with HOBA and the inability to say, "Thank you for a job well done." Hospital protocol, not to mention thousands of years of Arabian traditions, were being violated. But "...come the wars, and turn the rules around...." as Phil Ochs had once sung. There would be no official hospital gathering of work colleagues to say "Good-bye," the usual breaking of bread one last time, a few kind words, often actually sincere, and the "inevitable small token of our appreciation." No, that is not done with a member of the enemy's tribe.

With only ten minutes of work left, and the plane's departure looming three and a half hours away, I was called into the Beard's office. A couple of minutes later, his "First Lieutenant" arrived. The words "thank you" would never be uttered, of course, that was anticipated. The American School Board attitude had thoroughly metastasized. But I would receive that oft-cited token of appreciation, actually a *large* token. He pointed to his conference room table and said: "Some of your friends at work have given you this." I asked if there was an accompanying card, so I would know whom to thank. "No, there was not enough time to get a card." They understood well the circumstances of an expat's departure, knew all our belongings were packed long ago, and gone. That is why that token is always small. The large vase was utterly useless, one more carefully calibrated insult. They probably suspected the ultimate disposition of this vase—to enliven the drab little room of the Bangladeshi security man at our housing complex.

Departure under these circumstances meant there was nothing to lose. I decided to push one more matter, just to see what would happen, for I was leaving with my wallet lighter than it should have been—the hospital still owed me money. It is a long convoluted story, similar no doubt to what happens to employees in many a US corporation. Many verbal promises, but more importantly, with enough commitments in writing that I would have won the case in any US court of law. The clearest part of the case involved illegal deductions from my paycheck totaling a rather trivial US$ 600. I had pushed the matter previously in a formal grievance hearing. The deductions were such a clear-cut violation of Saudi Labor Law that even the beards running the hearing had to shrug, and say, "Yes, you are right, we owe you the money, and it will be paid." The Beard, in his position as Chief Operating Officer for the hospital put it in writing in a directive to Finance to pay this amount.

So, in addition to this large token, I asked him about my 600 bucks, and the fact that it had not been paid. What could he possibly say, I wondered? It was like he had attended drama school, because he clearly deliberated before answering. Eye contact was made, with his calm level gaze. And he said:

"We can do anything we want, just like you do at Gitmo."

We were hitting bottom in that vortex.

On that note I took my leave. Off in the vehicle that we had owned for ten years, the vehicle of so many desert trips, which we sold to the Filipino head maintenance man at a local garage. He had let me drive the vehicle until my departure. I raced home, gave the vase to our residential gate guard, loaded the suitcases, and bade a final farewell to the villa we had lived in for six years just off of Olaya Street, in the same area where I had first camped in the "full desert" when I arrived in 1978.

We drove to the garage, where a Filipino was assigned to take us to the airport. The Saudi who owned the garage was there. He was one of the many likable Saudis that I had gotten to know, a hard worker who had built up his own business, and a brother of one of my good friends at the hospital. I was soon launching our suitcases onto the x-ray machine at the airport, and the policeman looked at me, and said: *Tash ma Tash.* I smiled, acknowledging his recognition. Boarding passes in hand, the suitcases were checked, and we were in the passport line. I handed the immigration officer the four passports. He looked at my picture in the passport, then looked up at me again, and says those now familiar words: *Tash ma Tash.* He pointed at the Exit Only visa: "But why"?

I smile and shrug. "We all have to leave sometime."

Epilogue – An Entrance Only

For every exit there is also an entrance.

I snatched a few hours of sleep on the plane, but I awakened as the plane began to descend through the cumulus clouds. Summer solstice approached: it had already been light for an hour and half in these far northern climes. The Saudia flight is among the very first scheduled to land at Charles de Gaulle airport at 6:15. With the normal prevailing western winds, the plane is coming in from the east, and below are those place names from previous conflicts, Verdun, St. Michel, the Somme, the Meuse, and so many others. Names that denote another tribal conflict that has finally been put to rest. As it had 33 years previously, an airplane had come to carry me away from the conflict, or at least the very front lines of that conflict. Soon we would be driving along in our rental car, on the A-104, one of the perimeter expressways of Paris, to the A-6, and on to the A-7. All of this is familiar; the rest areas every 20 kilometers, each with its own children's play area. Another culture, other priorities. Some seven hours after beginning this drive, the *"La Porte de Soleil"* (the door of the sun) will loom up, a rest area on the A-7 which announces the entrance to Provence.

Wisdom can come from many sources. Why should I be surprised that it would come from a man who had once handed me a copy of *Mind Walk,* though we never had those philosophical discussions implied? On that long drive down to Provence, I had the opportunity to think about the Beard's last statement to me. He could easily have said: "We Saudis have simply come down to the level of you Americans."

It was a concept with which I would have to come to terms as I again re-entered American life three weeks later. There was certainly elation in coming home again, to enjoy the sheer immensity of the country and one's ability to travel within it, without a travel letter.

There was the openness and willingness of people to speak to you, to acknowledge one's presence in a friendly way, on the hiking and biking trails, just as was captured in *Tash ma Tash*. There was that simple ease of living and availability of things, obtaining books and magazines in a land where the censorship is more subtle.

Paris and I were in the car one day when she asked me, "Don't you miss it"? I tried to give her a balanced answer, citing the things I missed, but emphasizing what a relief to be stopped at a light and no longer be worried about whether the guy next to me might shoot me because I was a Westerner. I told her that it was also an immense consolation not to concern myself with what she was wearing.

Thanks to the Internet I continued to observe developments in our one-time safe oasis, deep in the desert. Week after week it was the same *Cry, The Beloved Country* story. South Africa had avoided tearing itself apart in a horrendous civil war. The war in Saudi Arabia hadn't reached the level of violence seen in some other countries, but it was relentless. The last weekend in May we had traditionally journeyed to Dhahran, so John could play baseball in Kingdom-wide championship games at Aramco.

One year we stayed at the very upscale Oasis compound. It was there the fanatics attacked, killed, and then decapitated a Swede and placed his head on the compound wall. Another of the victims was Frank Floyd Jr., who had been a department head in Engineering at King Faisal Specialist Hospital in the mid to late '70's. Although the fanatics were surrounded, somehow they arranged to "slip away," yet another sign of collusion with the security forces.

The same collusion was seen on the other side of the country, in Yanbu, where we had once spent a week scuba diving. The body of an executed Westerner was dragged through the streets, tied to the back of a pick-up truck. In Riyadh another Westerner was stopped at a fake police checkpoint, on the very same road that I had traveled so many times transporting John to and from baseball or roller blade hockey. The road passed in front of Imam University, the hotbed of fanaticism that had bred so much hatred. That Westerner's head was later found in a freezer during one of the compound raids by the security forces.

But in far, far greater numbers, it was the Saudis themselves who bore the brunt of the attacks, particularly the security forces. Those hapless foot soldiers were being killed weekly, in incident after incident, and they had no hope that an airplane would come and carry them away one day. Like the soldiers who had fought in the American Civil War, they were in "for the duration."

As a counterbalance to the joys to be found on America's bike paths, and the exhilaration obtained from climbing the surrounding mountains, I would have to come to terms with some inescapable aspects of American life. Granted, some elements had always been there. It had most certainly been brought home to me, from my year's personal experience in Vietnam, how ready we were to intervene in the affairs of other countries under the "we're just here to help you out" angle. This had happened in so many countries that almost no American asked could name them, and certainly they could never list the pretexts used at the time. There was the "Quiet American" himself, Donald Rumsfeld, insufferable in his smugness, the certainty that he knew best. There was the continually promoted idea that under the guise of "the war on terror" we could do whatever we wanted throughout the world, unrestrained by our own laws, or international laws to which we had subscribed. In a historical blink of the eye we went from a period in which the entire world stood beside us to a time when even our best foreign friends could only shake their heads in disbelief at our behavior.

We chose to live temporarily in an upscale part of the city so that John could complete his senior year of high school in a public school with a "good reputation." It was the fall of 2003, and in one of his classes the discussion was on the latest Iraq war. When he voiced objections to the invasion, the teacher called him a "communist." Yes, the old Joe McCarthy stand-by. I guess "*mullah*" or "terrorist" would just have been too much of a stretch. Once again, though, as he had done with the *mutawaa*, he didn't need any help from his parents. He calmly replied, "No, I am the real patriot."

But America has its own "beards," like Rush Limbaugh. In small doses I could listen to him, trying to gain insights into what makes the underbelly tick. I continue to wonder if he really believes what he rants about, or whether he just thinks of himself as the "Leni

Riefenstahl of this administration." One day I was listening to the car radio and Rush had his "Camp Gitmo" t-shirts, and songs, on the theme that Gitmo is really just a Club Med, and no one should dare criticize what we do there. The fundamental thought that innocent individuals have been held against their will—and tortured—for a period longer than the American involvement in the Second World War is never allowed on the radar screen. One only needs to incant "war on terror" and "9/11" and "we can do anything we want, just like you do at Gitmo." Later in the show, oblivious to the irony, Rush bemoans his personal legal problems and sharply criticizes a Florida District Attorney for waging a vendetta against him and assuming that he is guilty until proven innocent. He intones over and over and over again, as is his style, *"Whatever happened to innocent until proven guilty"*? Yes, Rush, what happened to it?

This right-wing talk-show mindset is even espoused, in a slightly more refined form, in the *New York Times.* David Brooks' column is often replete with denunciations of the Arab "mindset," sometimes with modest qualifiers: "Our mind-set is progressive and rational. Your mind-set is pre-Enlightenment and mythological...."— ".... of their dysfunctional neighbors, the Palestinians, with whom they used to share such an intimate feud."— "The Palestinians richly deserve to be left behind." His words are skillfully crafted to the purpose of blaming the other side, to blame the victim, and never to see the denounced traits within ourselves.

It has taken us 600 or 700 years to evolve a judicial system which banished practices that were acceptable in the Middle Ages. This system includes the right to confront one's accuser, and hear and refute the evidence presented against the accused. The American "beards" reduce our hard-won civil rights and values to "legal niceties." When one believes in burning witches, one empowers a type of person to find them. It becomes a quick ride down that slippery chute of historical development back to the Middle Ages.

The counter-terrorism official said there was an "absolutely incontrovertible match" of the fingerprints. From his job title alone, you know he is a hard-nosed, no-nonsense sort of guy, and almost certainly he is actually a male. We've seen him on thousands of action shows and movies, sacrificing his personal life in the pursuit of the bad guys, stopping that atomic bomb within seconds of detonation. He is an American hero. If he says it's so, it must be. The fingerprints belonged to Brandon Mayfield, a soft-spoken, be-speckled lawyer, a family man with three children, living quietly in Portland, Oregon. He had not been outside the United States for ten years. On the surface, he seems like an unlikely candidate to have masterminded the horrific Madrid train bombings in 2004, which killed almost 200 people. There is the circumstantial evidence, though, after all, he *is* a Muslim, and he has provided legal services to a few of his co-religionists. Mr. Mayfield was never tortured while he was detained for two weeks. But then again, no one heard an atomic bomb ticking in Portland either. With eyes lowered, and a bit of a shuffle in their walk when FBI officials released him, some "errors" in their "solid incontrovertible evidence" were cited. A fact that Spanish authorities had pointed out from the very beginning.

Another victim of the witch-hunt mentality is Maher Arar, a Canadian citizen who was arrested while transiting New York City and sent to Syria to be tortured. A couple of years later Canadian and American authorities admitted that his arrest was a mistake.

As Brandon Mayfield and Maher Arar so well know, before embracing a return to the Middle Ages as the "tough guy" solution, you might want to reflect where the finger might be pointed next, even if you are white, even if you do speak English, even if you are non-Muslim. It is a very old lesson, and thus for the most selfish of motives, ones that our Founding Fathers understood well, it is best to live by a set of laws that guarantees certain inalienable rights.

***

The very last veterans of the "Great War," World War I, are now fading away. The German infantrymen that Remarque depicted had entered the war with enthusiasm, yet the mud of the trenches, the constant shelling, the poisonous gas and numerous other horrors eventually led them to ask the hard questions—ones that should be obvious to anyone. "Why are we doing this?" "Who is responsible for starting this?" "Are there other alternatives?" It would take another "great" war before Europe found the way to live in peace.

The vast majority of the world's population has been sheltered from the horrors of the current conflict, and thus the urgency to ask the same questions may appear less. But mankind's advances in technology have increased our destructive capacity by magnitudes upon magnitudes over what was available during World War I. And it is now possible that only a few dedicated people, working in concert, can deliver this mayhem, killing as many people, or more, than were killed during all the previous wars of the 20th century.

Having a conflict that lasts for at least two or three generations greatly increases the odds that such mayhem will occur. One does not need to be in the trenches to realize that the alternatives should be examined and chosen, in order to bring the current conflict to an end.

Acknowledgements

The book is the result of the combined efforts of the vast assembly of people who chose to live in Riyadh during its period of dynamic economic and social transformation. There were the Saudis, a few of whom were actually born in Riyadh, many more migrated from other areas of the Kingdom. They were often gracious hosts, ready with a nod and a wink, to accommodate the foreign workers, particularly the Westerners, whom they had invited to their country. There were also the Western expatriates, who for a diversity of reasons, chose a "different career path," some of whom found adventure and a change of outlook. And there was the much larger group of expatriates from non-Western countries, who labored and retained their dreams of a better life when they returned home. The world goes to Riyadh, as Al Stewart once sang.

My family, Mary, Paris and John, not only provided the respectability which opened many doors that would have remained closed, but shared their personal observations and helped shape the book.

In order to record this experience in Saudi Arabia, three people made invaluable contributions. My wife, Mary Miller Jones, was charmed by weekends in Yabrin, a honeymoon near Umm Lajj and carries indelible images of a life and place so different from her birthplace. For much of her life she has toiled in the legal environment, ensuring that words, and their meanings, are used correctly. She has worked tirelessly on this project, helping record those images.

The two other individuals also understood what was important and relevant versus what was not, possessing a remarkable understanding of the English language, its nuances and subtleties. First, there is my daughter, Paris Taza Jones, who at age five understood the words of

Leonard Cohen as we drove across the Russian steppe. I should have known then that she could get the words right in depicting her own "inertial reference frame."

Secondly, there is my friend, confidant, and sometimes adversary on the tennis court, Dr. Jens Sieck. We shared many of the same experiences, and he provided essential balance to those experiences as well as to the vibrancy of the English language. As to those competitive and aggressive instincts which often afflict mankind, we agree that they are best dissipated on the tennis court.

The power of their insights was vital and simultaneously humbling.

Selected Bibliography

Ali, Abdullah Yusuf. *The Holy Qur'an (with commentary)*. Damascus: Dar Al Mushaf, 1938.

Baldwin, James. *If Beale Street Could Talk*. New York: Penguin Books, 1974.

Bell, Gertrude. *The Desert and the Sown*. London: Virago Press Ltd. 1985.

Blanch, Lesley. *The Wilder Shores of Love*. London: Abacus, 1984

Brooks, David. "What Palestinians?" *New York Times* (November 17, 2005)

——————— "Drafting Hitler." *New York Times* (February 09, 2006)

Cuddihy, Kathy. An A to Z of Places and Things Saudi. London: Stacey International, 2001.

Dowd, Maureen. "Frederick's of Riyadh." *New York Times* (November 10, 2002)

Ehrenreich, Barbara. *Nickel and Dimed: On (Not) Getting By in America*. New York: Henry Holt & Co., 2001.

Ellison, Ralph. *Invisible Man*. New York: Signet Books, 1964.

Fall, Bernard. *Hell in a Very Small Place: The Siege of Dien Bien Phu*. New York: Vintage House. 1968

——————— *Street Without Joy*. London: Pall Mall Press Ltd., 1964

Faludi, Susan. *Backlash: The Undeclared War Against Women*. New York: Crown Publishers, 1991.

Fehrenbach, T.R. *This Kind of War: Korea: A Study in Unpreparedness*. New York: Giant Cardinal, 1964.

Friedman, Thomas. "A Traveler to Saudi Arabia." *New York Times* (February 24, 2002)

——————— *From Beirut to Jerusalem*. New York: Farrar Straus Giroux, 1989.

Fromkin, David. *A Peace to End All Peace: The Fall of the Ottoman Empire and the Creation of the Modern Middle East.* New York: Henry Holt & Co. 1989

Greene, Graham. *The Quiet American.* New York: The Viking Press, 1956.

Holden, David and Johns, Richard. *The House of Saud.* London: Pan Books Ltd, 1982.

Horne, Alistair. *A Savage War of Peace: Algeria 1954-1962.* Middlesex, England: Penguin Books, 1979

Hosseini, Khaled. *The Kite Runner.* New York: Riverhead Books, 2003.

Huntington, Samuel P. *The Clash of Civilizations.* London: Touchstone Books, 1997.

Hussain, Lubna. "If You Don't Look Ahead, Expect Chaos Everywhere." *Arab News* (June 24, 2005)

Joyce, James. *Ulysses.* New York: Vintage Books, 1961

Lacey, Robert. *The Kingdom: Arabia and the House of Saud.* New York: Avon Books, 1981.

Lawrence, T.E. *Seven Pillars of Wisdom.* New York: Anchor Books, 1991.

Lewis, Norman. *A Dragon Apparent: Travels in Cambodia, Laos and Vietnam.* London: Eland Books, 1951.

Moorhouse, Geoffrey. *The Fearful Void.* Bungay, Suffolk, England: The Chaucer Press, 1975

Myrdal, Gunnar. *American Dilemma: The Negro Problem and American Democracy.* New York: Harper & Co., 1944.

North, Oliver L. *One More Mission.* New York: Harper Collins, 1993.

O'Brien, Tim. *The Things They Carried.* London: Flamingo, 1991.

Paton, Alan. *Cry, the Beloved Country.* New York: Scribner, 2003.

Remarque, Erich Maria. *All Quiet on the Western Front.* Greenwich, Conn: Fawcett Publications, 1958

Riefenstahl, Leni. *Coral Gardens.* New York: Harper & Row, 1978.

Roy, Jules. *La Bataille de Dien Bien Phu.* Paris: Albin
    Michel S.A., 1989.
Said, Edward. *Covering Islam: How the Media and the
    Experts Determine How We see the Rest of the
    World.* New York: Pantheon Books, 1981.
———————— *Orientalism.* New York: Vintage Books,
    1979.
———————— *Reflections on Exile: and other Literary and
    Cultural Essays.* London: Granta Publications,
    2000.
Saint-Exupery, Antoine de. *Wind, Sand and Stars.* New
    York: Harcourt Brace & Co., 1939.
Thesiger, Wilfred. *Arabian Sands.* Middlesex, England:
    Penguin Books, 1974.
———————— *The Life of My Choice.* Glasgow: William
    Collins Sons & Co. 1988.
Twain, Mark, *The Innocents Abroad.* New York, Dover
    Publications, 2003
Walker, Dale. *Fool's Paradise.* New York: Vintage
    Departures, 1988.
Wylie, Laurence. *Village in the Vaucluse.* Cambridge,
    Mass: Harvard University Press, 1974.

Glossary of Arabic Terms and Place Name

There is no generally accepted system for transliteration of Arabic words into English. For example, "Olaya" can also be rendered as "Ulaya" or "Aulaya." While working at the hospital, I was involved in projects to standardize the transliteration of Arabic names into Roman alphabet letters. No agreement was reached on such matters as the number of m's in "Mohamed" ("Mohammed") or the placement of the "Al" in front of the last name, thus "Al-Zahrani," "Al Zahrani," and "Alzahrani" were all utilized.

The Higerian (Hegerian) calendar is lunar based, and is "subjective," based on the sighting of the moon by "two Muslims in good standing." This is particularly relevant in determining the commencement and conclusion of the holy month of Ramadan. There may be varying dates utilized in different countries, based on the particular sightings. The subjective nature of the calendar means that it is impossible to publish an official calendar for the following year— attempts to do so are generally hedged with the qualifier: "operational."

PBUH means Peace Be Upon Him, and is traditionally added after the Prophet's name, thusly, Prophet Mohammed, PBUH.

In the Kingdom of Saudi Arabia, the only word in Roman letters whose spelling is officially determined is that for the holy city: Makkah. The various secular uses of "Mecca" in the West, including betting parlors in England, were the underlying basis for this determination.

A form of "Arablish" developed in the Kingdom among the expatriates and the Saudis who worked with them. For example, adding an "s" to the end of an Arabic word to

mean the plural was generally understood, though not correct in proper Arabic.

abaya: traditional black external cloak worn by women (called a chador in some Middle Eastern countries)

abu: father of

Ahlan wa Sahlan: traditional expression of welcome, literally "May you arrive as part of the family, and tread an easy path (as you enter)."

alf: thousand

Allah: God

Ameeriki: American

bas: only or enough

bayt: home

bisht: external cloak worn by men, often for formal occasions

Eid al-Fitr: holiday period at the end of Ramadan

Eid al-Hada: holiday period in conjunction with the annual pilgrimage to Makkah

fayn: where

fil: at the

ghutra: traditional cloth head covering for men (called a kufiah in some other Middle Eastern countries)

haram: forbidden

hajj: pilgrimage to Makkah, one of the five pillars of Islam

Hejaz: the western region of Saudi Arabia; ruled by the Ottoman Empire for centuries prior to the creation of the Kingdom of Saudi Arabia

Hijerian: calendar based on the lunar year, approximately 354 days – start date is the day of Mohammed's emigration from Makkah to Yathrib (Medina), corresponding to July 16, 622 AD

ijhaza: leave of absence (vacation)

Ikhwan: The Brotherhood

inta: you (female)

iqama: residency permit

itnaan: two

Jahaliya: the period before the Prophet Mohammed, PBUH, the "time of darkness."

Al Jazeera: The Peninsula

kabeera: large or old (female)

kalaas: finish

karim: generous

kharbaan: broken, non-functioning

khawaja: a term used to denote Westerners in Saudi Arabia

la: no

lau samaat: a more formal form of please

maajnoon: crazy

mafi mouk: no brains

mafi mushkila: no problem

Mahdi: The Guided One – prophesized redeemer

Majlis: a legislative assembly, or a room utilized for entertaining guests

Marabah Palace: principal residence of King Abdul-Aziz ibn Saud

maut: dead

min: with

min fadluck: please

mudeer: director

mush quais: not good

Musmak Fort: main fort in Riyadh which was seized by Abdul-Aziz ibn Saud in 1902, thereby ending a period of rule of the city by the Rashid tribe

Mutawaa: *"religious police"* Formal name of the organization translates as "The Society for the Preservation of Virtue and the Prevention of Vice." At one time, in the '50's and '60's, the term was an honorific, but in the late '90's and beyond, generally a term of contempt, by both Saudis and Westerners, for religious fundamentalists.

Nedj: the central region of Saudi Arabia; the area which was not formerly ruled by the Ottoman Empire, unlike either coastal area incorporated in the Kingdom of Saudi Arabia.

ragum wahead: number one

Rub Al-Khali: Empty Quarter, the southeastern portion of the Kingdom, with undefined borders with the United Arab Emirates, Oman, and the Yemen.

sabbah: seven

as Salaam Alaykoum: peace be upon you (traditional Arabic greeting)

saleh: prayer time

Shia: literally one of the followers of Ali, the son-in-law of the Prophet Mohammed, one of the largest denominations of Islam, 10-15% of the Saudi population is Shia, mainly in the eastern province

Sunni: the largest denomination of Islam, over 80% of the Saudi population adheres to this denomination

shwarma: Middle Eastern sandwich, composed of Arabic (pita) bread and chicken or lamb

souk: area of small shops – market place

soura: picture

takassusi: specialist

Tash ma Tash: foam, no foam (very popular Saudi TV show)

talatah mia: three hundred

taza: fresh

thobe: a loose, long sleeve ankle-length garment traditionally worn by Saudi men

Tihama: narrow low-land region on the west coast of Saudi Arabia

umm: mother of

wa: and

waled: boy. In Saudi Arabia the word is used loosely and could refer to grown men, if used by their elders. In Lebanon such usage would be considered a serious insult.

wasta: connections or influence

zojhatak: your wife

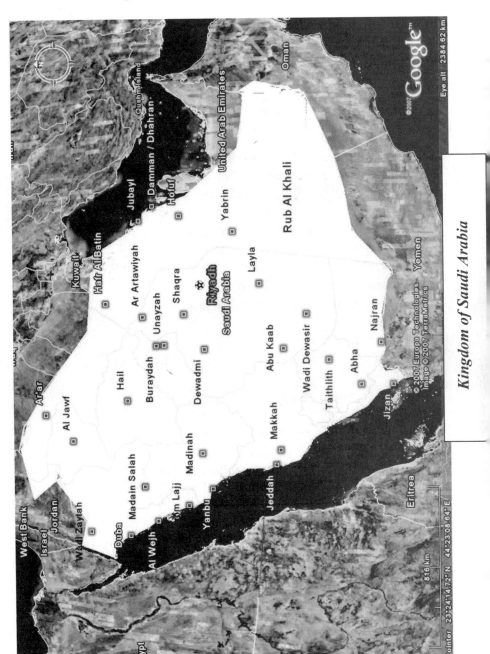

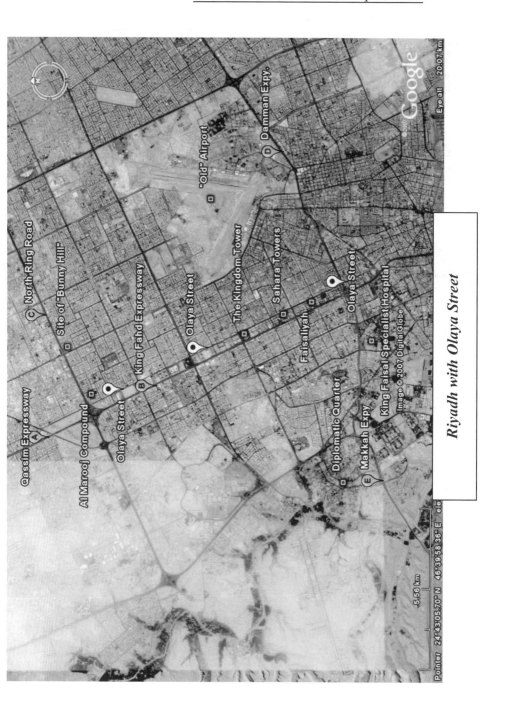

Riyadh with Olaya Street

King Faisal Specialist Hospital and environs

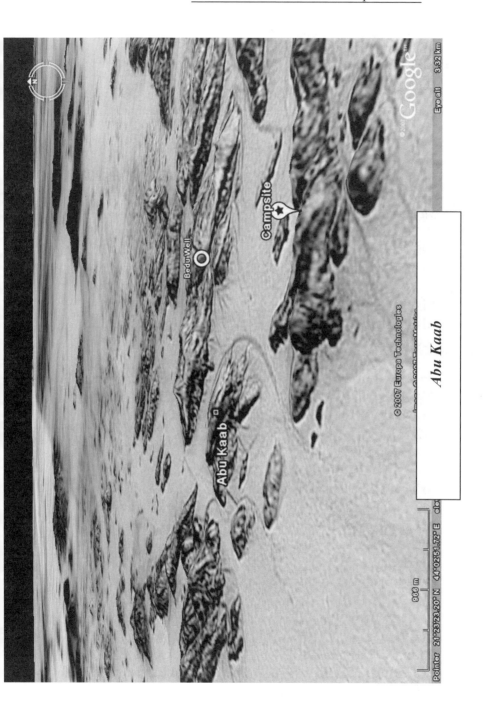

Abu Kaab